ARTIFICIAL

INTELLIGENCE

IN

FINANCE

4 books in 1

STOCK MARKET INVESTING FOR BEGINNERS

OPTIONS TRADING FOR BEGINNERS

PYTHON FOR BEGINNERS

PYTHON CRASH COURSE

JASON TEST MARK BROKER

The new comprehensive guide to master applied artificial intelligence in Physics.

Learn Machine Learning and computer programming with a complete crash course

CONTENTS

ARTIFICIAL INTELLIGENCE IN FINANCE 1

STOCK MARKET INVESTINGFOR BEGINNERS.. 19

introduction... 20

1.   the abc of stock market 22

What is the stock market?... 23

Who Integrates It? 23

Role of the Stock Exchange.. 24

How Does The Stock Market Work?... 25

Can I Invest In The Stock Market From Home? 27

Invest in the stock market: What platform to use?...................... 29

How much money do I have to invest in the stock market? 29

Can I start investing in a stock simulator? 31

2.   The Mechanics of Owning, Buying and Selling Stocks............. 32

Buy Shares to Become A Shareholder 32

Buy and sell stocks with online brokers 33

Purchase and sale orders for shares... 34

When is it the best time to buy shares on the stock exchange? 35

When is it a good idea to sell the shares on the stock exchange? 36

How long do you have to hold stocks in a short-term strategy? 38

How long do you have to keep stocks in a long-term strategy? 38

When should the shares be resold? 39

What shares can be purchased or sold online? 40

What stocks to invest in? 40

3.   Who is a Broker& How to Choose One 42

Stockbroker: What is it? 42

Stockbroker: Functions 43

Characteristics of a Stockbroker 43

How to choose the right stockbroker? 45

A Background Check Is a Must 45

Interviewing multiple runners is a must. 46

Check out these red flags. 47

Do your homework with references. 48

The Bottom Line 48

4.   How to Assess Risk and Volatility 50

Individual risk assessment 50

Systematic risk assessment 51

Standard Deviation 52

Beta 52

Value at risk 53

Conditional Value at risk 53

What is Volatility? 54

Implied Volatility 56

Historical Volatility 57

5. **Top Indicators of a Winning Investment 59**

Trend line 59

Simple Moving Average 60

Rate of change 62

Relative strength Index 63

Moving Average Convergence Divergence 64

Bollinger Bands 65

Fibonacci Retracements 66

All about Technical Indicators 66

6. **Basic Investment Techniques 71**

10 Basic Investment Techniques for Beginners 72

1. Set a Goal 72

2. Early Investment is Beneficial 72

3. Invest a Constant Figure Automatically 73

4. Don't Invest Too Much 74

5. Do Your Homework on Investment 74

6. Don't Pay High Commission 75

7. Don't Invest in One Place/Stock 76

8. Invest in Long-term Options 77

9. Keep an Eye on Your Portfolio 77

10. Continue Research 78

Final Words 79

7. **What You Should Know About Taxes 81**

The Long-term Capital Gains Rate Criteria 82

Reducing Tax on your Stock Sales 82

Experimenting with the Wash Rule 84

Deduction of Capital Losses... 85

Other Deductible Expenses in Investment 86

Final verdict 87

8. **All about the Bull & Bear Market................................... 88**

High Gross Domestic Products 90

Rising Stock Prices 91

Longer Stock Trading 91

Lower Unemployment Rates 91

The Bull Market History 92

The Bear Market Indicators 93

The Bear Market History 94

9. Common stock exchange terms and what they mean 98

What is the Stock Market? 98

1-Annual Report 99

2- Arbitrage... 100

3-Averaging Down 100

4- Bear Market... 100

5- Bull Market 101

6- Beta 101

7- Blue Chip Stocks 101

8- Bourse.. 101

9- Broker 102

10- Bid.. 102

11- Close 102

12- Day trading 103

13- Dividend 103

14- Exchange.. 103

15- Execution 104

16- Haircut 104

17- High 104

18- Initial Public Offering... 105

19- Leverage 105

20- Low 105

21- Margin 106

22- Moving Average 106

23- Open 106

24- Order 107

25- pink sheet stocks 107

26- Sector... 107

10.   Tips and tricks for investing in the Stock Exchange 109

1- Invest in Index Fund 109

2- Focus on Mutual Funds 110

3- Timing the Market.. 110

4- Set Goals.. 111

5- Five Golden steps of trading to learn: 111

6- Have a balance of investments 112

7- Think for long term... 113

8- Buy value stocks 113

9- Diversify investments among sectors 113

10- How much risk you can take?....................................... 114

11- Control your emotions 114

12- 360 Degree View 114

13- Automate stocks.. 115

14- Say no to leverage 115

15- Choose one sector... 116

16- Risk vs. Return 116

17- Buy low sell higher 116

Final Word 117

CONCLUSION 118

OPTIONS TRADING FOR BEGINNERS 119

introduction.. 120

1.   options trading basics 122

What Options Trading is? 122

Uses of Options 123

Derivatives.. 123

Options Trading Characteristics 124

All Options Expire 124

All Options Have a Strike Price 125

Option Contract Multiplier 125

Types of Options 125

What is Call? What is Put? 127

Buying and Selling... 129

2.   why trade with options.. 131

The Benefits of Options Trading 131

Options have Low Risk... 131

Options are More Cost-Effective 133

Options Offer Higher Returns 134

More Alternatives with Options **135**

Why Options are a Better Choice? **136**

Hedging.. 136

Speculation 137

How does Options Trading work? **137**

Types of Options **140**

Options Liquidity & Expiry Time **140**

How to Read Options Table? 141

3.   Major option trading concepts **143**

History of Option Trading **144**

Risks In Options Trading? **145**

Stock VS Option 146

Option Trading Platforms 147

Option Practicing Method **148**

Strategies for option trading **150**

Buying calls 150

Buying puts 150

Covered calls.. 151

The Worth of Option Trading... **152**

Option Trading VS Stock Trading **153**

Risk in Option Trading **154**

Option Account 155

What Is An Option Account? **155**

The Right Broker 156

The Best Broker 156

Best platforms **156**

4.   **Options Trading Myths and Misconceptions**

Misconception #1 Trading and Gambling are same 159

Misconception #2 Should only invest in Call and Put Option.............. 160

Misconception #3 Option selling is more profitable 160

Misconception #4 Put Option expire worthlessly 161

Misconception #5 Option trading is a zero-sum 162

Misconception #6 Options trading is easy 162

Misconception #7 Trading in Tax-deferred account 163

5.   **Top Options Trading Strategies** **164**

Buying calls **164**

Buying puts **166**

Covered call **167**

Iron condors 169

Bear calls **170**

Jade lizard **171**

Collar option 172

Diagonal spread 174

Butterfly 176

6.   Top Qualities of a Successful Options Trader 178

Options Trading 178

      Why people tend to go for options trading? 178

      Top Qualities of a Successful Options Trader 179

      Control on Emotions 180

7.   How to Select the Right Option for a Major Gain 186

Look for the Right Option 186

Frame your Purpose 187

Trader's Payoff 188

Analyze Volatility 188

Recognize Events 189

Make Your Strategy 189

Launch Parameters 190

How to make money with Options Trading 191

Making Money with Options Trading in 2020 195

Making most out of options 197

Indirect Strategies:.. 197

Mental strategies:.. 198

8.   Important Tips & Tricks about Options Trading........................... 199

Follow a Well Defined Exit Plan 201

9.   Important FAQs of Options Trading.. 206

Is there any definition of options? 206

How to gain maximum profit in options trading? 207

What happens in a case when options contract expires?.................... 207

What is the difference between strike price and stock price? 208

What is naked call? 208

What is American contract? 208

What is an European contract?... 209

Which one is more profitable European contract or American contract?209

So an American style contract is exercised more but is it more profitable?.. 209

When should you start options trading? 209

How much should you invest in options trading? 210

When should you exercise your options?... 210

Best strategy of options trading? 211

What is a short put and long call strategy?........................ 211

How an option writer makes money? 211

How do investors lose money in options trading? 212

CONCLUSION 213

PYTHON FOR BEGINNERS 214

Python code optimization with ctypes.................................... 235

Finding the Perfect Toolkit: Analyzing Popular Python Project Templates245

How are broad integer types implemented in Python?........................ 257

Create a bot in Python to learn English.................................... 268

The thermal imager on the Raspberry PI 288

Finding a Free Parking Space with Python 300

Creating games on the Pygame framework | Part 1............................ 322

Object-Oriented Programming (OOP) in Python 3.................................. 352

Conclusion 382

PYTHON CRASH COURSE 385

DAY 1 387

DAY 2 392

DAY 3 412

DAY 4 425

DAY 5 450

DAY 6 463

DAY 7 478

CONCLUSION 495

STOCK MARKET INVESTING

FOR BEGINNERS

THE BIBLE OF STOCK MARKET TIPS & TRICKS

Learn how to trade for a living with solid risk-management strategies. Use techniques based on trader psychology for your investment in options and forex. Earn extra income, create your source of passive income and get your own financial freedom.

INTRODUCTION

Did you know how many companies are registered with NYSE (New York Stock Exchange) and how much has been invested overall?

Here is a rough estimate: According to recent data, more than 3,000 companies have been registered, while the overall investment in just one stock exchange (NYSE) is about $15 Trillion.

Think of the other stock exchanges.....

The value of the international stock exchange is said to be $80 Trillion, Big Money – yeah – that means bigger gains...if you are in the game and (can play it correctly).

Now the question is how to learn it? Simple, follow the guidelines given in this comprehensive book, and you will be ready to play.

What's more interesting is 52 percent of Americans are Stock exchange investors. That shows how lucrative this market is.

So, before you start investing, read to learn the ABC of the stock market. It is written after doing research and is reviewed by some of the most successful investors.

Hope you would like this effort and enjoy reading and applying the strategies given in this book. In the end, if you ask me what that one thing that I should tell you as an expert to keep in mind (before beginning) is – it is: always remember: "a good Investment is always boring!"

"If investing is entertaining, if you're having fun, you're probably not making any money. Good investing is boring."

– George Soros

1. THE ABC OF STOCK MARKET

When we talk about investing in the stock market, we must understand that it is more than buying and selling shares. This activity can also be linked to other financial instruments where it is possible to operate in the short, medium, or long term.

The investment method used in the stock market is called "invest" if it is long term or "trading" if it is short.

Stock trading has become popular in this area of the stock market. This activity can be started online from anywhere in the world and consists of the sale and purchase of financial assets.

Trading consists of buying or selling an asset, then reselling or repurchasing it, and obtaining the respective profit. The advent of online trading has allowed many to invest in the stock market with little money, without owning large amounts of capital.

To manage the stock market, it is important to document yourself and study well the type of investment you are going to make.

What is the stock market?

The stock exchange is an organization where transactions of different financial instruments are carried out through authorized intermediaries. This institution provides the facilities for its members, brokers, or operators to negotiate the purchase and sale of securities.

The stock exchange originates from the City of Bruges, Belgium, within the Van der Burson family of bankers. These organized meetings in his palace to make commercial operations or to transact assets, and they had like shield three bags of skin. Then in 1460 in Antwerp, Belgium, the first modern stock exchange arose, for years later, expanding to other countries.

Who Integrates It?

The stock market has been made up of companies, organizations, or public and private entities, which are the applicants for capital.

Savers or investors who are the capital providers and intermediaries, brokers, brokerage houses, etc. also participate.

For companies to be able to list their securities on the stock market, they must publish their financial statements to determine their financial situation. When a company makes an offer on the stock market, anyone can know the information and performance of the company.

The stock exchange works like a large market or mall where stocks are bought and sold daily. Companies are listed on the stock exchange because it allows them to obtain new capital without having to borrow or borrow.

In this medium, any company can quote, as long as it meets the standards and the minimum investment requirements.

Role of the Stock Exchange

The time has come to show you what you want so much to know. Get ready to know the aim/mission of the stock market in any part of the world:

- Facilitate the transactions of the resources so that a better allocation of them is feasible.

- Support transactions by providing legal certainty.

- Guarantee liquidity, since assets such as shares and securities are converted into money.

- Inform truthfully and permanently concerning the values, operations, financial statements of companies, among other things.

- Contribute to the growth as well as the development of the capital and securities market.

- Organize the stock market through stock market operations.

How Does The Stock Market Work?

Below I will show you how the stock market works internally. Undoubtedly, this is information that you must know before entering this wonderful and fluctuating financial world. Do you want to know them?

When a person has to buy or sell part of a company, he does it through the stock market.

If the company sells its shares for the first time, it makes a public offering known as the "primary market".

For a company to grow, it needs additional capital that requires the contribution of new partners.

Shares are issued to find these partners that are sold in the so-called public offering to those who are interested in investing. When a public offer is made in the stock market, the company is made public, and the interested party obtains the shares.

Subsequently, this shareholder can, in turn, sell his shares in the future if he decides, according to his convenience. In the same way that other investors buy it, they also evaluate the updated information of the company for their convenience.

Analyzing the information allows the feasibility of a good offer to change significantly from one day to another.

The purchase and sale price of shares is set by free-market laws, that is, supply and demand.

Those who buy set the purchase price and those who sell do the same; this is how operations are carried out, both actors setting their stance.

The shareholder always expects to earn periodic dividend earnings, or by selling his shares at a higher price. The holder is an investor who, by acquiring a bond, expects to generate regular interest or profits at the end of the term.

Stockbrokers are responsible for conducting transactions between sellers and buyers of shares. Investments in shares are considered variable income, while investments in debt as fixed income.

Can I Invest In The Stock Market From Home?

Here I tell you everything! Investing in the stock market may seem like a complicated task and only for large entrepreneurs, but in reality, anyone can do it. I only recommend that you study very well what it is and of course you go to the experts in the stock market.

Thanks to the internet, this market can be accessed more easily from home or mobile by different applications. However, just because it is easy to invest in the stock market online does not mean that it is easy to obtain earnings by shares.

Investing in the stock market online maintains the principle of buying and selling shares; it is done through online brokers.

Benefits are obtained without the need to be in a specific place to operate the exchange, from where you are.

The online brokers will be the tool that will help us gain access to financial markets to invest in the stock market. You can invest in national securities and also in any company in the world, from small to large companies.

These so-called brokers can be obtained on web pages, applications, and other means such as banks (which allow investing from home).

The procedure is generally as follows:

- Open an account in a broker, the platform for trading your preference.
- You will obtain the corresponding username and password (if applicable).
- Each account will be associated with a bank account, where the money you will use for purchase and sales orders will be. The bank account will enter the money from the sale of shares, collection of dividends, and any other operation.

- Each operation will generate its commission, and you must bear in mind the brokerage costs, administrative expenses, and stock fees.
- Brokering costs are generally based on a percentage of what is invested for the services received. The costs or administration expenses depend on the country where you open your account; the commissions vary due to different factors.

Invest in the stock market: What platform to use?

There are many platforms to invest in the stock market. Below I will mention some of the most popular brokers or online trading platforms to invest or trade.

However, don't stop to decide! Take your time to try until you get the one that makes you feel safe and comfortable according to your needs.

How much money do I have to invest in the stock market?

You may have in mind that to invest in the stock market, you need to have a lot of money, but it is not.

I have good news for you, and it is that you do not need a lot of money, although I cannot give you a specific figure. Anyone can invest in the stock market on their own, without having as much money available to start.

When you invest more money in the stock market, it does not mean higher profitability; it is recommended to think in percentage terms, in terms of investment. You should start with little money to experiment, and then increase the investment according to the results obtained.

My primary recommendation is that you should save. That is, you need to have the ability to save to generate money, which you will then invest consecutively.

It is essential to make it clear that initially, your goal should be to gain experience and train. It is a complicated world, where many people end up losing a lot of money. Which occurs because they do not form before fully entering the stock market investment.

You should also take into account the impact in terms of money that the associated commissions will have on your investment.

Remember the commissions for a capital increase, custody of securities, purchase, and sale, collection of dividends, etc.

Can I start investing in a stock simulator?

A stock market simulator is a computer program with a very advanced interface that allows you to learn how to spend money in the stock market online. It has all the necessary tools to practice in real-time as if you were in the stock market.

It can support you as a fundamental tool to start trading in values and make some decisions without any risk! These simulators can be found in some specialized brokers or banks, and they are complex applications that are being commonly used.

Operating a simulator can avoid many headaches, helping you to train and learn, to have good knowledge. It enables you to get familiar with the interface handling play money, seeing the results of your decisions, to jump to reality.

"Unless you can watch your stock holding decline by 50% without becoming panic-stricken, you should not be in the stock market."

— Warren Buffett

2. THE MECHANICS OF OWNING, BUYING AND SELLING STOCKS

"If you aren't thinking about owning a stock for ten years, don't even think about owning it for ten minutes."

- Warren Buffett

The use of stock shares, whether it is getting dividends or speculating on their listing, is an increasingly popular and interesting practice. Of course, the risk of loss is also present, but depending on how you buy and sell your shares, this risk may be decreased. If you are wondering how to buy and sell stocks to large companies that are listed directly online, the following explanations may interest you.

Buy Shares to Become A Shareholder

A large part of individuals and institutions that buy securities do so to become a shareholder. It is the simplest use of stocks and their main objective. Indeed, when a company issues shares, it is possible to be a buyer directly online.

However, for shares already listed, this must go through an intermediary that can be an online agent or an online bank.

Of course, it is possible to buy shares directly from sellers who bought these shares themselves in the same way that you can resell your shares.

Buy and sell stocks with online brokers

People who wish to buy and sell shares on the stock exchange can do this from their homes. They can do so through an online trading platform proposed by a Forex broker. These Forex brokers make available to investors simplified trading tools called CFDs that allow speculation in the stock market.

These CFDs or Contracts for Difference allow you to buy a batch of shares on the stock exchange at a certain price and then sell it when the price has reached a level interesting enough to give you a profit on the difference.

However, the real advantage of CFDs for buying and selling shares on the stock exchange lies in the leverage effect, which allows you to multiply your investment by 100, 200, and sometimes even 400.

In this way, you can generate significant benefits when operating lots of larger stocks over a short period.

For example, if Apple shares are at €40 and you want to buy 100 lots, in theory, you would need an investment of €4,000. However, if you use a lever effect of 1:200 you can buy these 100 lots for just 200 euros.

Similarly, if this share goes to € 42 and you resell the lot of 100 shares, your profit will be 100x2, that is, 200 euros. It means that in a few minutes, you can double your investment.

Purchase and sale orders for shares

The Forex trading platforms that allow you to buy and sell shares on the stock market also allow you to enjoy practical tools to place your orders or program them in advance.

Thus, when scheduling a sell order for a certain price level, you no longer need to follow the market live, as your positions will automatically close at the right time. This method can be used to make profits, but also to limit losses with the "stop-loss" order that triggers the sale of your shares below a certain limit.

CFDs also allow positions to be taken directly for the sale of the securities, which means betting on the drop in prices.

When is it the best time to buy shares on the stock exchange?

Buying shares on the stock exchange can be an attractive investment, but it is not about buying any stock at any time. Indeed, the purchase of shares on the stock exchange is, first of all, a decision that must be made following a strategy. But then, when is it better to buy stocks?

When it comes to equity stocks, and to create a stock portfolio, it is preferable to buy the shares of long-listed companies to know in advance the potential of each security in terms of long dividends term. You can also choose to buy the shares of the innovative companies that issue their securities for the first time to be part of their success, although this is a bit riskier.

When it comes to online trading using CFDs, buying stocks is, first and foremost, a matter of finding the right time. Indeed, from a trading platform, you can access numerous international stock securities. But be careful: you should only buy a title if you think that your price will increase over time and in a more or less long term. In this way, you can obtain benefits by reselling the most expensive shares of what you have bought them.

Therefore, we advise you to buy shares on the stock exchange under the following conditions:

- the stock follows a strong and lasting bullish trend;
- a major event has just, or is going to, influence the share's upward price;
- technical indicators announce that the trend will remain bullish or a bullish reversal of a negative trend, and
- The sector of activity from which the share comes experiences strong growth.

When is it a good idea to sell the shares on the stock exchange?

Now we will be interested in cases of sale of shares on the stock exchange. A sale can be made to recover the money to invest it again or simply to pocket the profits if the corresponding title has increased in value.

Indeed, if you own some stocks in your stock portfolio whose dividends are becoming less interesting, it would be a good option to get rid of them to add more profitable stocks. You can also sell your shares to pocket profits because they have greatly increased in value since you purchased them.

When it comes to stocks trading on an online trading platform, things get a little complicated. Of course, you can re-sell the shares you have bought, but you can also directly sell a security without ever buying it. This method consists of investing in the price of these shares.

CFDs offer the possibility of investing both in the purchase and sale of shares on the stock exchange so that every opportunity can be taken advantage of even when the market is bearish. Thus, you can sell a share when:

- its price follows a strong and lasting downward trend;
- an event will take place or has taken place, and there is a good chance that it will lead to a fall or fall in the price of this asset;
- one or more technical indicators announce a sharp decline or bearish change for a stock, and
- the sector of activity from which the corresponding action comes suffers a major economic crisis.

How long do you have to hold stocks in a short-term strategy?

If you trade short term, or even concise term, you obviously will not hold your shares too long. A strategy like Day Trading, for example, will require the resale of your lots before the end of the session.

In this specific case, it is sensible to use a crowbar effect or bet a significant part of your capital to generate a substantial profit in just a few hours. Do not set yourself too ambitious a target, as you risk not being able to achieve it in time and suffering a bearish correction before leaving the platform you are speculating on.

If you trade for several days, you will only keep your shares until you reach a realistic target of a few max points. Consider setting a stop order in the right place so that your position closes on time.

How long do you have to keep stocks in a long-term strategy?

For more long-term strategies, it is necessary to take into account the possibilities of bearish reversals in the price of your shares.

These micro-movements should not force their positions to close before reaching their goal.

In effect, you will have to use stop and limit orders at the same time. The latter must be established far enough from its opening price so that its position remains open in the event of a possible correction. You should also think about having enough capital in your trading account to be able to cover these types of cases.

When should the shares be resold?

Apart from achieving the goal that you have set, some particular cases will push you to sell your shares without waiting any longer.

For example, when the price of the stocks you are following passes below a critical point indicating a strong probability of decline, it is better not to wait and close your position so as not to risk losing more money. These levels can be determined by the levels of technical support observed in the charts.

Likewise, if you follow the economic news of a company whose shares it operates, some posts may create a risk, and sometimes it is preferable to sell your shares before they expire.

What shares can be purchased or sold online?

For some years now, the offer of Forex brokers regarding CFDs for stocks has increased considerably, and now many titles can be accessed from the trading platforms we have.

Of course, you will find Spanish, European and international stocks. All the actions proposed on these platforms are part of the large international stock indices. They are, therefore, especially popular, volatile thanks to precise strategies based on technical or fundamental data.

What stocks to invest in?

As you will no doubt have observed, the actions proposed by brokers on their trading platforms are very numerous and, therefore, it is becoming increasingly difficult to choose which assets to trade.

So what stocks should you invest in? Although investing in the stock market is not an exact science and it is not possible to foresee exactly which stocks will be profitable and which will be losers, it is

sensible to analyze the sectors of activity that may experience
strong   growth.

3. WHO IS A BROKER& HOW TO CHOOSE ONE

Do you know what a stockbroker does? What are the main functions it performs? If you are not familiar with the answer to these questions, we invite you to read the following post, in which we will clarify everything about it.

Stockbroker: What is it?

The main task of a stockbroker is to advise other people who do not have sufficient experience to carry out operations in the diverse financial markets.

The stockbroker stands out for having good knowledge of finance and playing an active and main role in the stock market. It could be said that the stockbroker acts as an intermediary. It is the person who is between the broker and the investor who is interested in buying or selling.

The stockbroker guides and advises his clients in finance so that they can obtain the best possible returns. It is also in charge of managing the purchases, and the rest of the operations carried out by its clients. So it can be said that a broker's work cycle begins when one of his clients buys an asset and ends when he sells it and definitively closes the transaction.

Stockbroker: Functions

Among the functions performed by the stockbroker, we can find:

- Intervene in the purchase/sale of assets and the management of securities.
- It is placing of new securities in the market (Public sale offer, or also known as IPO). This refers to when a company is interested in starting to go public; it should be addressed to the broker, who will be in charge of finding a buyer for its shares.
- Inform and advise the client and companies.

Characteristics of a Stockbroker

We already know before that a stockbroker is the link between supply and demand in the stock market. Now, we will see the characteristics of the stockbroker and his trade:

- It is a commercial activity that can be carried out by any type of person.
- As it is an activity that anyone can exercise, not everyone can enter to carry out stock movements and transactions, because yes, no, it must go through the acceptance of a regulator. This process requires different requirements, including A minimum age, a specific level of education on the subject, accredit such knowledge if possible.
- The broker is under strict supervision at all times, promoting the good performance of the work without malicious news.
- The stock market regulator will constantly require the financial status of your account. Likewise, you are required to maintain a stable amount of equity.
- The agent will receive a commission according to the specifications of the agreement, this varies depending on the number of operations carried out, and may receive a fixed commission on their services, without the results of the operations affecting their heading, or, you can choose remuneration according to the percentage of their results.

How to choose the right stockbroker?

Investing is not as simple as buying and selling stocks, so the help of a professional is invaluable. A proficient stockbroker will devise a plan to grow your money while keeping your goals, risk tolerance, and time horizon in mind. Unfortunately, all stockbrokers are not created equal.

There are the bad, the good, and the ugly when it comes to investing. Choose the wrong broker, and it can cost you a lot of money on investment losses and unnecessary fees.

A Background Check Is a Must

You need your broker to be licensed and registered in the state in which you reside, yet you also want to ensure you have the right credentials, enough experience. And there are no major breaches of compliance.

All of that information is available by contacting your state's securities regulator. The American Association of Securities Administrators provides a list of contact information for state regulators here.

Equally, important is how the professional is paid. Stockbrokers can be paid a percentage of their invested assets, an hourly rate, a fixed rate, or a commission on the shares they sell to them.

Unlike financial advisers who have a fiduciary duty to take into account the best interests of their clients, brokers cannot earn a commission on the sale of particular stocks, bonds, or mutual funds and can earn a commission. Often it is better to turn to a feed adviser or stockbroker who does not earn a commission. Because they do not receive paid commissions, they have no incentive to drive one action or investment idea over another.

Interviewing multiple runners is a must.

A lot of thinking and searching should be done to choose a doctor, and the same diligence must be applied to finding a stockbroker. It means in addition to checking your history; You must interview multiple brokers before making a decision. It is particularly important because you want to feel comfortable with the person who handles your money.

When interviewing potential brokers, there are some key questions to ask. First, know how the broker is paid and what he can expect to pay in fees. After that, you want to know how your agent will contact you and how often.

Nothing can sour a relationship faster than an unresponsive stockbroker, especially when you're uncomfortable with an investment or when the markets are trading. Each broker will offer different investment services and products, so you also want to know what their fees are charging you. For example, does the broker offer online tools to verify your accounts, communicate, and analyze your portfolio?

Also, does the firm give you access to property research and third-party research on individual stocks, different industries, and market analysis? If you're interested in real estate or international investments, you want to make sure that the agent you go with not only offers investments in those areas but is also well-trained to invest in those industries.

Check out these red flags.

The way your agent acts during the interview can tell you a lot about that person. The goal of investing is to achieve a goal that is unique to you. At the initial meeting, your broker should ask you about your goals, risk tolerance, and time horizon. But if he or she is advocating a specific investment idea or making guarantees on return instead, you should raise red flags.

If the broker doesn't take the time to know your goals and is only interested in telling you what they can do for you, it's a telltale sign that the broker has their interest in your heart, not yours.

Do your homework with references.

Often one of the finest ways to find a good stockbroker is through word of mouth. Ask your family, friends, coworkers, and other acquaintances that they use for their investment advice, and you should be able to get a list of some names.

A referral can be invaluable, especially when it comes to someone you trust, but don't take the recommendation blindly. You need to do your due diligence, which means checking the agent's background, uncovering the fee structure, and interviewing the person to ensure their personalities identify themselves. After all, many of the investors who were scammed by Bernie Madoff and his Ponzi scheme blindly invested on the recommendation of a friend.

The Bottom Line

Investing in the stock markets can be very complex and time-consuming and often requires the help of a professional. But while a stockbroker can provide invaluable service if your money grows, not all stockbrokers are created equal.

There are the good, the bad, and the ugly. Eliminating those falls on the investor and to do that requires a bit of homework. From consulting the agent's background to asking key questions before hiring someone, there are many steps to choosing the right agent for your particular financial situation.

4. HOW TO ASSESS RISK AND VOLATILITY

Assessing risk is a step by step process and is a basic part of the risk management of an organization. However, risk management is also conducted on behalf of an individual as there are several types of risks; hence multiple ways and purposes are served to conduct a risk assessment or risk analysis. Mainly, two types of risk are undertaken in casual way, and that includes:

Individual risk assessment

Within individual cases and transactions, the risk is always involved. Risk can be assessed and analyzed in case of interaction between a physician and patient, a teacher and a student, a buyer and seller, and so on. It means whenever individuals interact with each other for any purpose. Individual risk can happen to occur between both sides.

However, individual risk assessment is affected by several factors like behavioral, psychological, ideological, religious, and others depend on the purpose of an individual's interaction with each other. Individual risk assessment affects rationally the whole process for which individuals interact with each other, and dealings and transactions are made among people.

So, there may be several requirements for individual risk assessment just depending on the nature of the task to be done by individuals, transactions to be made between them, and interaction is done among individuals. Whatever the purpose or reason for meeting individuals with each other, risk assessment and analysis becomes necessary to run the process smoothly.

Systematic risk assessment

Systems risk assessment or management can be seen in larger scenarios and broader sense. It can also be said an organizational risk assessment process that may require multiple problems, functional issues, and safety hurdles, etc.

Well, systems can be of two types like linear and non-linear. Whatever the type of system, several types of problems may occur over there, and it becomes essential to assess and analyze risks involved in each system. Risk can involve at all scales; from nuclear technology to food safety system and organizational or systems risks is evaluated on different parameters and requirements.

So, how to assess risk is another important point of our discussion, and the process of risk assessment involves identifying the amount of risk in a system. According to statistical and mathematical parameters, there are different ways to assess risk, and some of these are used commonly, but some are not used in routine life. Commonly used measurements of risk assessment include:

Standard Deviation

Standard deviation is a commonly used method for assessing and calculating risk; it measures the dispersion of data from its expected value. This particular method of assessing risk is used in the commercial industry, where investors have to make decisions about making investments or not. The current and expected rate of return is measured and compared for important decision-making in the industry.

Beta

Beta is another one important tool to measure risk value in both individual and systems risk management processes. It is a mathematical and statistical term that is used to calculate the expected and current value of risk involved in any system or individual interaction. If a system has a beta value of more than 1, it would be considered the risk involved in the stock market.

Value at risk

The level and value of risk are analyzed with the help of this mathematical tool, and it is also commonly used in measuring risk in the stock market. The maximum potential loss of an organization is judged using this value at risk method, and important business decisions are made according to the results of the assessment of risk in the industry and stock market.

Conditional Value at risk

This is another important and commonly used way to calculate and assess risk in the industry and stock market. Basically, tail risk is assessed using this tool, and it is also helpful in understanding the current condition of the stock market and other industries.
Risk management and risk assessment are categorized in two ways; systematic risk assessment and unsystematic risk assessment. Systematic risk is assessing risk about the market, and it also affects the overall security of the market.

However, systematic risk assessment is considered unpredictable, but hedging can be helpful in mitigating the risk of the industry. For example, unfair political affairs can affect a large span of industry and stock market, and this can be said a systematic risk involved in the stock market and other related industries of a country. Put options technique is used to sort out this type of risk.

Unsystematic risk is all about risk is involved in a particular organization, company, or sector. This type of risk is variegated, and it can be mitigated by the asset diversification process. A particular stock, company, or industry can be affected by this type of risk.

What is Volatility?

Volatility is a particular mathematical and statistical term that is used in measuring the dispersion of a security system, a company's rate of return, and the stock market index. In most business and commercial cases, if the volatility is higher, the risk is also considered higher in the particular industry.

Multiple statistical tools are used to measure volatility in the commercial sector and the stock market. Volatility represents the current value of assets of an industry, and important business decisions are made, and strategies are formulated according to the recent condition of the company's finances.

Volatility is also referred to as the amount of risk that is involved in security and other systematic approaches of an organization. If the volatility of an organization is lower, it would be considered that the security value will not fluctuate at once.

Traders, analysts, and risk managers use different techniques and tools to measure and assess volatility in the stock market index position. Often high volatility is considered a sign of high risk involved in the business sector and stock market sector.

Trade and business become riskier if the measuring parameters show high volatility in the stock market index. Volatility is measured by commonly used statistical tools like standard deviation, Beta, and variance.

Standard deviation is a common statistical tool that is used to measure market volatility, and Bollinger Bands is used by traders and investors to make decisions and formulate strategies in the stock market.

Maximum drawdown is another one important tool to assess volatility in the stock market, and it is useful in calculating the index points in the stock market as well. Stock price volatility is also measured by the drawdown method of assessing risk and volatility.

A beta is also a common tool that is used to measure the stock market volatility and also helpful in determining the diversification and benefits of other assets of the industry and stock market.

Regardless of measuring tools for assessing volatility, it is also important to discuss the types of volatility in the stock market and other market sectors. There are two major types of volatility that go hand in all market sectors and the stock market, and they include:

Implied Volatility

Implied volatility is known as projected volatility, and it is used to determine metrics of the stock market and other option traders. Having implied volatility, traders and investors are able to determine the right position of industry and stock market, and they can go ahead in all of their business dealings and transactions.

In this way, traders are also able to calculate the probability of the current stock market index and related trade and industry. However, implied volatility does not work in scientific affairs; hence there is not forecasting about how the market and industry will move forward in recent conditions.

Having implied volatility, traders cannot rely on the past performance of the organization and rate of return to move on in existing market conditions. They have to make estimates about the potential of the options in the stock market.

Historical Volatility

Historical volatility is also referred to as statistical volatility, and it gauges the fluctuations of security approaches after measuring and assessing price changes over. The rise in historical volatility means the price of a security will also move to the top than its normal range.

This is the time when traders and investors expect some unusual changes in the stock market and other market sectors. If historical volatility drops down, traders are not able to move on ahead in making decisions about business development or making any investment in the industry or stock market.

Whatever the types and categories of Volatility in the stock market, it can be assessed and measured by well-known statistical tools and approaches like standard deviation, co, efficient, Beta, and making a bell-shaped curve in diagrams of measuring volatility. Investors and traders used to compare different tools of measuring and assessing volatility, and it remains helpful for them to deal with different approaches to volatility.

Volatility and risk go hand in all business sectors and stock market industries. If the volatility of the stock market is high, the risk is also higher, and if volatility goes down, then there is a low risk for making investments in the stock market.

Investors and traders need to have the most reliable and valuable tools for measuring and assessing volatility and risk involved in their business industry and the stock market. And remember a tip:

"I will tell you how to become rich. Close the doors. Be fearful when others are greedy. Be greedy when others are fearful."

– Warren Buffet

5. TOP INDICATORS OF A WINNING INVESTMENT

When it comes to stocks, people are always afraid of losing their money because of the lack of the right strategy. You can make your investment secure by applying different strategies. Some people try to learn about indicators of a winning investment, which helps them to grow their business.

If you follow the indicators in the right way and wisely, they will minimize the chances of loss and can help make more profit. These indicators are helpful for both long term and short term investment. All these indicators are present on stock market websites.

Some top indicators of a winning investment in the stock market are mentioned below:

Trend line

Type

Trend indicator

Computation

When three rising price bottoms are connected, they make an uptrend, and when three falling price bottoms are connected, they make a downtrend.

Signals

When stocks are showing above an uptrend, it means that the market is positive and bullish, but when stocks show below a downtrend, it indicates that the market is negative or bearish.

Takeaway

If you are planning for the investment, but when the market goes above, then the downtrend line. If you are looking for profit or avoiding the chances of loss, then sell when market prices go below the downtrend line.

Simple Moving Average

Type

Trend indicator

Computation

A simple moving average is simply the average fluctuation of the stock market in a selected period. Investors use this method for the long term and short term investment. People who set a plan to invest for the short term calculate average fluctuation for the last ten days.

Traders who plan for long term investment calculate average fluctuations in the stock market for the last 100 or sometimes more than 200 days.

Signals

If the stocks remain on top than long term indicators in which investors applied a simple average method of 100 to 200 days, then the stock market is considered to be positive and bullish.
So it makes it easy for the traders to have a sense of making the right decision to invest at the right time.

Takeaway

When stocks approach long term moving average, then this is the perfect time to make your investment in the stock market, but when prices go below then moving average, then this is a time to sell. This technique is really helpful for making your money secure in stocks.

Rate of change

Type
Momentum indicator

Computation
When we talk about stocks, we must have to pay close attention to the rates which are changing with time. Rate of change is one of the best indicators which is used to check for the percentage change in prices in the selected period. Most commonly, traders use 14 days rate of change indicator, which helps them to understand better.

What it signals
After calculation, the positive rate of change indicates than the stock market is now positive, and prices are rising. The negative rate of change means the stock market is negative or prices are falling.

Takeaway
Fluctuation in the rate of change indicates that stock prices will make possibly turnaround. When prices are rising, but the rate of change is not affected, it indicates the reverse of trend.

Relative strength Index

Type

Momentum indicator

Computation

The relative strength index is based on the average ratio of high prices when stock rates rise. It also includes the average ratio of low prices when the stock market falls. This indicates how much a price can rise and fall on average. On the graph, it is plotted between 0 and 100.

What does it indicate?

You will have all the information about the relative strength index by Paying close attention to the graph. If the graph rises above then 70 to 80 it indicates that stocks are overbought. If the graph falls below 30 to 20, it signals that stocks are oversold.

Takeaway

Set up a plan to make the investment if the relative strength index goes (above) than 30 to 40 twice consecutively. Sell to make a profit or avoid loss when the relative strength index goes above than 70 to 80 twice consecutively.

Moving Average Convergence Divergence

Type
Trend and momentum indicator

Computation
Convergence Divergence is a difference between twelve and twenty-six-day moving average.

What does it indicate?
If you are searching for the best way to have an idea of an upward trend and downward trend in the stock market, then moving average convergence divergence indication can help you.

If the rate of moving average convergence divergence is increasing, then this indicates an upward trend. If it is falling, it indicates a downward trend.

Takeaway
Most commonly nine days, moving average convergence divergence is considered for buying and selling stocks. Make investment when it goes above than 9-day moving average and sell when moving average convergence divergence reaches below than nine days moving average.

Bollinger Bands

Type

Fluctuation, Trend, Momentum indicator

Computation

Bollinger bands indicator is composed of three lines. The first one is 20 days moving average second one is the upper band, and the third and last one is the lower band. The two bands upper and lower are plotted in such a way that they act as two standard deviations, and their core is moving average.

What did it indicate?

If you are interested to see the trend, it is indicated by the moving average. Now the gap between these two bands, which are upper and lower, signals the fluctuations in the stocks.

Takeaway

When prices start reaching the upper band during high fluctuation in the market shows stocks are overbought. On the other hand, when prices start decreasing or falling towards the lower band due to a high rate of fluctuation, this indicates that the counter is oversold.

Fibonacci Retracements

Type

Trend indicator

Computation

Percentages 23.6%, 38.2%, and 61.8% are considered the golden ratio in the stock market, which is based on the Fibonacci number series.

What did it indicate?

Whenever a fall occurs in stocks, most often stock market retraces stock prices to an extent before it happens to the beginning of the next trend. Many investors believe that these retracements occur almost close to the Fibonacci numbers golden ratio.

Takeaway

Occurring of retracement at 23.6% indicates the strong trend of upward retracement or downward retracement. Typically retracement ends on 38.2%. If the retracement goes over than 61.8%, this is the indication that the trend is over.

All about Technical Indicators

Some technical indicators are listed below:

Trend indicators

This is one of the most advanced techniques to grab an idea of market trends such as upward trend, downward trend, and sideways trend.

Momentum Indicators

When traders want an in-depth analysis of trends, momentum indicators help them out to have a better understanding of the market. They just act as warning signals. In some cases, they might be giving the right information. It does not mean that all reduction in market momentum will lead to the trend reversal.

Volatility Indicators

Understanding of fluctuation of stocks in the stock market is a goal of every person who has invested in stocks. Volatility indicators help to understand the unpredictability of the market. It is mostly measured in standard deviation.

Volume indicators

Volume indicators play a key role in making a decision, whether it is a perfect time for making the investment or otherwise. Small traders focus on this indicator because as soon people start selling volume decreases and rates also fall, then they consider it the best time for investment.

After some time, people start buying once again and rates start rising, and they consider it the best time for selling with big profits.

On-Balance Volume

On-Balance volume is the most advanced technique used by professional and experienced traders. It is a more in-depth analysis of volume indicators. The on-Balance volumes gather all the information about the volume and setup all this information on a single-line indicator.

Now, this indicator adds up the volume on up days and also subtracts the volume, which is on down days. As a result, it assists in calculating the cumulative buying and pressure of selling.

It also tells us about the trends. The escalation in prices leads to the rising of On-Balance volume. Drop down in prices leads to the falling of On-Balance volume.

Average Directional Index

After knowing trends, it is most important to learn the concept of trend strength. Usually, it is graphed on a single line with the value ranging from 0 to 100. It is the most powerful technique which helps the investors to have a better understanding of a stronger zone.

Average Directional Index helps traders to build more confidence and aggressive position.

When the values on the graph reach above 20, it indicates the rise in the average directional index, and it represents that trend is getting stronger.

Relative Rotation Graph

This is one of the unique indicators which is used to visualize trends in the relative strength of even more than one or multiple securities against each other.

This helps to indicate relative outclass performers in the market and tell you to pay attention to the specific area of the market, which deserves the most. According to the most expert people in stocks, the relative rotation graph indicator helps to build a portfolio.

Final words

Indicators are simply the warning signals that give you certain information about different things, such as trend reversals. These can be used to have a deep understanding of the stock market. Before working on any indicator and going for the live trade, you just need to gather all the information related to that specific indicator.

 Each of the indicators can be used in many ways. Also, it can provide you with more in-depth information as long as you try to research it. It may be a tricky process for beginners who are just starting or have not started yet.

6. BASIC INVESTMENT TECHNIQUES

Investing a portion of your earnings is always a smart decision, especially in a world where nothing is permanent.

You never really know when you might end up needing your investments or savings. You don't always end up in need of them, but when you do, having a backup investment plan managed properly is a great way to sum up, your lifetime earning efforts. This way, when the hard time comes, you can be sure that you didn't work hard all your life to simply end up with nothing at all.

However, when you aren't very familiar with investment techniques, and you're more of a novice in this phase, you might end up investing your earnings in something useless or a waste of money.

Now to avoid such situations as a newbie in investing your earnings, its better you go through the basic techniques. This way, you can be sure that you'll end up investing your precious savings in something that's actually worth it.

You might think of looking for sources to help you learn these basic techniques, right? Well, you don't really have to go anywhere else, as we've got you covered with just the right basic techniques you'll need to start as a beginner in this. So let's not waste any more time and just go ahead to discover some such basic techniques.

10 Basic Investment Techniques for Beginners

1. Set a Goal

When you start investing your money, you need to firstly think of what you really want from your investment. This means that even if your basic motto is to earn money through your investment.

You should mainly determine what your income is along with your financial condition, how much you can really invest according to your circumstances, and how much profit you would need.

2. Early Investment is Beneficial

Yes, it is true, whether you're a college student or studying in high school, the sooner you consider investing in something that benefits you, the more it will get easier for you to invest with time.

This simply means that your earnings would increase over time, while the investments you make would also benefit you with the passage of time. Hence, with all these aspects, starting early would help you invest less money in the future and again more of the profit.

So it doesn't matter how less you can invest in the first place or what options you've got with the least of your savings or earnings; it's all going to benefit you over time. So just go for it as early as possible!

3. Invest a Constant Figure Automatically

Often we consider stalling and storing our money for some uses and needs, whether they're important or just something we're keen to invest in. And in such situations, we often utilize our investment money in such ways, ending up with no money to invest at all.

This gives the least motivation for investing further, and sooner when you'll notice, you'd probably forget about investing at all. But since it is really important for the upcoming time of your life, its better you go for an automatic investment option.

This way, the money you set aside for investing every month would be automatically taken from your account through brokerage service firms or automated investment services. Also, with this, if you even forget about the investment money, these services would make them don't.

4. Don't Invest Too Much

Now considering investing a great amount of your savings or earnings with the idea of having it doubled or profited into a figure that would leave you overwhelmed is good – and also something we all think of.

When you do start investing anything anywhere, it's important you snap yourself out of those fantasized dreams and get realistic.

This means that you can't go with investing a great number of your earnings without keeping your basic expenses in mind. Since you aren't sure of when the profit might arrive, and these bills are more of a constant paying need.

Hence, starting small with your investments, while calculating the money you'll need for your needs is certainly a great way to manage your earnings while also investing them.

5. Do Your Homework on Investment

Yes, we all need this, quite aware of everything basic when it comes to investment. But that's certainly not enough when you're getting ahead with choosing options and managing the dealing process on your own. Since this is more of official business, and you can't just act amateur and new in this, even when you are.

Hence, studying the basic terminology on making the right decisions and furthermore on stocks, bonds, funds, CDs, and other such investment options – is really important.

This way, you won't only learn about investment options and what suites you according to your position, but you'll also learn how you should deal with your investment and make decisions according to the market efficiency.

All this homework would certainly benefit you in the beginning, as well as for future investment needs.

6. Don't Pay High Commission

Remember this, when you go to professionals to help you look for investment options that would profit you well, you might end up being scammed by these professionals. This isn't something obvious, but as a newbie, you might end up facing these situations. Hence, to avoid it, it's important you don't blindly trust professionals who would take a high commission from you for the investment options and further process.

In this way, you might end up paying a large commission to the professionals, while being rewarded with the least of profit afterward.

Hence, before you trust any professional and their commission demands blindly, its better you study on them and research on the investment options they offer you with. This would keep you safe from any kind of loss.

7. Don't Invest in One Place/Stock

Well, investing in stocks doesn't always result in large profits, but also leads you to equal losses. However, it's in your hands if you need to limit your losses and keep it all neutral.

For this, you can always look for investment options that are completely different from what you are already investing in.

This way, when one market ends up going down for a while, the other would be up. Hence, you won't just be left with loss only, but rather both profit and loss. This would be a way of diverse investment for you, keeping you benefited with your investment at all times.

8. Invest in Long-term Options

This is highly beneficial, and that is why some top investors recommend beginners and everyone looking for basic investment techniques to always invest in long-term options. This mainly means that when you consider the short-term profits offered by a company and only do timely research on it, you might not end up gaining profits with that investment option for long.

So instead, investing in what might keep you happy and pleased for the next ten years, despite the ups and downs, are certainly the right companies you should look for. Hence, when you research on any company or investment option, make sure it is based on solid fundamentals as well as a strong and consistent long-term prospect.

9. Keep an Eye on Your Portfolio

Now before you start thinking what this basic technique is mainly referring to, let's get to the point here. So keeping a specific portfolio carried in terms of your investments is very good.

However, you can't always invest in the same place and never really go for a change. Because most of the time, we find options that are much better in the profit or the previous ones just don't profit us much anymore.

Hence, keeping track of your portfolio and changing your investment options every time the economic market changes would certainly be a smart move. This way, you can stay away from the investments that are giving you loss, even when they once offered you great profit.

And also, you can explore new options from time to time and make the most out of your money through these options.

10. Continue Research

As mentioned several times earlier, learning more on the economic market and what goes on in the present time is always a smart move in terms of investment.

This means that even when you've invested your money somewhere and have learned the most of that aspect and what's trending, you don't have to stop there.

But instead of that, reading and studying about the things you've invested in while also staying intact with the market trends sometimes, along with the global economic change – all would surely help you make smarter decisions in the future.

Final Words

Investments are the smart way everyone plans to save and benefit from their income nowadays. Whether you are old, a young entrepreneur, or just a student, you've surely come across multiple investment options several times in your life.

As much as it all seemed pleasing, beginners find investing their money anywhere a lot frightening too. A simple reason for that is the fact that they might end up losing their precious earnings or savings.

But even if you are new in something, it shouldn't be what stops you from taking a step forward. Instead, leaning the new ways of making more profit and the tons of options you've got today to invest in; is always a great way to spend your money as well as time.

Now that you've even got some basic techniques that can help you get started and going in your investment journey, there's really nothing more you should be worrying about. So without having any second thoughts, just go ahead and apply these techniques for your better future!

Pro Tip:

"Patience is the key when you are investing in the stock market."

7. WHAT YOU SHOULD KNOW ABOUT TAXES

The stock market is a great place to pour in your savings as an investment. As only with some basic skills and knowledge on this market, you can make a great profit out of it. However, that's surely not all to what it is, as there are losses too.

But that's mainly what the stock market mainly revolves around; the losses and the profits. It's never really the same, and as much as you invest in it, the more you get to have a hold on this aspect. However, learning just about the basics of what might result in a loss and what would profit you are not the only thing one should study. As when you're a beginner, you'd probably end up in situations that would ask you to understand more than just that.

Now, this can refer to a lot when it comes to learning everything about stock markets, but what I'm mainly referring to are the taxes.

Now whether you're a newbie in the stock market or someone who was around for a while now, learning the role of tax here is essential.

As only this way, you can be sure to make better investments in the right stocks; while understanding the tax criteria according to your position. So for a clearer view on everything about tax in the stock market, let's discuss some basics below.

The Long-term Capital Gains Rate Criteria

This tax rate is mainly applied to your profit, which is less in comparison to the rate that is applied to your other income that applies a tax. As an example, if your tax rate is 15%, you're most likely to pay a tax of 5% on your stock's profit.

Whereas, if you've got a tax rate of 25% to pay, then your profits tax rate would be 15%. However, this tax rate is mainly applied to the profit kept for a year or more, which is gained by the sale of your stock.

But that's not the tax rate applied to the profit from stock selling that is kept for less than a year. As instead, when you've got profit stored for less than a year, you're more likely to pay the tax rate for it, which is equal to the ordinary tax rate you pay on your income.

Reducing Tax on your Stock Sales

Here is a point to remember, when you determine the profit of your stock sale in a specific calculations method, you are more likely to understand the exact meaning of the variables in the formula. This mainly means that you can plan the exact amount in a way that you reduce the liability of the tax, when you sell your stock.

Now, most of the time, we consider the full amount of the check received after selling stock to be the one that we should pay a tax on. However, that's certainly not the complete truth, as there are ways you can subtract the amount of tax you pay according to how much you can.

A simple formula to get this done is to subtract the basis of your tax amount to the sales you've received, and you'll get a deductible loss or a taxable profit you can eliminate from this profit of yours. This way, you won't really end up losing too much of the unexpected tax from your profit, especially when you don't even want to.

Now one might consider how they can really reduce the sales proceeds in all this calculation so that you don't pay too much tax, right?

Well, a simple and obvious way to do that is to pay some commission to a broker who would help you get through this. So instead of paying too much on the tax, you can pay a little in order to make sure you can get along with this formula of reducing your sales tax.

Next, is the basis in the formula just mentioned? Well, if you're still wondering what that might refer to, and then you can consider it to be the main cost of the stock you'll be selling. However, that's not all, as it can also include the dividends that you've reinvested in the stock or the commissions you pay to the opposition.

Yet, in some cases, if you've inherited a stock, then the basis would simply be determined as the fair market value of the stock after the date of the decedent's death. Also, if you've received the stock as a gift to you from someone, then you can consider the basis to be a lower amount of the fir-market value, according to its value, at the time the gift was sent to you.

Experimenting with the Wash Rule

Now you might have heard of this rule in the stock market, but understanding it from a closer perspective is also very important.

Since we're mainly discussing taxes in the stock market, this rule also revolves around just that.

However, it's mainly the practice of selling a stock for profit when you're in the position of gaining loss from it, and when you do sell it and gain the profit, you buy it back instantly.

Now, this isn't really what the rule mainly is, but rather where you can apply it in your stock affairs. Hence, with the help of the 'wash rule,' you get to prevent the loss you'd get on the sale of a stock if you buy its replacement stock in the time period of 30 days.

This mainly helps you get out of the limitations applied by the IRS; that doesn't allow an investor to claim the loss after selling stock and then buying it again in less than 30 days. Hence, when you've got the 'wash rule,' you can make less loss through a stock.

Deduction of Capital Losses

When you face losses in your stock market, you are allowed to deduct an amount with respect to the losses from your tax returning amount. Now as much as this is a benefiting factor of the stock market, you're also supposed to face some limitation here.

This means that you are only allowed to gain a specific amount of your losses through the tax return every year. Hence, no matter how many stocks you sell at a loss, you are going to be able to deduct only $3,000 per year. And the rest of your loss would be taken forward to provide to you in the coming years.

However, if you're willing to first calculate all your losses and gains through this specific limitation and understanding how what you'll be ending up with, you can always apply the capital losses against the capital gains you achieve — both in the present year and the one's coming afterward.

Other Deductible Expenses in Investment

Often we don't pay attention to a specifically less tax deduction from our profits, which is mainly the commission of the brokers in the stock market. However, these aren't just any brokers, but rather the one's who either manage our mutual fund account or simply provide us with advisory services in the stock market. And so, this tax amount is deducted as a fee for their services offered to us.

But if you don't feel like allowing the deduction of this fee, then you've always got a long-term option of having these fees deducted back to your account. This deduction to provide your fees back to you can take place as an investment expense on Schedule A, which would be possible on your tax return.

Now in terms of understanding the exact amount deducted from your profit for the brokers fees, you'll need to do a little work. This doesn't mean proper research and study on it, as most of the broker fees depend upon the 1099s of year-end statements – where you can find a statement provided on the total charged fee for a year.

But since many brokers do not follow this criterion, you might simply have to contact your broker and ask them for how much fee you paid. This way, you can have a clear idea of how much you would want to take back as the deduction.

Final verdict

Almost everyone nowadays considers the stock market as a great source of investment and profit income. And so, we'd quite often notice how most of the surrounding people are a part of this market. And why not? When there's such a huge stock market available for you to invest, and gain profit from, there's hardly any reason one should step back from it.

However, even with all the pros on might consider this hugely benefited market, there are certainly some loopholes one should consider before stepping into it. Now one obvious one here might be the fact that you might lose just as much as you would gain (unless you don't master the investing techniques). But other than that, the tax factor in the stock market is also something one should study about; before you end up noticing that your profits have lessened.

Now keeping that in mind and the fact that not many consider the taxing of their stocks to be as important of an enlightening subject for them as others in this aspect, we've aligned everything important you should learn about. Now keeping that in mind and the fact that not many consider the taxing of their stocks to be as important of an enlightening subject for them as others in this aspect; hence, just go ahead; and make the most of it!

8. ALL ABOUT THE BULL & BEAR MARKET

Incorporate the world; you must have heard the words Bull and Bear; this is a general description for dual market conditions rise and down. Simply, a bull market is just about the market is on the rise, and its economy is sound and stable, whereas a bear market describes the down condition of the economy in which stocks are in decline in value.

This particular name and the term is used to describe what markets are doing in general, and what its positions in the current situation are. Bull and Bear also narrate about appreciation and depreciation of market value. Investors and traders are also given names as Bullish and Bearish according to the particular market conditions.

Bull and Bear both names are just phrases that indicate the current condition and situation of the market; hence, the behavior and mentality of investors and traders can also be judged in a particular scenario. If the market is the Bull, the investors would be named as Bullish, but if the market is bear, then they would be called Bearish.

There is a historical background behind these particular terms and names of market conditions, and they are related to the psychology and gestures of both animals bear and bull. However, it is also said that actual expression for these terms is just unclear right now, but it can be described according to the bull and bear's action.

For example, a bull is always seen to attack by its horns upwards while the bear is analyzed the attacking swap its paws downwards. So these factors can be considered for giving names to market conditions; up and down.

Actions of both animals are related metaphorically to the market conditions. If the economy is up, it would be considered a bull market, and if the stock goes down, it would be named as a bear market.

Whatever the origin of these phrases and terms, they are interesting and seen to be rational in the corporate world. Our next discussion would be based on all about the bull and bear market. What market conditions and indicators can fall in both types of terms or categories? So, keep reading the following lines for the interesting narration of the bull and bear market.

Some usual indicators of the bull market include:

High Gross Domestic Products

This is simply a usual indicator for a well-established, stable, sound, and flourishes economy as it is bull market condition. In this particular condition, GDP remains high; hence consumer spending is also upward.

Rising Stock Prices

Rising stock prices leave a very good impact on the mentality and behavior of people associated with bull market conditions, and they get more confident in making investments in the industry. Prices and rates are also increased in this particular market condition.

Longer Stock Trading

The whole environment and climate of the market last cool and hopeful, so investors feel free to busy their shares on more business sides. This is the reason this condition is related to longer stock trading terms.

Lower Unemployment Rates

In bull market condition, more and more people are hired on jobs, and there is no concept of unemployment. Up-gradation of business means there is a growth in the workforce, and most people are hoping to be a part of the good ear of industry.

Another good point of bull market conditions is that it remains longer than bear market conditions. Not only this, but the average total return for a bull market is also seen to grow. If we see a global scenario of bull market conditions, we can find notable examples of bull market conditions in the corporate world historically. Like:

The Bull Market History

The 1940s-1950s

It was a time after post second World War, and it was the bull market condition when the US economy was at the top, and most of the soldiers were returned to their homes.

1980s-2000s

This was also a golden period for US economic conditions, and it was a bull market when a 600% average return rate was determined to be gained in the overall corporate world.

Today

US economic conditions have consistently grown up since 2017. This is also said to be a golden era of the corporate world in the United States as jobs are always available over there, average returns for investment have grown up, investors are always ready to put their part in trading activities and business.

So this is a bull market in a nutshell; however, whatever the condition of the bull market is, it can exist with a bear market. Further, we are going to describe the same information about the bear market. So don't leave it without reading the following lines.

In contrasts to the bull market, a bear market is just all about going down, getting pessimism, the condition of trade is stagnation, trends are down, people are not confident and insecure, stocks are sold rather than buying, etc. This is a bear market condition where there are no jobs, no hope, no business planning at all.

The Bear Market Indicators

Some usual indicators for the bear market include:

Fall down of Market Prices

Investors and traders become bearish in a bear market, and they are not willing to buy a new share of the business that results in complete fall down in market prices, and stability of industry as well.

Complete Unemployment

Unavailability of jobs or relatively low rates of employment is a clear sign of bear market. Fall down of companies and shareholders results in layoffs and downfall of the workforce as well.

Shorter Stock Trading

In the bear market, stock trading conditions get more bearish, and investors do not buy and sell stock shares. The industry stops at all.

Although a bear market is seen to be very bad, it does not last long at all. A study by Morningstar reveals the fact that average bear market conditions last just for 1.4 years in the history of the corporate world.

Regardless of indicators and facts about the bear market, there are several notable examples of the bear market that last in the history of the US economy.

The Bear Market History

1929s

During this session of the year, the US economy was seen to be paralyzed entirely as there were no jobs; people get homeless and lost wellbeing. Not only America but the entire world was impacted by the bear market conditions in the United States in 1929.

The 2000s

This was the time when there was a severe downfall of tech companies in the United States, and it was called a bear market.

2008s

2008 was the time for the housing market crash. This was a severe bear market as there were no jobs, homeowners lost their homes and traders get empty and fail to even think about investing in stock shares. This bad bear market is felt till now the United States has come into the bull market.

Investors and traders are always seen scary about the bear market as it is a scary and empty region in the corporate world, but it does not last long as we have seen in the previous history of the United States economic survey and information.

From our discussion put above, you can now better understand a clear difference between the Bull and Bear have. Both conditions are contrary but go hand in hand with each other.

You know, up and downs are parts of life, and everyone has to go through both of these phases, whether it relates to the personal life of an individual or it is associated with a corporate world. We can say that the Bull and Bear market reflect the general overview and behavior of practical life.

Don't you think that this particular term or name of market conditions be pretty much interesting? These market conditions are associated with the attack actions of two animals Bull and Bear.

Well, the importance and existence of both the Bull and Bear market are undeniable, but both animals are remarkable for their incredible and unpredictable strength to attack and defense. Some facts reveal the evidence of Bull and Bear market concept from the era of Elizabeth and ancient times when bull and bear were together to entertain the people come in the crowd.

The fight between Bull and Bear are famous in this regard, and this is the reason both market conditions are named accordingly.

So, what does bull and bear market means for you become important to ask after giving you solid facts and information about bull and bear market? Hopefully, this would be pretty much enough about the bull and bear market. Good luck with your investment!

9. COMMON STOCK EXCHANGE TERMS
AND WHAT THEY MEAN

If you are planning to start investing your money in the stock market, then there are some common stock exchange terms that you must know. These terms are very important in understanding of the behavior of the stock market.

You should also have known the basics before diving onto the live trade. If you want to become a successful trader, these terms will assist you in achieving your goals and building your career in the stock market.

What is the Stock Market?

In short, any exchange allows people to buy and selling of stocks and give permission to companies to issue stocks to people. Stocks represent the company's ownership or equity. Shares are the units of the company. When people invest in the stock market, it means that they have bought shares of one or more than one stock.

What does the stock exchange terms mean?

Stock exchange terms are slang specifically for industry security. Professionals and expert traders use these terms to talk about different game plans, patterns, charts, and many other related elements of the stock market industry.

Common stock exchange terms are listed below:

1-Annual Report

The annual report is specifically made by the company for its shareholders. This report is designed in such a way that it attracts the shareholders. The annual report carries all the information about the company's shares and their game plan for the present and future. When you are going through the annual report, you are gathering information about the company's financial situation.

2- Arbitrage

This is one of the most advanced terms in the stock market, which every trader should know. This refers to buying stocks at a low price from one market and selling at a higher rate on another market.

For example, sometimes a stock ABC trade on $50 on one market, and the same stock on the other market trade on $55 so traders buy shares on low price points and sell them on higher rates to make the profit.

3-Averaging Down

When stock prices fall, and you plan to buy stocks on lower rates, your average buying prices decrease. This strategy is used most commonly in the stock market. After buying, you plan to sell those stocks shares when the stock market rebounds.

4- Bear Market

A bear market is opposite to Bull market. It means that the overall market is negative or falling. In this stage, the market falls up to 20% the quarter after quarter. This is one of the scariest situations for big investors because their investments are at great risk.

5- Bull Market

Bull Market is opposite to the bear market. Bull market meant the rising of the stock points. In this stage, people start investing money in the stock market because they were positive behavior.

6- Beta

This is the whole relationship between the stocks and the overall market. If stock ABC has a beta of 5.5, it means that for every one-point movement in the market, the stock ABC moves 5.5 points and vice versa.

7- Blue Chip Stocks

These are the stocks that large backup companies and leading industries. Blue-chip stocks are well known for their management and sound records. This expression is thought to be derived from casinos where blue gambling chips are used.

8- Bourse

In short, Bourse is a modern and more advanced name of the stock market. It means where people gather for the purchasing and selling of stock shares. Most commonly, it refers to Parries stock exchanges or non-US stock exchanges.

9- Broker

Many people who are beginners and don't understand the behavior of the stock market, that make contact with different brokers. These brokers are experienced traders who have sound knowledge of tradingstocks. These beginners contact these brokers and ask them to buy and sell stocks for them. Brokers charge high commissions for these services.

10- Bid

Bidding is as common and simple as we do in freelance and other daily projects. In stock market bidder, who is a buyer bid for a specific share. Bid means the buyer willing to buy the share on his desired rates. The bid is made according to the asking price of the seller.

11- Close

Simply this refers to the time when trading will stop, and the stock market will close. Its timings vary from country to country. Each stock market has its own time of closing and opening. After closing the stock market, it is not available for live trade.

12- Day trading

This is one of the most advanced terms in the stock market. Day trading refers to buying and selling of stocks shares on the same day. This method is used by many experienced traders.

After buying shares, people wait for the next day to sell them at much higher rates. But there are 50/50 chances that they may end up with profit or loss. So, Day trading is a smart strategy, but it requires a lot of experience to make profits.

13- Dividend

Many companies offer incentives to attract more traders to their company. Some companies pay their shareholders one of their earnings portions, which are called the dividend. Some companies pay dividends annually or quarterly. Not all companies offer a dividend.

14- Exchange

Exchange refers to a place where thousands of investments are traded daily. There are many popular exchanges in the world. New York Stock Exchange is one of the most popular exchanges in the world, which is present in the United States of America.

15- Execution

We are familiar with this term in the sense of computer where it means the completion of a task. In the stock market, it also acts the same as in the said case. When a trader buys or sells stock shares, after completion, it is said that the transaction has been executed.

16- Haircut

The haircut is the most known term used in the stock market. It is the slight difference between the bids made by the buyer and the asking price of the seller.

17- High

High indicates the milestone reached by the stocks. It points out that the specific stock has never reached such a high price before. In the stock market, there is also one other high. This high is used to demonstrate the milestone reached by stocks in a specific period. It may be fortnightly or in 30 days.

18- Initial Public Offering

Initial Public Offering means that when a company decides to expand its business and offers its stocks available for the public. The Securities Exchange Commissions is responsible for issuing Initial Public offering and is very strict against its rules.

19- Leverage

Leverage is considered the riskiest and dangerous game tom plays in the stock market. After having your complete research, you decide to borrow shares from your broker and set up a plan to sell them on higher rates. If you successfully sell those shares on higher rates, you again return those borrowed shares to the broker and keep the difference.

20- Low

Low is opposite to high. It indicates that the specific stocks have never fallen to this price before. Low is also demonstrated for a specific period may be weekly or monthly.

21- Margin

Margin is almost the same as that of leverage. It is also considered one of the riskiest game. It is an account that allows you to borrow money from the broker to invest that money into the stocks. Now the difference between the loan which you borrowed from the broker and rates of the securities is called margin.

Margin is not for beginners; even the most experienced traders fail to apply this strategy.

22- Moving Average

Moving average is the average price of the stock shares at a specific time. 50 and 200 are considered the best common time frames to study the behavior of the moving average.

23- Open

Simply open refers to the time when the stock market is open for the live trade. Traders start buying and selling of stocks according to their plans. This varies from country to country. Every stock market has its own time to open and close.

24- Order

Order is the same as bid, but in the order, you decide to buy or sell stock shares according to your plan after deciding your order to sell or buy the stocks. For example, if you are willing to buy 200 shares, then you have to make an order.

25- pink sheet stocks

Many beginners take start with pink sheet stocks. If you are just planning to invest in this stock market, you most probably have listened to pink sheet stocks. These are penny stocks and are traded on a small scale, and each share price is $5 or even less than that. Because these are the shares of smaller company's, you will not find them on the big markets such New York Stock Exchange.

26- Sector

There are dozens of companies that belong to the same industry. These companies are available publically in the stock market to buy their shares. These stocks groups which belong to the same industry are called sectors.

Many experienced traders trade in a single sector, such as cement or steel. There are many advantages to investing in the same sector because it is much easy to predict the fluctuations.

10.   TIPS AND TRICKS FOR INVESTING IN THE STOCK EXCHANGE

Almost everyone is searching for a shortcut, which leads them to success. Its human nature, we always look for miracles that can change everything. When it comes to the stock market, people are scared of losing their investments. They find ways that could become beneficial for them to secure their investments and make a profit.

Avoiding loss in stocks is not an easy task, and even sometimes, experienced traders fail to achieve their goals. With time by learning more and more about stock market behavior is the only way to get success.

There are some pro tips and tricks for investing in stock exchange which every trader should know:

1- Invest in Index Fund

One of the most important tips for investing is to invest in index fund instead of looking to invest in individual stocks. It also depends upon your goals, but investing in individual funds is not a good approach.

If you are taking stocks on a serious note, then investing in index fund in a specific sector can be a great way to build your portfolio. It also helps to focus on one thing. There are some important points to remember while investing in index fund. These are expense ratio and assets in total.

2- Focus on Mutual Funds

It is a well-known saying that putting all eggs in one basket is always the worst choice. When you are planning to buy some stocks shares, do remember not to invest in single stocks. Always find good growth mutual funds and put your money in it. This approach is the most secure one, but it seems boring and time taking. But many people love to focus on mutual funds. This technique helps to minimize the chances of losing investment.

3- Timing the Market

Many beginners think there are sometimes when the selling or buying of stocks can make them profits. They all end up losing their money. Learning market volatility is not an easy task. Some experienced traders also believe that timing the market is not a good way to dominate in the stock market. You have to experience about market fluctuations and sell or buy stocks accordingly. There is no best and worst time to buy or sell stock shares.

4- Set Goals

Setting up goals is always the best method that every person should follow, which leads to success. People without goals are like blind people. Before diving into the stock market, first, you should set the goals of your investments. When you have set a long term plan, then you will have a better understanding of what to do and how to reach the destination.

5- Five Golden steps of trading to learn:

- Setup:A setup is composed of a high probability pattern to follow on the chart. It also ensures the reason why you are considering a trade. You need to track them to make sure that how consistent they are.

• Strategy: There must be a way to trade the setup and the perfect plan for it, which seems to be working. Beginners should always work on the strategies and spend time on it.

• Entry: Entry can make a big difference. If you enter the right way, then you will end up making a profit. On the other hand, the wrong entry will lead you to make run out of money.

• Stop: There should always be a stopping point when you are going through live trade. This whole thing should be pre-planned, and you should know why you are going to stop.

• Profit Target: When things start getting right in your favor, you sometimes make bad decisions. Instead of regretting later on, make decisions to set a profit target.

6- Have a balance of investments

There are three types of investments, which are low, high, and moderate risk investments. All these investments have some pros and cons. Keeping a balance between these three risky investments can be a wise approach. If you are just starting, then prefer to invest in low-risk investments.

As soon as you get some experience, move to the moderate and then high-risk investments. Low-risk investments can make you small profits, Instead of losing all of your money in high-risk investments, consider low and moderate risk investments.

7- Think for long term

We always look for short term methods which can make big profits. But in reality, these things are nothing. So always plan for the long term. Try to invest your time in learning the behavior of the stocks to make more profits in the long run.

8- Buy value stocks

Value stocks mean stocks that are established with minimum variations. If you want to get success in the stock market, you need to learn the volatility of the stocks. Buying value stocks can make your investments much safer and secure. While looking for value stocks, consider their earning ration and price to sales ratio.

9- Diversify investments among sectors

No one can predict the stock market uncertainty. A sudden change in the country or even abroad can affect the stock market. This sudden change may be a political activity, a storm, a disaster, or any unusual thing. Diversification of investments among sectors is a proven way to minimize the chances of losing investments.

10- How much risk you can take?

Before start trading, you should make your mind clear that how much risk you can take. There are some pros and cons of this strategy. This strategy helps to have a better understanding of your game plan. Whether you are going for long term or you have made your plan for the long term in both cases, you need to be clear about how much risk you can bear.

11- Control your emotions

One of the key activities to achieve your goals in the stock market is to be patient. The stock market is considered one of the most uncertain market. No one knows what will happen in the next minute. People lose millions in seconds.

To control your emotions at that time is a hard task. But to become a mature trader, you must value stocks and able to see your pocket running out of money. With a relaxed mind, you can set a plan B and C to get things in the right direction.

12- 360 Degree View

Experienced traders always dive deep into learning more about stocks every day. This is the reason because of which you gain more and more experience. Whether you are buying or selling stocks shares, you must be aware of what you are doing.

You must be clear about what its outcomes will be. There must be some strategies for the sudden uncertainty to keep you stable in the market.

13- Automate stocks

Automating your stocks is a key activity to gain more experience in the stock market. It also helps to build your security and play on the safe side. If you are not willing to do it manually, then Robo-Advisors are always there to assist you. When you have a habit of regular investments, then you also avoid timing the market strategy.

14- Say no to leverage

Leverage simply refers to start investing in stocks by borrowing money. There are many ways to borrow money. For example, you can also borrow from brokerage firms. Some people who are new to the stock market use this method to start their stock market journey. There are bright chances of their failure because of high risks are involved. This strategy can do work for you when you have gained much experience in stocks.

15- Choose one sector

Investing in one sector can be a better approach. Professional traders always invest in one sector. There are many advantages to investing in one sector. If your focus is on one industry, you will learn more in a short time. You will also start getting familiar with the fluctuations in the industry.

16- Risk vs. Return

Simply, more risky investments always have chances of big profits. On the other hand, less risky investments have small profit margins. So, you have to be clear with your game plan that how much return; you are willing to have. People always make foolish mistakes and goes for high-profit margins and lose their money. So instead of regretting at that time, invest in between high and low-risk investments.

17- Buy low sell higher

This is the most well-known method which almost all the traders apply. But some people get wrong with this strategy, and instead of making a profit, they end up with the loss. One of the most important factors to consider while buying low price stocks is to calculate their standard deviation.

If the stocks in which you are interested in buying to have a 15% standard deviation, you are good to go. It will be a better strategy if your stock standard deviation falls below then 15% in a short period. There are bright chances of that specific stock that now it will go up.

Final Word

Many people believe that stocks are a scam, but if you set up things in the right direction, then these stocks can make you more profit than any other business in the world. All you need is not to focus on investing your money in the stock market, but you need to invest your time to learn the stock market. No one can ever predict with 100% surety about the stocks.

But by gaining more experience, you can understand the behavior of stocks and learn about the fluctuations. Before going for the live trade, considers all the above-mentioned tips and tricks for investing in the stock market to make your journey in stocks successful.

CONCLUSION

Thank you for downloading my book on stock market investment. It is a self-help book for newbies who want to start as investors and make money. Filled with top rules, regulations, important terms, and strategies that one should know before jumping into the investment game, the book encompasses all the beneficial information needed for new investors.

Here is one question for you, may I ask? What did you learn from this book? Can you recall?
Here is what I tell everyone to remember while investing in the stock exchange:

"Rule number one: Don't lose money. Rule number two: Don't forget rule number one."

Warren Buffett

How can you make this sure? Follow the set of advice, suggestions, and guidelines given in this book. Hope you found it helpful and worthy to keep. Please do not forget to give us your feedback, so we can improve further.

THANK YOU, HAPPY INVESTING!

OPTIONS TRADING

FOR BEGINNERS

Trade for a living and earn extra passive income. Invest from home, learn how to swing trade stocks. Tips on risk management. Get financial freedom with a positive ROI in 7 days

---

MARK BROKER

INTRODUCTION

Out of many misconceptions, one that surrounds many markets is options are risky. Well, if you ask an options trader, he won't agree to this. The reason is if options trading were risky, it would have been an obsolete concept in the market. Why are more and more traders and investors jumping into this business?

There is just fear that makes people think that options are not profitable. All you need to do is grab all the concepts carefully and apply them when needed. Moreover, make sure you pick the right strategy and at the right time.

"Investing should be more like watching paint dry or watching grass grow. If you want excitement, take $800 and go to Las Vegas." - Paul Samuelson

Have some patience since investment is no joke! According to a ballpark estimate, a beginner needs at least one to two years to become a highly successful trader.

You can rely on this beginners' guide book on options trading that contains all the basic concepts, tips, techniques, solutions related to options trading. Read the theory carefully and then implement the concepts given in it one by one. Here is an authentic mantra to options trading:

Whenever you make a trading strategy, think it through at least three times before your final call – this is the real recipe to success!

1. OPTIONS TRADING BASICS

"Never invest in a business you cannot understand," says Warren Buffett, the famous American Investor, and we agree to him! That's why we shall start from scratch for you in this book.

In this chapter, you will learn the basics of Options Trading with examples. We suggest you take notes of the new concepts you come across in here so you could absorb more than expected.

Here is a Pro Tip: Focus on the concepts and terms given in this. This will help you grab the basics really well. So, shall we start?

What Options Trading is?

At first, options trading looks overpowering, but it is very easy to understand if you start from scratch. By that we mean if you start from concept to concept.

Basically, traders' portfolios are created with different asset categories. For instance, they may be ETFs, stocks, mutual funds, and bonds, etcetera. Options are sort of an asset category with many frills. Meaning, they can give you more benefits than ETFs and stocks.

Uses of Options

Options can make a trader powerful. It is because they can add to a trader's income, leverage, and protection. For every investor, there is an option scenario present. For instance, one can use options as a beneficial hedge against a falling stock market in order to limit the losses. They can also be utilized to make recurring earnings. Besides, options are also used for 'speculative purposes' like betting on the movement of stocks, etcetera.

With bonds and stocks, there isn't anything such as free lunch. Options are also not different. It involves risk, and investors should be well-aware of this.

Derivatives

Derivatives are considered as a 'bigger' group of securities – and options belong to them. A derivative's price is 'derived' from something else. For instance, ketchup is the derivates of tomatoes, and fries are the derivative of potatoes. Similarly, a stock option is the derivates of stocks, while options are derived from financial securities.

Some of the examples of derivate include puts, calls, mortgage-backed securities, futures, swaps, forwards, and more.

So, what you understand by options?

- Options are basically contracts. They allow buyers the rights (not obligations) to purchase or sell (in case of a call or put) a specific asset at a certain price or before specified expiry date.
- Investors use them for generating income, hedging risks, or speculating.
- They are called derivatives. The reason is options derive their value from underlying assets.
- A (stock option) contract typically has 100 shares of (an underlying) stock, but they may be written on any type of underlying asset from currencies, bonds to commodities.

Options Trading Characteristics

All Options Expire

Remember, all options expire one day. This means they 'DIE' after the expiration day. This expiry could be after two days or two years. Meaning, traders need to think about the expiry time before buying an option.

Stocks can be held for life, on the other hand.

All Options Have a Strike Price

There is a 'strike price' for every option. This is the prince in which an option can be converted into 'shares of stock.' For instance, if there is a strike price set for an option at $109. You can use the option to buy/sell shares of stock at this strike price.

Option Contract Multiplier

Let us suppose there is a share of stock with a price of $105. It can be purchased at $105. When an option is $6.00, It CANNOT be purchased at $6.00. You would rather need $600 to buy this.

The reason is options can be traded with 100 shares of stock. Meaning, you need to multiply an option price with 100 to attain its 'premium.'

Types of Options

Options trading has immense upward potential with limited risk. There are two main types of Options.

- Call Options

Call option price shows an upward movement when the stock price increases, and it starts to go down when the stock price goes down. Meaning, you can say that it is directly proportional to stock prices.

Call Option Price moves with the Stock price!

One can share 100 shares of stock with the strike price of a Call Option. Let us suppose that there is a rental apartment, and its price is $200,000. You want to purchase this apartment, thinking that its value will be doubled after some time. However, you do not want to pay the full price of this apartment.

What to do?

You can purchase a 'Call Option' for this apartment. This option will allow you to make this purchase (of amount $200,000) in 24 months. But this process will involve a contract, and you will have to pay for that contract.

This financial contract is known as 'Option.'

So, the strike price of this option will be $200,000 with the expiration date of 24 months. The advantage of this is if the apartment price rises during this period, it won't affect you (you will not have to pay extra on that).

Now, let us imagine that the opposite happens. The price of the apartment does not increase in value. Rather it decreases after 24 months to $150,000.

In this case, you are not forced to buy the apartment because you have the option not to buy it. With the decreased price of $150,000 in mind, you will not opt to purchase it at the strike price of $200,000.

Since you paid for the contract at a minimal price (the contract), you only lose that. Now compare this loss with the option to buy the house by paying the full price at once. You would have lost $200,000 or (at least $50,000), wouldn't you?

What is Call? What is Put?

A call option allows an investor the right to purchase stock, while the put option allows him to sell it. Here is an example of the Call option. A person may be interested in purchasing a new apartment in a new building under construction near his locality. However, he would only want to pay for it once the construction work is complete.

That person can take advantage of his purchase option. Through option, he can purchase it from the owner in the next four years at (let us say) $400,000 as a down payment. This cost will be called "premium."

Here is a put example. Suppose you buy a home, and with that, you also purchase a homeowner's insurance policy. This policy helps to protect your property against damage. You have to pay a premium for this for a fixed period of time. This premium is highly valuable, and it helps to protect the insurance holder in case of a home accident.

Suppose, instead of an apartment, your asset was index investment or stock. So, if a trader wants to buy insurance on his S & P 500 Index, he can buy put options.

Suppose again that you foresee bear market in the future, and you do not want to lose more than 10 or 11 percent in that Index. If the Index trades at $2800 (for instance), you can buy a put option, which will make you eligible to sell the Index at $2550 at any point before the expiration date.

This will help reduce your loss. Even if the market drops at zero, your loss would not be more than 10 percent, in case you hold the put option.

Buying and Selling

Options allow you to do four things:

- Sell Calls
- Sell Puts
- Buy Calls
- Buy Put

Keep these four scenarios in mind because this is important when you enter the trading business. Purchasing stock offers a long position for investors. But buying a call option can extend your position (it can make it even longer). Short selling offers a shorter position. In an underlying stock, selling an uncovered call also gives a short position.

Similarly, buying puts also makes a short position for you in the underlying stocks. While selling naked puts offers you a longer position.

Remember that buyers of options are known as holders, and sellers of options are known as option 'Writers.'

1. There is no obligation on call and put holders to buy or sell. They have their rights. The only risk for them is to spend money on buying premium.

2. However, it is important to call and put writers to buy and sell in case their option expires. This means they can make more, but they also have a higher risk level than holders.

2. WHY TRADE WITH OPTIONS

Options trading first started in 1973. They can give a lot of benefits to individual traders, though they have a reputation for being risky. Well, you must be thinking, what are those benefits, aren't you? Here is the answer to this.

The Benefits of Options Trading

Although options have been around for quite a time now, most investors still 'fear' using them. The reason is less information and incorrect use. Meaning, if you have good knowledge of all the basics of options (like we are providing here), you are more likely to succeed as an investor.

Individual investors should be aware of the correct usage and benefits of options before blindly following the rumors that options are 'risky.'

Options have Low Risk

Some situations call for high risk for buying options than having equities. However, there are also scenarios when using options trading becomes the best strategy. This also depends on how properly you use them. Options need low financial commitment than equities. Moreover, they are impervious, which promises less risk.

Another quality of options is compared with stocks; options are safer. They are protected by stock-loss order. This order helps to halt losses under a predetermined price indicated by the trader. However, the nature of the order also matters a lot.

Let us suppose a trader purchases a stock investing $50. He does not want to lose more than 10 percent; he places a $45 stop order. It becomes a market order when the stock trades below this price. This order can work during the daytime, not during night time.

For instance, stocks close at $51, but the next day, you hear bad news about stocks like the company owner lies about earnings or there is embezzlement noted. Stocks might open down at $20. If this happens, this price would be the first trade below the investor's stop order price. The trader would sell at this price ($20), locking in the loss.

For his protection, if the trader had bought the put, he would not have suffered from that loss. Options do not close when the market goes down and closes. This happens with stop orders. Meaning, stop orders close if the market shuts down.

Options keep the traders covered 24/7. Stop orders cannot provide insurance 24 hours. This is why options are considered as a 'dependable form of hedging.'

Options are More Cost-Effective

With greater leveraging power, options can help save you a lot of money. You can attain an option position the same as you obtain a stock position. To buy 200 shares of a stock worth $80, you have to pay $16,000, for instance. But if you want to buy double calls worth $20 (representing 100 shares contract), the total expenditure would be $4000. How?

Try this formula: 2 contracts multiply by 100 shares divided by contract x $20 price in the market. You will have an additional $12,000 for use at your discretion.

Although this is not so simple, it requires a good understanding and good strategy. You will need to pick the right call at the right time to buy for mimicking the stock position in the correct manner. This strategy is known as Stock Replacement, which is not only viable but also cost-effective and practical.

Let's suppose you want to buy Schlumberger (SLB), thinking that it might increase in value in the next few months. You think you should buy 200 shares and the company is trading at $131. So, your overlay would be $26,200.

Instead of investing such a heavy amount, you could pick options to mimic the stocks and buy a call option called, August – using only a $100 strike price for $34.

If you want to acquire a position equal to the size of 200 shares that are mentioned above, you need to purchase double contracts. Your total investment for this would be $6,800, instead of $26,200. (Here is how: double contacts x 100 shares/contract x market price of $34). You can also get interested on this or use your money for another investment.

Options Offer Higher Returns

Options trading promises higher percentage returns. Traders do not need a calculator to find this. They can invest a low amount and get a higher amount back.

Let us consider the above use case to compare the return on investment. Traders need to purchase stocks for $50 and an option for $6. Suppose options price changes by 80 percent (of the stock price). If stocks move up to $5.5, a trader will get a 10 percent return. But the option would gain 80 percent of the stock price of $4.5. A return of this kind on $6 investment amounts to 67.5 percent, which is much better than a 10 percent profit on stocks.

More Alternatives with Options

Traders can find more investing alternatives with options. They are highly flexible. There are many strategies to recreate synthetic option positions.

These positions offer investors a plethora of ways to obtain their investment goals. Besides synthetic positions, options have many other alternatives. For instance, many investors work with brokers who charge a little margin for shorting stocks. Other traders work with them (brokers) who do not wish to short stocks.

The incapability to do the downside when required limits traders and investors. However, no broker can rule against traders for buying puts in order to 'play the downside.' This is a big benefit for investors.

Options also allow traders to trade the 'third dimension' of the market. Interestingly, they can even trade-in 'no direction,' stock movements, and during volatility. Mostly, stocks do not show 'big' moves; but investors have the edge to trade in stagnation too. Thus, options can only offer multiple alternatives that can give them profit in all types of markets.

Why Options are a Better Choice?

Still, if you want to know why options are a better choice, read this out:

Hedging

The main purpose of inventing options was hedging. It helps to reduce risk. So, take options as your insurance policy. Like you insure your car and home, options can ensure your investment in case of a downfall movement.

Suppose a trader wants to buy something related to tech stocks. But he also wants to limit his loss. The trader can do these easy throughput options, which give him two benefits: minimize risk and maximize profit. Short selling can also reduce loss at the time of a downturn.

Speculation

The ability to predict the future price is speculation, as its name hints. You might think that the price of a stock would go down in a day, based on technical or fundamental analysis. He might sell the stock or sell put after the speculation.

This has got an attraction for many investors to call options because it offers leverage. A call option (out of the money) may cost only some cents of a few dollars compared to the $100 stock's full price.

How does Options Trading work?

When weighing option contracts, it is important to determine the future probabilities. Options get costlier when there is higher predictability in the future. For example, when a stock value rises, the call value also increases. This is crucial to understand the value of options.

A shorter expiry means a lower value of an option as the chances of price rise diminish as the expiry comes near. If a trader purchases an out-of-money 1-month option, while stocks do not move, it losses its value. It is because time is money when it comes to options trading. This wasting con of options is called 'time decay.'

Similarly, if a trader buys an option with a longer expiry; the chances of price movement for that option becomes brighter and brighter as there is enough time for the price to get bigger.

The price also goes up with volatility. When the market is uncertain, the odds get higher. If an asset's volatility goes up, price swings maximize the probability of substantial movements both up and downwards.

Higher price swings also up the chances of an occurring event. It means, the higher the volatility, the greater the options price. Volatility and options trading essentially linked to each other in a way.

On many exchanges, a stock option allows you to buy/sell 100 shares. This is why you should multiply your premium with 100 to get the final amount.

Check out this Example of Investment Table:

	June 1	June 21	Expiry Date
Stock	$67	$78	$62

Price			
Options Price	$3.15	$8.25	No Value
Contract Value	$315	$825	$0
Paper Loss/Gain	$0	$510	-$315

Most of the time, holders make profits by closing out their positions. Meaning, a holder sells their option; while a writer buys his position back for closing. Not more than 10 percent of the options are executed, and 60 percent are closed (traded out), while 30 expire without having value.

In options, fluctuations can be understood by "time value" (intrinsic and extrinsic value). Their premium is the combination of time value and its intrinsic value. Intrinsic value is the sum above the strike price.

Time value indicates the added value a trader needs to pay above the intrinsic value. This is a time value or extrinsic value. Therefore, the option price in the above example can be considered as:

Time Value +	Intrinsic =	Premium

$0.25	$8.00	$8.25

In practical life, Options trade at (some level above) the intrinsic value. It is because the chances of an event's happening can never be absolutely zero – even if it is never in the cards!

Types of Options

There are two major types of options: American and European. The first type can be exercised at any time between the purchase date and expiry. Moreover, Us-based options have a higher premium. The early use feature commends this.

But European options can only be exercised on and near their expiry date. Most of the options on the exchanges belong to the second type.

There is also another type called Exotic Options that are actually a variety of payoff profile from vanilla options. Exotic options are typically meant for professional investors. Other types of options include Binary, Asian, Knock-out, Barrier, and Bermudan Options.

Options Liquidity & Expiry Time

There is another way to categorize options – by the time duration. Short term options expire with 12 months. Long term options have a greater expiry time. They are known as LEAPS or Long-term Equity Anticipation Securities. They are like regular options with typically longer time duration.

Options can also be categorized by their expiry time. Many option sets expire on Fridays, every week, every 30th or 31st of a month, and on a daily basis. There are also quarterly based expires for ETFs and Index Options.

How to Read Options Table?

It is not possible to do options trading and lack the know-how of reading options tables. Here is how you can read the options table without difficulty.

• You will notice a term "Volume (VLM)" in the table. It indicates the total number of contracts traded in the most recent session.

• You will also hear 'Bid' and 'Ask.' A bid is the most recent price at which the traders wish to purchase an option. While, an 'ask' is the most recent price at which the market wishes to sell an option.

- Implied Bid Volatility (IMPL BID VOL) refers to uncertainty in speed and direction of price in the future.

- Delta is the predication or probability. For instance, there are 30 percent chances of expiration of a 30-delta.

- Open Interest (OPTN OP) signifies the grand total of contracts for a specific option. OPTN OP reduces when the open trade closes.

- Gamma (GMM) is called the speed of an option. It can also be called the movement of delta or predication.

- Vega and Theta are two Greek values used in Options trading tables. Vega represents the amount at which an option price is likely to change. Theta represents the degree of value downward change in an option price during a passing day.

- The 'strike price' is a term used for price at which someone buys/sells underlying security if wishes to use options.

3. MAJOR OPTION TRADING CONCEPTS

Options trading is a term that is used in stock exchange the simple definition of options trading is that 'it is the contract between two parties in which the stock option buyer(holder) purchases the right but not the obligation to buy or sell shares of the underlying stock at a predetermined price from/to the option seller (writer) within a fixed period.'

Options offer alternative systems that allow the investor to take advantage of the exchange and trading underlying protections. There are different types of procedures, including different mix options, hidden resources, and different derivatives.

A question will come into your mind that why a person needs options trading at all, options trading is the most efficient method used in the stock exchange, and it predates the modern stock exchange by a large margin.

So, one must not think that it is just a scam created by some group of people to manipulate minds to earn money because whenever a common person thinks to invest money in the stock exchange he or she is confused by terms like these, so let us tell you that what options trading is.

History of Option Trading

Some believe that it was the Greeks who gave the idea of option trading. Long before the modern world, humans were trying to decide the prices of different goods, and that's how different methods of trading were introduced into the world.

Let us revise from scratch here...

We will give you a simple example to understand what options trading is but for you to understand we want you to focus on the example with an empty mind, for example, you want to buy stocks for $4000 and you go to the broker, but the broker gives you an exciting offer that you can buy stocks for $4000 now, or you can give a token of 400 and reserve your right to buy it at $4000 after a month, And even if stock increases in value at that time. But the token amount will be non-refundable.

Now you think that it is possible that the stock will increase its price to 4020 at that time and you can even buy it after the increase in price, and since you have only paid 400, so you have the rest of the money to use elsewhere. Now you can wait easily for a month and decide by acknowledging the stock prices after a month that if you want to buy the stock or not.

Now, this is what you all an oversimplification, and this is options trading. In the world of trading, options are used as instruments, just like a musician needs a different instrument to get the perfect song; a broker needs options to make a perfect sale. And its price is mostly derived from stocks.

We assure you that if you read the article to the end, you will perfectly know what option trading is, and we will also tell you different strategies used in options trading.

Risks In Options Trading?

Most strategies that are used by options investors have limited risk but also limited profit, so options trading isn't a method that will make you rich overnight.

Options trading may not suit all types of investors, but they are among the most flexible of investment choices.

Options in investment are most likely used to reduce the risk of a drop in stock prices, but a little risk is involved in every type of investment. Returns are never guaranteed investors look for options to manage risks for ways to limit a potential loss.

Investors may choose to take options because the loss is limited to the price you pay for the token money. And in return, they gain the right to buy or sell stock at there at their desirable price, so options in trading benefit a lot to the investors.

Different Strategies Used In Option Trading

Traders often know very little about strategies used in options trading and jump to trading options, knowing the different strategies may lower the risk of potential loss in the market, and traders may also learn to limit the risk and maximize the return. So with a little effort, traders can learn how to take full advantage of the flexibility and power that stock options can provide.

Stock VS Option

One must think that why is there a need to trade in options when someone can trade simply too, to this thought confuses many of us so here is the answer

The options contract has an expiration date, depending on what type of options you are using. It may be in weeks, months, or even in years unlike stock, because the stock has no expiration date.

Stocks are usually defined by numbers, but on the other hand, there are no numbers in options.

Options drive their value from something else. That's why they fall into the derivative category, unlike stocks.

Stock owners have their right in the company (dividend or voting)on the other hand options have no right in the company

Some people may find it difficult to understand the method of options though they have even followed it in their other transaction, for example (car insurance or mortgages).

Option Trading Platforms

if a person wants to trade options, he or she must have a brokerage account, and for that, he or she will want to understand what they what before they sign up with a broker. Each platform is unique and has its pros and cons. So a person must learn more about the best options trading platform to determine which one may be the best suited for their needs.

If a person wants to find the best trading platform, he or she must review different brokerages and options trading platforms. A person must consider different factors like competitive pricing, high tech experience, good for a variety of trader needs and styles.

Some of the best options trading platforms for 2020 are:

TD Ameritrade: Best Overall

Tastyworks: Runner-Up

Charles Schwab: Best for Beginners

Webull: Best for No Commissions

Interactive Brokers: Best for Expert Traders

Option Practicing Method

1. Stocks are purchased, and the investor sells call options on the same stock which he has purchased. The number of stock

shares you have purchased should match the number of call options you have sold.

2. After buying the stock shares, the investor buys put options to gain equal shares. Married acts as an insurance policy against short-term losses call options with a specific strike price. At the same time, you will sell similar call options at a higher strike price.

3. An investor purchases an option with cash from outside, while simultaneously works an out of the cash call choice for a similar stock.

4. The investor purchases a call option and a put choice simultaneously. The two alternatives ought to have a similar strike cost and expiry date.

5. The Investor purchases the call option out of cash and the put choice simultaneously. They have a similar termination date; however, their strike cost is extraordinary. The expense of the

information strike ought to be not exactly the expense of the call strike

Strategies for option trading

Options traders use several strategies to make a profit from this business. The different ways of strategies are used to get profit, which involves using the many alternatives and combinations. The most common strategies are covered calls, iron condors, buying calls, and buying puts. Option trading provides advanced strategies.

Buying calls

Buying calls or long call strategy is used when an investor increasingly buys calls and sets an option on the exact underlying asset with fixed date and price. The investor uses this strategy when they are feeling bullish and confident in an increase in some stock price. In this type, the investor increases the risk as he can face a huge profit or loss, but it's always unknown which way the stock goes.

Buying puts

Usually, the investor uses this strategy when they are bearish on some stock; for example, the investor is confident in a particular stock and had a good understanding of stock but doesn't want to take a huge risk, so he uses short selling strategy.

The put option gets an increase in value when the price of the asset falls. As the market falls, the profit increase in short selling. The risk is not confirmed as the trades return with leverage. But on the off chance that the basic Ascent past the option prices, then the option will expire uselessly.

Covered calls

This strategy provides a small change in the price, the profit is not that big, but the risk it involves is less. The covered call buys 100 shares of stock and then sells one call option per 100 shares. Covered call strategy gives a chance of profit to the investor and also reduce the risk. The share is protected by this call when the price of the stock decreases.

Iron condors

In this strategy, the trader sales a put buys another for a low price and uses them to buy a call then sell the call at a high price after some time. If the stock price is kept somewhere between two puts or calls, then we make a profit. The loss comes with possibilities, one if the price increase suddenly and the other is if the price decrease suddenly, it is spread that causes this condition. This strategy is used by neutral traders or in a neutral place.

Several other strategies are used, which are:

- Broken butterfly
- Iron butterfly
- Jade lizard
- Bear call
- Calendar spread
- Protective put

The Worth of Option Trading

When we buy a bike or car, we want to protect them; the insurance is used for the safety of the car. So just like insurance, the option gives us safety. We invest money and buy shares now we want to protect our investment, for this we use options.

The option provides us good protection of our money. For example:

We bought the 100 shares at the rate of 150 dollars, which Worth 15000. We have invested and now have the risk of a decrease in price. We buy the option to remove risk from our shoulders, and the guy gets paid now assume the risk. Likewise, we buy the put option for 500 dollars. If the stock increases with the rate of 170, we will get the profit, even buying an option of 500.

But if the stock price decreases with the rate of 130, we still are stable, the loss won't affect us as we have the contract on the option which has the same price. We can sell the shares at the same rate we bought, so in that case, by using the option trade, the chance of loss is very low. It provides a lot of ways to gain profit in trading.

Option Trading VS Stock Trading

An option trading is not stock trading. Well, both of them are trading, but they are quite different. Many people don't even know about the options trading; it's just another type of trading. Few things make the difference between the option trading and stock trading, here is these point.

• In options trading, the value is taken by someone else and had a contract with it. It does not get the values on its own. This is completely different from stock trading. Option trading belongs to the derivative category.

• In stock, the numbers are definite, but an option, the numbers are not definite.

• The options trading use the contract, which has the expiration date, the person has no meaning after the expiry date. The date can be in months or years according to the option there are using. Stock trading has no expiration dates.

• In options trading, the owner has no right in the company. They have no affair of any kind related to the company. In stock share, they had the rights to the company.

Risk in Option Trading

The risk involves in option is not as much as people think. Trading does involve risk. Its procedures work along with the risk. In option, the risk can contain only in few things.

• The options trading use many strategies with these strategies. Each has its own risk. The few options work on the spontaneous increase and decrease process. This sometimes gives a big loss to the investor.

• The option involves a lot of complexity. This trading is bot difficult to understand. The strategies of its self are complex. Those who are a beginner in option do not understand it well and invest the money with the little knowledge which results in a loss.

• The other problem with the options trading is that it has the expiration date, which can cause you all you invest if the contract expires. This is one big factor in this trading.

Option Account

For option trade, you need an options account. Before you make an account, you need to fill the agreement with your broker. The broker will know your investment and your trade. He will generate the strategy according to the level of trading you want. The broker will guide you about options trading and its policies.

What Is An Option Account?

The account that is used to access the option trade is an options account. The broker gives access to the user for an options account. For all the trading, the brokerage account is used; it does the selling and buying. After giving all details, you will be able to open the account.

The broker tells the two type of account which you want to open, the real money and demo money account. After all the procedures, your account will ready for trading.

The Right Broker

Before choosing your broker, you check in on him. Always choose the one with an authentic source. The information you provide him should be protected. Always check the payment and its cost. Aim for the right option.

The Best Broker

- Schwab Brokerage ($0.65 per options contract)
- E-trade ($0.65 per options contract)
- Ally Invest ($0.5 per contract traded)
- TD Ameritrade ($0.65 fee per contract)

Best platforms

Options trading is a high-level risk. It needs to be protected from fraud. When selecting the platform, you must select the best one.

There are many best platforms available in the market; there has a good reputation, such as.

• Charles Schwab, this platform is best for the beginner. If you are a beginner, you should choose this platform. This platform gives more understanding to users.

• TD Ameritrade is the best platform for the options trading in the world. The cost is low and no account minimum requirements

• Tastyworks provide trading access to different devices. It allows PC, laptops, and mobile phones. It is one of the most high-tech platforms.

Webull platform gives no commission

Options trading is not meant for beginners who have zero ideas about the market. So if you are just starting your journey with the stock market, you may have to spend some time learning the basic concepts of options trading.

When we talk about stocks, it's all about investment and turning that investment into profit. So it requires strong knowledge and experience to make some big profits and avoid loss.

4. OPTIONS TRADING MYTHS AND MISCONCEPTIONS

There are many myths and misconceptions related to the term "Options Trading" not only in the stock market but also for the public. Options trading is known to be risky; according to Mike Bellafiore, the Co-Founder of CMB trading, "Trading is a sport of survival, reinvention, and perseverance, even for the successful trader."

Indeed, in the stock market or business, there is no such thing as assurance; there is always a risk involved with putting your money into something. The stock market or business is always about numbers and good strategies. If your strategies and numbers are right, you are in it for the long haul; otherwise, you will end up with nothing.

The winner of U.S. Investing Championship in 1984 Martin S. Schwartz says,

"A lot of people get so enmeshed in the markets that they lose their perspective. Working longer does not necessarily equate with working smarter. In fact, sometimes it's the other way around." in a trading business, you can use your shortcomings or failures for your future benefits as well; according to Brett Steenbarger, an active trader and a Ph.D. scholar, "we will never be perfect as traders. That's what keeps us ever-learning, ever-growing. Our main challenge is to use our shortcomings as inspirations, fueling continuous improvement."

There are many myths and misconceptions about trading.

Misconception #1 Trading and Gambling are same

The first and the most common one is trading and gambling are the two sides of the same coin. In trading, a trader goes through all the present, past data, and numbers whether gambling is a game of available odds.

Trading is about technical analysis you look into the details, risks, profit, gain, and the market, whereas gambling is based on fundamental values.

You put in your money in what you might think will happen. Also, gambling is an addiction, illegal, and also very toxic for your mental health and behavior.

Misconception #2 Should only invest in Call and Put Option

Options are the type of contract that allows the buyer to purchase or sell the underlying asset. To simplify it, the trader purchases a call option if he is expecting the demand of the underlying asset to rise within a certain deadline, and the trader opts for a put option if he is expecting the demand of the underlying asset to fall within a certain time period.

It is a misconception about the call and put option that it is the only profitable way of trading options, but in reality, the buying of calls and puts is highly risky in trading because you can never be sure about the demand of the underlying asset for that you need the proper analysis of the direction it is moving, its time frame and size of the move. You can analyze the size and the direction right, but if your options have expired before the move happens, then you may lose money.

Misconception #3 Option selling is more profitable

Option selling is basically giving someone the right, but not the obligation, to make you purchase 100 shares of a stock at a strike price before the expiration date. In simpler terms, they are basically paying to increase their flexibility, and you pay to decrease your flexibility. So when you are selling options, you are not only using the money in your brokerage, but you are also in debt. Option selling can be profitable if you play right by the rules, but there is also high risk involved in it.

Misconception #4 Put Option expire worthlessly

Option expiring worthless is when options expire from your trading account and cease to exist. There are a lot of misconceptions about 90 percent of the option expiring, but according to the report by The Chicago Board Options Exchange (CBOE), approximately, only 30% of the options expire worthlessly. 60% of the option positions are closed before their expiration, and 10% of the options are exercised.

Secondly, options expiring worthless, only work against the option buyers, but option writers still get their profit if the put option has expired.

Misconception #5 Option trading is a zero-sum

This is one of the oldest myths about option trading. It says that if a buyer wins, then the seller has to lose. But no, that is not true at all!

Options are given to manage the risk. They do not give you anything of value other than the choice to buy or sell assets. When you use options to hedge your risk, you are transferring your risk to someone else who is willing to hold on to it. So the options trading is not a zero-sum game.

Misconception #6 Options trading is easy

There is another misconception about options trading that people assume it is easy. According to the Charles Faulkner trader and an author he says "After years of studying traders, the best predictor of success is simply whether the person is improving with time and experience" you need years of experience, learning the market and its resources completely and strategies then you can be a successful trader.

Trading is rarely about "luck" it's all about good hand-on knowledge. People do not mostly have an in-depth knowledge of the options trading or stock market. It is more than just investing the money. All the experts in trading business have years of experience and knowledge, and they even use their failures as a weapon for their future success.

Misconception #7 Trading in Tax-deferred account

There is a common misconception about using traditional or IRA accounts for the trading option because they both will ease up the tax advantage, and It could be a perfect retirement plan, but there are certain limits to it. You can only invest to a certain limit through your tax-deferred account. You cannot use the money before retirement. After five years, you are only able to withdraw the income.

5. TOP OPTIONS TRADING STRATEGIES

The options trading utilizes a few strategies for financial specialists to benefit from trading. The various methods of strategies are utilized to get profit, which includes utilizing the numerous other options and combinations.

The alternative exchanging gives advance techniques. These systems help financial specialists to increase the most extreme benefits. The top strategy is used for different levels of trading. Many popular trading strategies are used in the market. These strategies are well known in trading and have numbers of users. The following are the top option trading strategies.

Buying calls

Purchasing calls or long call methodology is utilized when a financial specialist progressively purchases calls and sets a choice on the specific hidden resource with fixed date and cost. The investor expects more leverage than just owning the stock. The financial specialist uses this procedure when they are feeling bullish and certain about increment at some stock cost. The confidence of the investor prepares them to pick this option strategy.

In this sort, the speculators increment the hazard as he can confront the gigantic benefit or loss, but it's consistently obscure what direction the stock goes. If the stock goes up, the investor will get the profit, and if the shares price decrease, then the investor will face a big loss. Even the most experienced traders face loss at some point, but that does not mean it will only give loss.

The profit in it usually covers the loss of investors. For example, If the investor wants to buy a developing house, then he will purchase the buy call option by doing this he can pay the same price according to the contract as the cost of a house is 200,000 now as when the development will be complete, the cost of the house will be increased.

Suppose the price of the house incredibly increased after 2,3 years, and now the house is worth 400,000. The investor will pay the same amount, although its price in the market is double because of the option he can pay the same amount of 200,000 as written on the contract. The only thing the investor will be worried about is the expiration date.

Buying puts

In this options trading strategy, the investor has the legal right to sell the shares at the given price. The date is also fixed at a certain time. The buying puts give more authority to the investor.

Normally, the financial specialist utilizes this strategy when they are bearish on some stock; for the model, the speculator is positive about the specific stock and had great comprehension of stock yet wouldn't like to face an immense challenge, so he utilizes short selling procedure.

The put choice gets increment in esteem when the cost of benefit falls.

As the market falls, the benefit increment by short selling. The chance isn't affirmed as the trade return with leverage. But if the fundamental Ascent past the choice value, then the alternative will terminate pointlessly.

Mostly the traders are sure that the market will fall. They purchase the share to sell it at a certain time as they have the right to do so, the values of the share increase when the stock moves towards the other direction. It is a simple way to gain profit.

If you want the insurance on your shares in stock, you can buy a put option. If the investor has a share of 500 dollars, and he realized the market would lose the value. They can sell there share at a reduced price of about 475 dollars. The loss is reduced in this way.

Covered call

This strategy provides a small change in the price, the profit is not that big, but the risk it involves is less. The covered call buys 100 shares of stock and then sale one call option per 100 shares. Covered call strategy gives a chance of profit to the investor and also reduce the risk.

The share is protected by this call when the price of the stock decreases. In this strategy, the seller of the call option possesses the related amount of underlying instrument. In the covered call option, you can buy stock and sell the call option on Out of money(OTM).

The term buy-write is referred to when the call been sold at the same time with the purchase of stock. We get a small amount for call sales when we pay for stock shares. We have to sell calls to generate income in it. This option needs direct investment and calls to sell.

The investor uses this option strategy when they think the price will not further increase. We have to hold a long position. The chance of profit is low as the increase in price is not expected.

Suppose, the stock was trading at $200 on May 20th, 2014; The Leg 1 Buy 100 portions of the stock for $200 and Leg 2: Sell the 206 strikes June 26th, 2014 Call for $7.30, Lot size – 100 offers

The sum paid to take these two positions approaches - the Stock cost paid less call premium got, for example, $.20,000 (Stock buy) – $730 (Premium got) = $19,270

If the stock value ascends over the call strike of 206, it will be worked out, and the stock will be sold. In any case, the methodology will make a benefit since you are secured by the stock you own.

State, the stock cost at termination is $210.

In the event that the stock falls beneath the underlying stock price tag, your long position is at a misfortune. However, you have some pad from the call premium got by selling the call.

State, the stock falls and is at $190 on the lapse

Iron condors

In this strategy, the trader sales a put buys another for a low price and uses them to buy a call then sell the call at a high price after some time. If the stock price is kept somewhere between two puts or calls, then we make a profit.

The loss comes with possibilities, one if the price increase suddenly and the other is if the price decrease suddenly, it is spread that causes this condition. This strategy is used by neutral traders or in a neutral place. This is a simple options strategy.

The iron condors option does not require a big investment to start a trade; you can start the trade with a minimum amount. The investor relies on the stock to stay at some particular point. It is a small strategy that involves risk, but the investor invests in a small amount to maintain the risk.

Consider the stock is trading at the cost of $120, executing an Iron Condor trading procedure we will: Sell $100 Strike Put for $3.0 Sell $140 Strike Call for $3.0
With an expectation that the cost will stay inside these two strike costs that we booked so, we make a benefit. In any case, because of

the danger of boundless misfortune, we would ensure our situations by Buy Strike Put for $90 Buy Strike $160 Call for $2.

Bear calls

This option works on the procedure of sale and buy. The investor sells the call option and then purchases the calls at a high strike rate. This option uses the investment of the trader to get the profit income. The procedure works on limited levels. It uses two legs. These work on a 1:1 ratio to make the net credit.

Even though this is not a Bearish Strategy, it is actualized when one is bullish. It is generally set up for a 'net credit,' and the expense of buying call choices is financed by selling an 'in the cash' call choice. For this Options Trading Strategy, one must guarantee the Call alternatives have a place with a similar expiry, the equivalent hidden resource, and the proportion is kept up.

It, for the most part, ensures the drawback of a Call sold by safeguarding it, for example, by purchasing a Call of a higher strike cost. It is fundamental, however, that you execute the system just when you are persuaded that the market would be moving essentially higher.

The investor is expecting a small decrease in the stock. They sell the calls and then purchase the calls at high strike. The option works better when the volatility is high. The expiration date is good enough to handle things. The traders don't waste the expiry date, as it is important for the trading. The investor uses the long term to execute the process.

If the market is expecting the rise in stock, then the traders sell the one strike call and then buy another at the higher strike. The investor gets the profit by the amount of cost.

If the stock is expecting a sudden rise, then they sales the call and then buy the new ones which they even buy at a high rate, but instead of loss they gain profit, and then they buy more calls.

Jade lizard

In this options trading strategy, the traders sell short calls and put, and the underlying assets should not move. The cost collect in the results is great. All the options have the same expiration date. It minimizes the risk and maximizes the reward. Trading options maximize the risk in one direction.

The jade lizards option are a sort of Options Trading Strategy which is rehearsed by Traders to pick up benefit from their exchanges

If there should arise an occurrence of Straddles and Strangles, Lizards diminish the upside hazard. They are most valuable when basic stays or floats toward the strike. High benefits are created in high IV and non-bearish situations. This neutral strategy involves short calls and short put spread. It is a slow strategy; it does not increase suddenly. It uses the call cost and puts the cost at high volatility.

Let's suppose that the investor accepts this trade is a drawback chance. In the event that ABC stock moves above £25 per share, the financial specialist would lose $£1 on the call spread, yet gains £1.10 from the premium gathered for a net addition of £0.10.

The investor benefits from the exchange, except if the cost of ABC moves underneath the strike cost of the bare put by more than the top-notch that is gathered. In this model, the stock cost would need to dip under £18.90.

Collar option

It is similar to the covered call but has extra protective puts to protect the value of security between 2 bounds. The Collar Options Trading Strategy can be built by holding portions of the hidden all the while and purchasing put-call alternatives and selling call choices against the held offers.

One can support the expected drawback in the offers by purchasing the fundamental and, at the same time, purchasing a put alternative beneath the current cost and selling a call choice over the current cost. Buy one put option than lower the limit for protection; sell the call option at the upper limit.

Both must have the same expiration date and the quantity. The call and put options are out of money. The underlying assets price expired at a strike price of the short call option. The instability is surprising when the market is unstable at the point when the cost of an alternative ascent, there is a likelihood that the cost may fall and you may miss out on the benefit.

In such a case, the advantage should be secured. The option protects the losses a lot and decreases the chances of all loss, but with all the protection, sometimes it reduces the profit.

Let us guess that stock value rises to Rs 50In this case; the trader would have understood the estimation of his stock holding rise to (100*50) = Rs 5000.

As he is the seller of the Call option, he anticipated that the cost of the fundamentals should fall. In any case, its cost has, in certainty, risen. The Call option purchaser will practice his privilege and will purchase the Call alternative at the strike cost of 48, which is lower than the cost of the fundamental that is 50. So the option seller got (48*100) = Rs 4800 by selling the Call option.

For a Put alternative purchaser, an option is in the cash if the strike cost is higher than the cost of the hidden. For this situation, as the strike cost of 43 is not exactly the CMP of the hidden, which is 50, and along these lines, the option is rendered useless for him.

Net benefit from the exchange = Rs 5000 – Rs 4800+500 - 300 = 400

Diagonal spread

The diagonal spread option strategy uses many strikes and months. It works with the combined bits of a long call spread and a short call spread. Diagonal spread moves diagonally and also the names.

The option is presented in different rows and columns. In this options trading strategy, the short terms are sold, and long terms are bought. A transient shortcoming or Strength that you think would go up or go down once more, at that point, to the advantage of it.

The system is controlled on the short-side for risk, and if the market plays smoothly, it can become open-finished on the long side.

At the point when executed for cash, it permits edge necessities to be met. The investment is at high risk when it works quickly in our way. The diagonal spread has its setup, which we have to follow.

• The equal number of options is required.

• The options must have the exact underlying security.

• The options in the diagonal spread should have the same class.

• The different expiry dates are used.
• The two different strike prices.

In the diagonal spread, the bullish long call diagonal spread purchases the option with the lower strike rate and longer expiry date then sells the short date option with high strike rates.

Butterfly

The broken wing butterfly option is a bit similar to the butterfly trading strategy, but In this trading strategy, the calls and puts are much similar to directional strategy rather than the butterfly strategy.

Its sides have a different level of risk; the risk is different on each side. Usually, the profit occurs if the underlying expires at the short strike price. The broken wing butterfly option provides more profit than the butterfly option.

Futuresmag merits the credit for begetting the "Broken Wing Butterfly," an amazing option in contrast to the Butterfly, where the objective is starting an exchange at zero expense.

It is an amazing options trading which expands on the positive attributes of a Butterfly Spread. Dissimilar to the Long Butterfly, where one needs to pay another charge, Broken Wing Butterfly

Strategy is a net credit procedure, frequently rehearsed to build the likelihood of benefit.

Broken Wing Butterfly Strategy is equivalent to a Butterfly in which the sold spread is regularly more extensive spread than the bought spread. It has the similarity of long butterfly spread having the same strikes that are not much different from the short strike. It works when the option has all the puts or all the calls.

For example, the stock is trading at Rs100. You buy one 120 calls on ABC, you sell two 105 calls in ABC and purchase one 100 calls in ABC, So you get the net credit of Rs. 10.

6. TOP QUALITIES OF A SUCCESSFUL OPTIONS TRADER

'The key to trading success is emotional discipline. If intelligence were the key, there would be a lot more people making trading money'

– Victor Sperandeo

To be an options trader, certain qualities are required that are not at all difficult to achieve. To develop those qualities, you have to know about the options trading.

Options Trading

In options trading, the buyer has the right, when he wants to buy (in the case of a call) and when he wants to sell (in the case of a put) but he is not bound to buy or sell the certain asset at a specific price, as the name 'Options' suggest. The trader is also not bound to trade in some specific time. He has the total choice of what and when he wants to trade.

Why people tend to go for options trading?

Options can provide better income than any other job. It is not much different from the stock exchange. It is just like your own business; all you have to do is predict where the market and stock rates are going. You have to take a risk, but the income will be higher than you have thought. The end results can give a shock as market rates keep on changing every minute.

Top Qualities of a Successful Options Trader

Just like in any other business, there is a huge risk of loss. Every other person cannot be a good businessman. Many people have weak patience level, they lose their heart, and on failure, they leave the business or sell at a low price without giving another try.

The one who buys that at a low price takes it to another level. Similarly, everyone cannot be a good trader. Being a successful trader demands certain qualities. If you achieve those qualities, nothing can stop you from becoming one of the most successful options traders.

1.   Control on emotions
2.   Record keeping
3.   Finding the right strategy for you

4.   Consistency

5.   Learning from failures

6.   News interpretation

7.   Being yourself

8.   Patience

9.   Flexibility

10.   Risk management

These are a few qualities to make you a successful trader in options trading, and a positive attitude towards these skills can make you a professional options trader. Let's dig a bit more into these qualities to polish your personality a little more.

Control on Emotions

Mixing your emotions with your business can take you towards destruction. You have to manage your social life along with the real-life without tangling them with each other. You must be able to manage the happening in real life and happenings in the business. Not only that, but you must have total control over your mind and hold your nerves while doing the business.

Records Management

If you keep a record of whatever you do, next time you will be able to avoid the mistake you have made previously, and you will be able to see where you have gone wrong.

This habit will provide you information on your wealth to improving your odds of success. By keeping the records, you will be able to make up your previous losses. Records will also help you keep track of profit/losses for tax purposes, if applicable.

A Good Planner

Everyone has their own strategy (like the way of doing things). Some people tend to go for short sales and make multiple sales in a day. Others hit their luck after a long time and make a large amount by a single sale.

Even if they perform a single sale in a week, they can earn more than the one who makes many sales in a day. Once you find the right strategy for yourself, you have to stick with that strategy. It is crucial which strategy you are choosing for yourself. It is because in options trading, the right strategy and technique to trade will take you to the top, and the wrong will do the opposite.

Consistency

Nothing other than small chunks can be earned without consistency. You have to give a lot to achieve a lot. In the case of options trading, you have to invest your time to achieve experience. The more experience you get, the more you learn.

Like you learn when and where to put your money; and when to draw it out. Many people get back when they see smaller earnings, not knowing that smaller steps lead towards greater steps.

Learning from Failures

Just as most businessmen lose their money, similarly, every trader also faces losses. This is just part of the game! But a successful trader doesn't give up on his loss and try to avoid loss in the future from the experience he gained from his previous loss.

Then a time comes when he has learned every possible reason leading to his loss. In the future, he can cover up his previous losses by avoiding the same mistake.

News Interpretation

The traders must be able to interpret the news. If you are good at interpreting the news, you will have the exact knowledge to predict which is the product will give profit and when. If you can predict the future, you'll be able to raise your income by investing in a certain product.

You'll also be able to predict when to buy or sell the product to maximize your profit. Some news is just the hype; you have to be able to differentiate between the real news and the hype.

Do not Follow What Others are Doing

Everyone has their thinking. But once you come to the trade business, do not rely completely on others' strategies. In order to be a successful trader, you don't have to do what everyone else is doing. You have to be limitless and be yourself. You may come out of your comfort zone, but following your own passion will be the key to success. Your willingness to take risks will benefit you in being yourself.

Patience

Being a successful options trader demands a lot of patience. You have to be able to wait until; it's the right time to perform the action. It means, if you have to put your money into something, you have to wait until you think; it is the lowest price for a certain product. Similarly, while selling, you have to be patient until it reaches the highest amount of profits.

If you are not patient while trading; a huge loss may be on your way!

Flexibility

The rates of market changes every day; you have to be able to learn the changing dimensions of the market. You have to learn about the changing trends of the market and adopt newer strategies.

You have to be well aware of the relevant news and always believe yourself as a learner. You have to accept the losses as loss in any field of work is inevitable. You have to accept wherever the market is going, whether it suits you or not.

Risk Management

In options, you are playing in millions, so there is a huge risk. You have to manage how much risk you can bear at a certain time. Being limitless does not mean you have to forget about what you are risking while putting your money. If you allot a certain capital to an investment, you may be able to avoid a higher risk of loss but, the greater the risk, the greater will be the gains or losses.

Conclusion

If you have these certain skills or qualities, one day, you will be the most successful trader of the options trading. Just be patient and have consistency in your work. The doors of success will keep opening for you. The most important thing is believing in yourself; if you take larger risks and **have** belief in yourself, there is nothing you cannot do.

7. HOW TO SELECT THE RIGHT OPTION FOR A MAJOR GAIN

Starting from simple purchases to more complicated spreads like butterflies, options have a plethora of strategies. Moreover, they are available for a bigger range of currencies, stocks and commodities, futures contracts, and exchange-traded funds.

Often, there are hundreds of expiries and strike prices for each option. This poses a challenge for the novices to select the best option out of many. Here is how you can do that like a pro.

Look for the Right Option

Imagine, you already have an asset in mind that you wish to trade on, like a commodity. You picked it from stock screener through your insight and the insight of others (e.g. research). Regardless of the selection technique, after identifying your asset for trading, you need to follow these steps to achieve your goal.

- Frame your purpose of investment
- Determine your payoff
- Analyze volatility

- Recognize events
- Make a Strategy
- Launch parameters of options

These steps follow a logical process, which makes it easy to select the right option to trade on. Let us breakdown what these steps reveal.

Frame your Purpose

The base of getting into the trading business is finding the purpose of investment. Why do you want to start options trading? What is the purpose behind this? Do you want to make real money, or is it just a side-business? Ask yourself these questions. Make a notebook and write all the answers that you have.

Now you might be thinking, why so? It is because you need to be clear on this point. Using options to make real money is very different as compared to purchasing them for speculating or hedging.

This is your first step, and it will form the foundation for other steps. So, buckle up!

Trader's Payoff

In the second step, determine your risk and reward payoff. This should be dependent upon your appetite or tolerance for risk. Know your type – like if you are one of the conservative traders, using aggressive strategies for options trading might not be suitable for you. These strategies include purchasing deep out-of-money options in large quantities or writing puts etcetera.

Each strategy has a well-made risk and reward profile. You have got to keep an eye on it. And do not forget to assess your payoff at the end of the day!

Analyze Volatility

It is one of the most crucial steps in options trading. You have got to analyze implied volatility for sure. Compare it to the history of options stock volatility, plus the volatility level in the market.

This allows you to know about the thinking of other traders. Whether they expect the stocks to move fast or up in the future or not, if there is high volatility, there will be a higher premium too. In this case, options writing will be more suitable for you.

A lower rate of implied volatility means there will be lower premium – good for the purchase of options (if you think that the stocks will move more and so their value will increase as well).

Recognize Events

There are two main types of events: stock-specific and market-wide. Stock specific events include types like spin-offs, product launches, and earnings reports, etcetera. Market-wide events, on the other hand, are those that have a huge role in broad markets like economic data releases and Federal Reserve Announcements.

It is important that you know and recognizes each event type. Since they have a huge impact on implied volatility and, thus, can have a great impact on the price when it occurs. Recognizing events before they can help traders to make a bigger profit, determine the right time and the appropriate expiration date for your trade.

Make Your Strategy

The first four steps allow you to see clearly the way to your options trading business. Now you are in a good position to devise your own plan after knowing the events, implied volatility, risk, and reward pay off and your investment goal.

Suppose a conservative trader with a good portfolio wishes to earn a premium within some months. He should then use the covered call "writing" technique to achieve his goal. While an aggressive investor who foresees market decline within some months should purchase puts on main stocks so on.

Launch Parameters

After the fifth step is clear on your mind, try to launch parameters. For instance, you should establish the expiration time, option delta, and strike price, etcetera. Let us say a trader wants to buy the longest expiration date call. But he also wants to pay a low premium on it. In this case, the out-of-the-money call is the most appropriate for him. But for a high delta call, focus on in-the-money option.

In short, follow the given steps to make a good profit and establish yourself as a professional options trader in the market. Determine your objective of investment, analyze your risk and reward, assess volatility, think about the happenings, make your strategy, and then tailor your options parameters.

How to make money with Options Trading

An Option trader earns money by buying or selling or by being an option writer.

With options trading, you do not only buy or own stock in a company, but you are also in a position to sell that stock in the future. If you know the right strategies, you can earn above $100,815 through options trading. Learning the right strategies, knowledge about risks, learning the market, multiplying the profit, and building wealth will help you make more money with options trading.

Earning Money with options trading in 2020

We have enlisted some special Options Trading techniques that could help you understand and earn money better through Options Trading.

Recap

Before really getting into the business, you need to recap what options trading really is, what its terms are, and how it's done with minimum risks involved. In simple terms, options trading is buying and selling options contracts.

Options trading does not allow you to vote or receive dividends or anything else a (partial) owner of the company can do. It is just a contract between you and some other party that grants you the right to purchase (i.e., "call option") or sells (i.e., "put option") stock of a company at a certain price.

It is one of the most basic 'leveraging' tools available to investors who are looking to increase their potential profit by accepting the increase in risk that always comes attached to it.

There are some essential key terms that are normally used in Options Trading:

Stock

A stock option is a contract between the company and the stock option buyer to buy or sell 100 shares of the company at a determined amount within a certain time period.

Expiration

In options trading, there is a contract involved, and each contract has an expiration date. You can buy or sell your options before the expiration date, but once it crosses the expiration date, the contract has no value to it. In that case, only an option writer can earn.

Strike Price

A strike price is a price at which the commodity or asset is to be bought or sold when the option is exercised. For example, if the strike price is XYZ dollars for a call option, then you could exercise your contract by purchasing the identified stock at the strike price.

Premium

Options Premium is the price to be paid by the party who is purchasing the right buy/the right to sell, to the party that is selling the right to to buy/the right to sell, as a premium to enter into a contract for the risk of the option being exercised if the contract is in the money, that the writer (seller) of option is bearing while entering into the option contract. It depends on the strike price, the volatility of the underlying, and expiration date.

Call and Put Option

In options trading, there is a call and Put option A call is when you buy or purchase a stock and put is when you sell a stock. You can buy or sell a stock before the expiration date.

Underlying Asset

The underlying asset is reference security (stock, bond, futures contract, etc.) on which the price of derivative security like an option is based. For example, options are derivative instruments, meaning that their prices are derived from the price of another security. More specifically, options prices are derived from the price of an underlying stock.

Option Style

An option contract is made up of two different styles; American style or European style. Options can be practiced in a particular way, and both styles allow you to practice them differently. American style options can be used any time before expiration, whereas European style options can only be used on expiration dates itself.

Contract Multiplier

The contract multiplier states the quantity of the underlying asset that needs to be delivered in the event the option is exercised. For stock options, each contract covers 100 shares.

Relative Value

Selling a commodity at a higher price than the buying price and purchasing at a lower price than the market or what you sold it as.

Making Money with Options Trading in 2020

Option traders use different strategies to evaluate the trade. A list of tools is included in the process of evaluation.

The list might include; analysis, history, statistics, stability, debt, dividends, etc.

With a little reading, a trader can easily minimize his risk of losing his investment. Here are the top 10 strategies of how to make money through options trading:

Naked Call

A naked call is an options strategy in which an investor sells (a call option) without the security of owning the underlying stock.

Covered Put

A covered option is a strategy where the stock is bought or owned, and an option is sold. The underlying stock is bought, and simultaneously writes–or sells–a call option on those same shares. The Covered Put also has a higher profit in case the stock moves down to the strike price of the short puts.

For example, an investor uses his call option (buys) on a stock that represents 100 shares of stock per call option. For every 100 shares of stock that the investor purchases, they will sell one call option against it. This strategy is referred to as a covered call because, in the event that a stock price increases rapidly, this investor's short call is covered by the long stock position.

The formula for calculating maximum profit is:

Max Profit = Premium Received - Commissions Paid

Max Profit Achieved When Price of Underlying <= Strike Price of Short Put

Making most out of options

Options are like a business; not everyone can achieve high wages or income. To be a successful businessman, you need a certain type of mindset, few skills, and a little capital. While discussing how to make money through options, we don't have to only look onto physical strategies but also mental and indirect strategies.

Indirect Strategies:

Record keeping

Keeping proper records of your progress is really helpful for a successful practical life as well as for business. In options, you can track your progress, the weaknesses, and the reasons for these weaknesses. It will help you to learn from your mistakes and avoid them in the future.

Stay aware

Technology keeps on developing every day; each day, we see new innovation. To walk with others and avoid staying behind them, you must have access to the latest news and updates about technology and stay ready for what is coming next.

Stay updated

To be a successful options trader, you have to be updated on what is going on in the stock market and how and when prices are going to change. This way you will be able to predict the prices of the market and plan your move accordingly to avoid losses

Mental strategies:

Managing the risk

It is a famous saying, "Cut your coat according to the cloth." Applying this on options, you have to agree that don't put all your money into one product. Only invest as much amount for which you can bear the risk.

Managing time

No one can force you to put or call the money in a certain product until you yourself want to do so. Look for the perfect time to do so, invest only when you know it is a perfect time. The most important thing is patience. But keep track of the expiration date.

Separate practical and business life

To make progress as an options trader, never mix up your emotions with your business. If you are going through something bad in real life and getting frustrated, mind taking a break. A fresh mind can think well than the mind busy in solving other issues. Options trading is the game of the mind, so take a break and come back when you are relaxed.

These are the few physical, mental, and indirect strategies that we have discussed above. Hope, this will take you to the heights of success and make most out of options.

8. IMPORTANT TIPS & TRICKS ABOUT OPTIONS TRADING

An option trading is a part of trading that allows you to trade your market expectations while also control the risk that you are going to participate in this trading with. Now, if you get a better a clearer idea of how to rightly perform options trading, there are no limitations to it. This means that you can trade various strategies and seek profit in all sorts of market conditions.

However, this options trading doesn't mean that you have to trade the strategies of your complex trading options to seek profit from them. Instead, you can spend your money more effectively to gain profit by simply replacing your regular trading positions with the help of options.

A Little Insight:

With the start of 2020, the options trading activity has achieved a drastic increase. Now, if we calculate the increase in the options contracts in this year up until now, an estimation of a 53% increase has been calculated – in comparison to that of the same time last year. Hence, there can certainly not be a better time to head onto the trading options activity – if you're thinking about it.

However, understanding the trading options strategies and how it can be performed properly is very important. Therefore, even if you're a pro in trading, it's important to know the major and important tips regarding options trading. Now, these strategies and tips may change according to the conditions and criteria of the market.

But to give you a consistent answer of how you can firmly perform options trading, we'll discuss some tips below that might just do the trick. So without further ado, let's go ahead and discover some such tips!

Follow a Well Defined Exit Plan

Controlling your emotions while trading options can be crucial in terms of helping you achieve great profits. This crucial step can be defined by simply having a plan to work and always sticking to it. This way, you are well aware of the outcome you desire when following that plan, and you can surely achieve it. So no matter how much your emotions force you to change your mind and forget our plan while you're on it, make sure you don't!

Now when you make a well-defined plan, you can't miss on the exit planning here too. This exit plan doesn't mean that you are supposed to minimize your loss in terms of facing the downside of options trading. But instead, having a well-defined exit plan and a downside exit plan in advance can help you get out of the trade at the right time – even if the trade is going right according to your plan.

This is very important because options trading is an activity that faces a decay in the rates when the expiration date starts coming closer.

Educate Yourself

Trading options can be a complex activity in comparison to simply buying and selling stocks. And if you don't understand this activity well, there are chances that you might not be able to get anywhere in it. However, if you keep seeking knowledge and experience in this, you'll be better aware of how you can invest here and gain profit.

Now to get started in this, you need to have a proper assessment of your investment plan. This assessment can include your individual goals, the risk constraints, the time horizon, tax constraints, and the liquidity needs you have.

Don't Double Up for Past Losses

If you are thinking of doubling on an options strategy just because you want to cover your past loss, then you're surely not going to get far with this. A simple reason for that is that options in options trading are simply derivatives, and their prices properties aren't the same as the underlying stock holds them.

Therefore, even if it sometimes makes sense to double up just so that you can catch up on the loss you faced earlier (and because you follow this in the stocks), it doesn't mean that it will also serve you with profit when you're in the options galaxy.

Hence, instead of enhancing your risk, you should simply step back and close the trade. This way, you can cut more of your losses that might further come in the same trade, and simply go for a different opportunity. As a result, instead of digging deeper into the specific options category, you will be accepting your loss and saving yourself from a bigger downfall.

Manage Your Risk

Now the most important aspect here is the risk of the options trading. So when you go for options trading, you must understand how much risk you can take. Whether you're a beginner or someone who has been in the options trading for a while, having a certain risk assessment that you can handle is very important.

Once you have that, you can look into the different methods that can help you manage your risks. Now to manage the risks, you can go for different options throughout the life of the options contract – to manage the risks. These different options include:

Closing a Trade: this mainly refers to taking an offsetting position in the trade. So if you have purchased a call option in trading options, you can simply set the call option and close the trade for managing the risk on time.

Allowing an Option to Expire

This can be possible when a contract in trading options has reached its expiration date without being worked on. Here, you can also purchase or sell a call or put, according to the contract.

Roll out an Option

This is mainly the process of managing risk by simply closing an option that is near to the expiration date, and then simultaneously investing in a similar category of trade that has a distant expiration date.

Assignment

Lastly, another strategy of managing the risks in trading options is to simply go for an assignment. This is possible when you sell an option by simply receiving or delivering the shares that lie under the stock of that option.

Finally

Now trading options are quite a familiar trading aspect for many, but most of the new traders aren't very familiar with it. However, achieving great profits and success in trading options is something anyone can achieve. Only if you educate yourself in this, gain some experience, and righty follow efficient tips and tricks (as mentioned above) – you are sure to go far in trading options.

9. IMPORTANT FAQS OF OPTIONS TRADING

We tried to include all the basic and important frequently asked questions regarding options trading. Hope they help you understand the options trading better and if not. You can post your inquiries in the comment section.

Is there any definition of options?

Options are derivatives that are supported on the value of underlying securities such as stocks.

Options are putting down your money for the right to buy a stock at a specific price before its expiration date. There are two types of options; options buy or sell.

When an investor takes part in options, s/he is either buying or selling an options contract and is making a bet that either the underlying share will rise in price or fall in price before the expiration date.

How to gain maximum profit in options trading?

According to Allen Everhart, the best way to maximize profit in options trading is to just keep it simple. In his words, "I have come to appreciate buying deep-in-the-money/deep-in-time call options despite the disparagement this strategy gets."

Purchase a 70 delta call if you think the market is going higher - or put if you think the market is falling. You will not need to worry much about theta decay (there's a little, but not much) and you'll profit 80% of a $1 move on the stock or ETF at a much lower cost than an equivalent number of shares of stock, and there's no risk of being randomly exercised and having the stock (long or short) suddenly appear in your account the next morning!

When you have 200 short option positions on, and a dozen of them get randomly exercised overnight, you will appreciate the 'simple' approach to options trading.

What happens in a case when options contract expires?

In case if the contract reaches its expiration date and you have not yet exercised your right to options, then you will lose your right and premium. The contract becomes invalid.

The only person who will profit from this is the writer of the contract.

What is the difference between strike price and stock price?

A strike price is a price at which the owner of an option can execute the contract, whereas; a stock price is the last transaction price of at least a single share of an underlying.

What is naked call?

It's a strategy in which an investor writes a call option without having a position in the underlying stock itself. To set up a naked call, an investor simply sells a call option without owning the underlying stock. If s/he writes a naked call & the stock goes up 100 or 200%, the writer has to deliver, but it is a high-risk strategy.

What is American contract?

An American option is a version of an options contract that allows holders to exercise the option rights at any time before and including the day of expiration.

What is an European contract?

A European contract only allows you to exercise on the day of expiration.

Which one is more profitable European contract or American contract?

An American contract option allows the investor to exercise any time before the expiration date whereas, in European contract options during their

"exercise period" (usually right when they expire, but no earlier).

So an American style contract is exercised more but is it more profitable?

If I exercise my American contract before its expiration date, the investor might get more profit, but he/she might lose money too. Mathematically, there is no advantage, since an investor can make the same amount of profit on exercising its right on the day of its expiration.

When should you start options trading?

You should start options trading when you have enough investment and savings too. You need the proper knowledge, data, and strategies about the market. You should be able to not only predict but also implement the strategies at the right time.

How much should you invest in options trading?

It is advisable to start your investment with $5,000 to $15,000. Try not investing all of your savings or income on it since there is a high-risk factor involved in trading options.

When should you exercise your options?

According to Bill Bischoff, you should exercise your options put the very last-minute.

The last-minute is when the stock has risen to the point where you are ready to unload — or just before the option expiration date, whichever comes first. At the last minute or on the date of expiration, you know that there is no going higher than this, so you can easily exercise your options, although, on the last day, the tax cost is usually higher.

Best strategy of options trading?

According to Allen Everhart, there is no such thing is the best strategy. Everyday stock or market rate is different. Even the underlying asset or companies are different from each other too. You cannot apply one strategy to all of your options. However, all options trading strategies are directional.

What is a short put and long call strategy?

A short put and a long call are direction-ally the same. The shot put and the long call makes money when the stock goes up. But short put is known to be a little riskier than the long call strategy.

The short put can be exercised if the stock does not decline, and in that case, you can keep the premium of the option.

How an option writer makes money?

An option writer makes money when the stock or premium that has been bought reaches its expiration date without being exercised. In that case, the option writer gets to keep the entire premium.

How do investors lose money in options trading?

There is no one specific reason why an investor loses his/her money. There are different cases and scenarios. But the most common mistakes people make are they do not gather enough information or their lack of knowledge. Most people assume that it is a short way to become rich or may believe in "luck" too much.

CONCLUSION

thank you for downloading this book. The objective of writing it was to let amateurs, novices, and even pros understand the tricky and sometimes hard to digest concepts.

The language of this book is, therefore, simple, easy, and user-friendly (in a sense that anyone can grab the meaning). On top of that, we have added as many examples as we could with each new concept so that the reader does not get confused.

In the end, we would wind up from where we began from – 'learning the concepts of options trading might seem difficult – but once you grab them – they are yours!"

So, just remember, you have got to be patient, risk-tolerant, and a mindful planner when it comes to business. Have a great trade. May each of your investments give you more profit than you expected.

PYTHON

FOR

BEGINNERS

A crash course guide for machine learning and web programming. Learn
a computer language in easy steps with coding exercises.

JASON TEST

Design patterns are reusable model for solving known and common problems in software architecture.

They are best described as templates for working with a specific normal situation. An architect can have a template for designing certain types of door frames, which he fit into many of his project, and a software engineer or software architect must know the templates for solving common programming tasks.

An excellent presentation of the design pattern should include:

Name

Motivating problem

Decision

Effects

Equivalent Problems

If you thought it was a rather vague concept, you would be right. For example, we could say that the following "pattern" solves all your problems:

Gather and prepare the necessary data and other resources

Make the necessary calculations and do the necessary work

Make logs of what you do

Free all resources

???

Profit

This is an example of too abstract thinking. You cannot call it a template because it is not an excellent model to solve any problem, even though it is technically applicable to any of them (including cooking dinner).

On the other hand, you may have solutions that are too specific to be called a template. For example, you may wonder if QuickSort is a template to solve the sorting problem.

This is, of course, a common program problems, and QuickSort is a good solution for it. However, it can be applied to any sorting problem with virtually no change.

Once you have this in the library and you can call it, your only real job is to make somehow your object comparable, and you don't have to deal with its entity yourself to change it to fit your specific problem.

Equivalent problems lie somewhere between these concepts. These are different problems that are similar enough that you can apply the same model to them, but are different enough that this model is significantly customized to be applicable in each case.

Patterns that can be applied to these kinds of problems are what we can meaningfully call design patterns.

Why use design patterns?

You are probably familiar with some design patterns through code writing practice. Many good programmers end up gravitating towards them, not even being explicitly trained, or they simply take them from their seniors along the way.

The motivation to create, learn, and use design patterns has many meanings. This is a way to name complex abstract concepts to provide discussion and learning.

They make communication within the team faster because someone can simply use the template name instead of calling the board. They allow you to learn from the experiences of people who were before you, and not to reinvent the wheel, going through the whole crucible of gradually improving practices on your own (and constantly cringing from your old code).

Bad decisions that are usually made up because they seem logical at first glance are often called anti-patterns. For something to be rightly called an anti-pattern, it must be reinvented, and for the same problem, there must be a pattern that solves it better.

Despite the apparent usefulness in this practice, designing patterns are also useful for learning. They introduce you to many problems that you may not have considered and allow you to think about scenarios with which you may not have had hands-on experience.

They are mandatory for training for all, and they are an excellent learning resources for all aspiring architect and developing who may be at the beginning of their careers and who have no direct experience in dealing with the various problems that the industry provides.

Python Design Patterns

Traditionally, design models have been divided into three main categories: creative, structural, and behavioral. There are other categories, such as architectural patterns or concurrency patterns, but they are beyond the scope of this article.

There are also Python-specific design patterns that are created specifically around problems that the language structure itself provides, or that solve problems in unique ways that are only resolved due to the language structure.

Generating Patterns deal with creating classes or objects. They serve to abstract the specifics of classes, so that we are less dependent on their exact implementation, or that we do not have to deal with complex constructions whenever we need them, or that we provide some special properties of the instantiation. They are very useful for reducing dependency and controlling how the user interacts with our classes.

Structural patterns deal with assembling objects and classes into larger structures while keeping these structures flexible and efficient. They, as a rule, are really useful for improving the readability and maintainability of the code, ensuring the correct separation of functionality, encapsulation, and the presence of effective minimal interfaces between interdependent things. Behavioral patterns deal with algorithms in general and the distribution of responsibility between interacting objects. For example, they are good practice when you may be tempted to implement a naive solution, such as busy waiting, or load your classes with unnecessary code for one specific purpose, which is not the core of their functionality.

Generative Patterns

Factory

Abstract factory

Builder

Prototype

Singleton

Object pool

Structural Patterns

Adapter

Bridge

Composite

Decorator

Facade

Flyweight

Proxy

Behavioral patterns

Chain of responsibility

Command

Iterator

Mediator

Memento

Observer

State

Strategy

Visitor

Python Specific Design Patterns

Global object pattern

Prebound method pattern

Sentinel object pattern

Type Annotation in Python

First, let's answer the question: why do we need annotations in Python? In short, the answer will be this: to increase the information content of the source code and to be able to analyze it using specialized tools. One of the most popular, in this sense, is the control of variable types. Even though Python is a language with dynamic typing, sometimes there is a need for type control.

According to PEP 3107, there may be the following annotation use cases:

type checking:

expansion of the IDE functionality in terms of providing information about the expected types of arguments and the type of return value for functions:

overload of functions and work with generics:

interaction with other languages:

use in predicate logical functions:

mapping of requests in databases:

marshaling parameters in RPC (remote procedure call)

Using annotations in functions

In functions, we can annotate arguments and the return value. It may look like this:

```
def repeater (s: str, n: int) -> str:
return s * n
```

An annotation for an argument is defined after the colon after its name:

```
argument_name: annotation
```

An annotation that determines the type of the value returned by the function is indicated after its name using the characters ->

```
def function_name () -> type
```

Annotations are not supported for lambda functions
Access to function annotations Access to the annotations
Used in the function can be obtained through the annotations
attribute, in which annotations are presented in the form of a
dictionary, where the keys are attributes, and the values are
annotations. The main value to returned by the function is stored in
the record with the return key.
Contents of repeater . annotations :

```
{'n': int, 'return': str, 's': str}
```

4 programming languages to learn, even if you are a humanist

The digital age dictates its own rules. Now, knowledge of programming languages is moving from the category of "too highly specialized skill" to must have for a successful career. We have compiled for you the four most useful programming languages that will help you become a truly effective specialist.

Vba

If you constantly work in Excel and spend time on the same routine operations every day, you should consider automating them. Macros - queries in the VBA language built into Excel will help you with this. Having mastered macros, you can not only save time, but also free up time for more interesting tasks (for example, to write new macros). By the way, to automate some operations, learning VBA is not necessary - just record a few actions using the macro recorder, and you can repeat them from time to time. But it's better to learn this language: macro recordings will give you only limited functionality.

Despite its attractiveness, macros have two drawbacks. Firstly, since a macro automatically does all the actions that you would do with your hands, it seriously loads RAM (for example, if you have 50,000 lines in a document, your poor computer may not withstand macro attacks). The second - VBA as a programming language is not very intuitive, and it can be difficult for a beginner to learn it from scratch.

SQL

In order to combine data from different databases, you can use the formulas VPR and INDEX (SEARCH). But what if you have ten different databases with 50 columns of 10,000 rows each? Chances are good to make a mistake and spend too much time.

Therefore, it is better to use the Access program. Like VPR, it is designed to combine data from various databases, but it does it much faster. Access automates this function, as well as quickly filters information and allows you to work in a team. In addition to Access, there are other programs for working with databases (DBMS), in most of which you can work using a simple programming language - SQL (Structured Query Language). Knowledge of SQL is one of the basic requirements for business analysts along with knowledge of Excel, so we advise you to take a closer look if you want to work in this area.

R

R is a good alternative to VBA if you want to make data processing easier. How is he good? Firstly, unlike a fellow, it is really simple and understandable even for those who have never had anything to do with programming in their life. Secondly, R is designed to work with databases and has wide functionality: it can change the structure of a document, collect data from the Internet, process statistically different types of information, build graphs, create tag clouds, etc. To work with Excel files, you will have to download special libraries, but it is most convenient to save tables from Excel in csv format and work in them. By the way, it is R that the program was written with which we make TeamRoulette in our championships. Thanks to her, we manage to scatter people on teams in five minutes instead of two hours.

To learn how to work in R, first of all, download a visual and intuitive programming environment - RStudio .

Python

Python is an even more powerful and popular programming language (by the way, it really has nothing to do with python). Like R, Python has special libraries that work with Excel files, and it also knows how to collect information from the Internet (forget about manually driving data into tables!). You can write endlessly about Python, but if in a nutshell - it's a really convenient and quick tool that is worth mastering if you want to automate routine operations, develop your own algorithmic thinking and generally keep up with technical progress.

Unlike R, Python does not have one of the most convenient programming environments - here everyone is free to choose to taste. For example, we recommend IDLE, Jupyter Notebook, Spyder, for more advanced programmers - PyCharm.

You_can learn how to program in Python and analyze data using it in our online course "Python. Data Analysis". The consultants from Big4 and Big3 will tell you how to work with libraries, create programs and algorithms for processing information.

Well, as it were, let's go

Well, if you (You, He, She, It, They) are reading this means we are starting our first Python lesson. Hooray (...) Today you will learn how to code. And what's more, you'll learn how to code in Python. But to start coding you need Python. Where to get it?

Where to get Python?

But you think that now you can just sit down and cod. Well actually yes. BUT usually real hackers and programmers code in code editors. For working with Python We (I) recommend using a Jupyter Notebook or JupyterLab or Visual Studio Code. We (I) Will code in Visual Studio Code, but the other editors are no different.

Well, it's CODING time.

I'm too old for that

Everyone always writes the first code that displays "Hello World". Well, are we some kind of gifted? No, and therefore we will begin with this. In Python, the print () function is used to output text. To output "Hello World" we need to write the following:

```
1    print("Hello world!!!")
```

It's alife

Yes, you just wrote your first program. Now you are a programmer (NO).

Let's look at the structure of the print function. This function consists of the name - print, and the place where we throw what this function should output. If you want to display any text, you need to write it in quotation mark, either in single or double.

But now let's enter some text. For this, Python has an input function. To accept something, you need to write the following:

```
1    a=input()
2    print(a)
```

What does this program do for us? First we introduce something, at the moment we don't care what it is, text or numbers. After, our program displays what you wrote.

But how to make sure that we write the text before entering something? Really simple. There are two ways to do this.

```
1    print('            )
2    a=input()
3    print(a)
```

How can, but not necessary

If you run the second program you will notice that you have to enter data in the same line in which the text is written.

```
1    a=input(          )
2    print(a)
```

How to do

But this is not aesthetically pleasing. We are here with you all the aesthetes. And so in order for you to enter values on a separate line, you can do the following:

```
1    a=input(          )
2    print(a)
```

Like cool, but why?

As we can see, \ n appeared at the end. This is a control character that indicates the passage to the next line. But it's too lazy for me to write it down every time, and therefore I prefer to type everything in the line where the text is written.

But where to apply it? Very simple, you can take math. There are some simple arithmetic operations in Python that I will tell you about now.

Python has the following arithmetic operations: addition, subtraction, multiplication, division, integer division,

exponentiation, and the remainder of division. As everything is
recorded, you can see below:

```
1    6+2
2    6-2
3    6*2
4    6/2
5    3//2
6    3**2
7    3%2
```

I will finally learn how to multiply

If you want to immediately print the result, then you just need to
write an arithmetic operation in print:

```
1    print(6+2)
```

The result of this program will be 8

But how do we carry out operations with numbers that the user
enters? We need to use input. But by default in Python, the values
that input passes are a string. And most arithmetic operations
cannot be performed on a line. In order for our program to work as
we intended, we need to specify what type of value Python should
use.

To do this, we use the int function:

```
1    a=int(input("        : "))
2    b=int(input("        : "))
3    print(a+b)
```

We add up the two numbers that the user enters. (Wow, I found out how much 2 + 2 will be)

Python code optimization with ctypes

Content:

Basic optimizations

Styles

Python compilation

Structures in Python

Call your code in C

Pypy

Basic optimizations

Before rewriting the Python source code in C, consider the basic optimization methods in Python.

Built-in Data Structures

Python's built-in data structures, such as set and dict, are written in C. They work much faster than your own data structures composed as Python classes. Other data structures besides the standard set, dict, list, and tuple are described in the collections module documentation.

List expressions

Instead of adding items to the list using the standard method, use list expressions.

```
#Slow
    mapped = []
    for value in originallist:
    mapped.append (myfunc (value))

    # Faster
    mapped = [myfunc (value) in originallist]
```

ctypes

The ctypes module allows you to interact with C code from Python without using a module subprocessor another similar module to start other processes from the CLI.

There are only two parts: compiling C code to load in quality shared object and setting up data structures in Python code to map them to C types.

In this article, I will combine my Python code with LCS.c, which finds the longest subsequence in two-line lists. I want the following to work in Python:

```
list1 = ['My', 'name', 'is', 'Sam', 'Stevens', '!']
    list2 = ['My','name', 'is', 'Alex', 'Stevens', '.']

    common = lcs (list1, list2)

    print (common)
    # ['My', 'name', 'is', 'Stevens']
```

One problem is that this particular C function is the signature of a function that takes lists of strings as argument types and returns a type that does not have a fixed length. I solve this problem with a sequence structure containing pointers and lengths.

Compiling C code in Python

First, C source code (lcs.c) is compiled in lcs.soto load in Python.

```
gcc -c -Wall -Werror -fpic -O3 lcs.c -o lcs.o
    gcc -shared -o lcs.so lcs.o
```

Wall will display all warnings:

Werror will wrap all warnings in errors:

fpic will generate position-independent instructions that you will need if you want to use this library in Python:

O3 maximizes optimization:

And now we will begin to write Python code using the resulting shared object file.

Structures in Python

Below are two data structures that are used in my C code.

```
struct sequence
    {
        char ** items:
        int length:
    }:

    struct cell
    {
        int index:
        int length:
        struct Cell * prev:
    }:
```

And here is the translation of these structures into Python.

```
import ctypes
    class SEQUENCE (ctypes.Structure):
        _fields_ = [('items', ctypes.POINTER (ctypes.c_char_p)),
                    ('length', ctypes.c_int)]

    class CELL (ctypes.Structure):
        pass

    CELL._fields_ = [('index', ctypes.c_int), ('length',
ctypes.c_int),
                    ('prev', ctypes.POINTER (CELL))]
```

A few notes:

All structures are classes that inherit from ctypes.Structure.

The only field _fields_is a list of tuples. Each tuple is (<variable-

name>, <ctypes.TYPE>).

There ctypesare similar types in c_char (char) and c_char_p (* char)
.

There is ctypesalso one POINTER()that creates a type pointer from each type passed to it.

If you have a recursive definition like in CELL, you must pass the initial declaration, and then add the fields _fields_in order to get a link to yourself later.

Since I did not use CELLPython in my code, I did not need to write this structure, but it has an interesting property in the recursive field.

Call your code in C

In addition, I needed some code to convert Python types to new structures in C. Now you can use your new C function to speed up Python code.

```python
def list_to_SEQUENCE (strlist: List [str]) -> SEQUENCE:
    bytelist = [bytes (s, 'utf-8') for s in strlist]
    arr = (ctypes.c_char_p * len (bytelist)) ()
    arr [:] = bytelist
    return SEQUENCE (arr, len (bytelist))


def lcs (s1: List [str], s2: List [str]) -> List[str]:
    seq1 = list_to_SEQUENCE(s1)
    seq2 = list_to_SEQUENCE(s2)

# struct Sequence * lcs (struct Sequence * s1, struct Sequence *
s2)
common = lcsmodule.lcs (ctypes.byref (seq1), ctypes.byref
(seq2)) [0]

    ret = []

    for i in range (common.length):
        ret.append (common.items [i] .decode ('utf-8'))
    lcsmodule.freeSequence (common)

    return ret

lcsmodule = ctypes.cdll.LoadLibrary ('lcsmodule / lcs.so')
lcsmodule.lcs.restype = ctypes.POINTER (SEQUENCE)

list1 = ['My', 'name', 'is', 'Sam', 'Stevens', '!']
list2 = ['My', 'name', 'is', 'Alex', 'Stevens', '.']

common = lcs (list1, list2)

print (common)

# ['My', 'name', 'is', 'Stevens']
```

A few notes:

**char (list of strings) matches directly to a list of bytes in Python.

There lcs.cis a function lcs()with the signature struct Sequence * lcs (struct Sequence * s1, struct Sequence

s2) . To set up the return type, I use lcsmodule.lcs.restype = ctypes.POINTER(SEQUENCE).

To make a call with a reference to the Sequence structure, I use ctypes.byref()one that returns a "light pointer" to your object (faster than ctypes.POINTER()).

common.items- this is a list of bytes, they can be decoded to get retin the form of a list str.

lcsmodule.freeSequence (common) just frees the memory associated with common. This is important because the garbage collector (AFAIK) will not automatically collect it.

Optimized Python code is code that you wrote in C and wrapped in Python.

Something More: PyPy

Attention: I myself have never used PyPy.

One of the simplest optimizations is to run your programs in the PyPy runtime, which contains a JIT compiler (just-in-time) that speeds up the work of loops, compiling them into machine code for repeated execution.

Finding the Perfect Toolkit: Analyzing Popular Python Project Templates

The materials, the translation of which we publish today, is dedicated to the story about the tools used to create Python applications. It is designed for those programmers who have already left the category of beginners but have not yet reached the category of experienced Python developers.

For those who can't wait to start practice, the author suggests using Flake8,pytest, and Sphinx in existing Python projects. He also recommends a look at pre-commit,Black, and Pylint. Those who plan to start a new project, he advises paying attention to Poetry and Dependable.

Overview

It has always been difficult for me to form an objective opinion about the "best practices" of Python development. In the world of technology, some popular trends are continually emerging, often not existing for long. This complicates the extraction of the "useful signal" from the information noise.

The freshest tools are often only good, so to speak, on paper. Can they help the practical programmer with something? Or their application only leads to the introduction of something new in the project, the performance of which must be maintained, which carries more difficulties than benefits?

I didn't have a clear understanding of what exactly I considered the "best practices" of development. I suppose I found something useful, based mainly on episodic evidence of "utility," and on the occasional mention of this in conversations. I decided to put things in order in this matter. To do this, I began to analyze all the templates of Python projects that I could find (we are talking about templates used by the cookiecutter command-line utility to create Python projects based on them).

It seemed to me that it was fascinating to learn about what auxiliary tools the template authors consider worthy of getting these tools into new Python projects created based on these templates.

I analyzed and compared the 18 most popular template projects (from 76 to 6300 stars on GitHub), paying particular attention to what kind of auxiliary tools they use. The results of this examination can be found in this table.

Below I want to share the main conclusions that I have made while analyzing popular templates.

De facto standards

The tools discussed in this section are included in more than half of the templates. This means that they are perceived as standard in a large number of real Python projects.

Flake8

I have been using Flake8 for quite some time, but I did not know about the dominant position in the field of linting that this tool occupies. I thought that it exists in a kind of competition, but the vast majority of project templates use it.

Yes, this is not surprising. It is difficult to oppose something to the convenience of linting the entire code base of the project in a matter of seconds. Those who want to use cutting-edge development can recommend a look at us make-python-style guide. This is something like "Flake8 on steroids." This tool may well contribute to the transfer to the category of obsolete other similar tools (like Pylint).

Pytest and coverage.py

The vast majority of templates use pytest. This reduces the use of the standard unit test framework. Pytest looks even more attractive when combined with tox. That's precisely what was done in about half of the templates. Code coverage with tests is most often checked using coverage.py.

Sphinx

Most templates use Sphinx to generate documentation. To my surprise, MkDocs is rarely used for this purpose.

As a result, we can say that if you do not use Flake8, pytest, and Sphinx in your current project, then you should consider introducing them.

Promising tools

In this section, I collected those tools and techniques, the use of which in the templates suggested some trends. The point is that although all this does not appear in most project templates, it is found in many relatively recent templates. So - all this is worth paying attention to.

Pyproject.toml

File usage is pyproject.tomlsuggested in PEP 518. This is a modern mechanism for specifying project assembly requirements. It is used in most fairly young templates.

Poetry

Although the Python ecosystem isn't doing well in terms of an excellent tool for managing dependencies, I cautiously optimistic that Poetry could be the equivalent of npm from the JavaScript world in the Python world.

The youngest (but popular) project templates seem to agree with this idea of mine. Real, it is worth saying that if someone is working on some kind of library that he can plan to distribute through PyPI, then he will still have to use setup tools. (It should to be noted that after the publication of this material, I was informed that this is no longer a problem).

Also, be careful if your project (the same applies to dependencies) relies on Conda. In this case, Poetry will not suit you, since this tool, in its current form, binds the developer to pip and virtualenv.

Dependabot

Dependabot regularly checks project dependencies for obsolescence and tries to help the developer by automatically opening PR.

I have recently seen this tool more often than before. It seems like to me that it is an excellent tool: the addition of which to the project affects the project very positively. Dependabot helps reduce security risks by pushing developers to keep dependencies up to date.

As a result, I advised you not to lose sight of Poetry and Dependabot. Consider introducing these tools into your next project.

Personal recommendations

Analysis of project templates gave me a somewhat ambivalent perception of the tools that I will list in this section. In any case, I want to use this section to tell about them, based on my own experience. At one time, they were beneficial to me.

Pre-commit

Even if you are incredibly disciplined - do not waste your energy on performing simple routine actions such as additional code run through the linter before sending the code to the repository. Similar tasks can be passed to Pre-commit. And it's better to spend your energy on TDD and teamwork on code.

Pylint

Although Pylint is criticized for being slow, although this tool is criticized for the features of its settings, I can say that it allowed me to grow above myself in the field of programming.

He gives me specific instructions on those parts of the code that I can improve, tells me how to make the code better comply with the rules. For a free tool, this alone is already very much. Therefore, I am ready to put up with the inconvenience associated with Pylint.

Black

Black at the root of the debate over where to put spaces in the code. This protects our teams from an empty talk and meaningless differences in files caused by different editors' settings.

In my case, it brightens up what I don't like about Python (the need to use a lot of spaces). Moreover, it should be noted that the Black project in 2019 joined the Python Software Foundation, which indicates the seriousness and quality of this project.

As a result, I want to say that if you still do not use pre-commit, Black, and Pylint - think about whether these tools can benefit your team.

Subtotals

Twelve of the eighteen investigated templates were created using the cookiecutter framework. Some of those templates where this framework is not used have exciting qualities.

But given the fact that cookiecutter is the leading framework for creating project templates, those who decide to use a template that did not use a cookiecutter should have excellent reasons for this. Such a decision should be very well justified.

Those who are looking for a template for their project should choose a template that most closely matches his view of things. If you, when creating projects according to a precise template, continuously have to reconfigure them in the same way, think about how to fork such a template and refine it, inspired by examples of templates from my list.

And if you are attracted to adventure - create your template from scratch. Cookiecutter is an excellent feature of the Python ecosystem, and the simple process of creating Jinja templates allows you to quickly and easily do something your own.

Bonus: Template Recommendations

Django

Together with the most popular Django templates, consider using we make-django-template. It gives the impression of a deeply thought out product.

Data Processing and Analysis

In most projects aimed at processing and analyzing data, the Cookiecutter Data Science template is useful. However, data scientists should also look at Kedro.

This template extends Cookiecutter Data Science with a mechanism for creating standardized data processing pipelines. It supports loading and saving data and models. These features are very likely to be able to find a worthy application in your next project.

Here I would also like to express my gratitude to the creators of the shablona template for preparing very high- quality documentation. It can be useful to you even if you end up choosing something else.

General Purpose Templates

Which general-purpose template to choose in some way depends on what exactly you are going to develop based on this template - a library or a regular application. But I, selecting a similar template, along with the most popular projects of this kind, would look very closely at Jace's Python Template.

This is not a well-known pattern, but I like the fact that it has Poetry, isort , Black, pylint, and mypy .

PyScaffold is one of the most popular non-cookiecutter based templates. It has many extensions (for example, for Django, and Data Science projects). It also downloads version numbers from GitHub using setuptools-scm. Further, this is one of the few templates supporting Conda.

Here are a couple of templates that use GitHub Actions technology: The Python Best Practices Cookiecutter template, which, I want to note, has most of my favorite tools.

The Blueprint / Boilerplate For Python Projects template, which I find pretty interesting, as the ability it gives them to find common security problems with Bandit, looks promising. Also, this template has a remarkable feature, which consists in the fact that the settings of all tools are collected in a single file setup.cfg.

And finally - I recommend taking a look at we make-python-package template. I think it's worth doing it anyway. In particular, if you like the Django template of the same developer, or if you are going to use the advanced, we make-python-style guide instead of pure Flake8.

How are broad integer types implemented in Python?

When you write in a low-level language such as C, you are worried about choosing the right data type and qualifiers for your integers, at each step, you analyze whether it will be enough to use it simply intor whether you need to add longor even long double. However, when writing code in Python, you don't need to worry about these "minor" things, because Python can work with numbers of integerany size type .

In C, if you try to calculate 220,000 using the built-in function powl,

```
#include <stdio.h>
#include <math.h>

int main (void) {
  printf ("%Lf\n", powl (2, 20000));
  return 0;
}

$ ./a.out
inf
```

you will get the output inf.

But in Python, making this easier than ever is easy:

```
>>> 2 ** 20,000
39802768403379665923543072061912024537047727804924259387134 ...

... 6021 digits long ...

....
6309376
```

It must be under the hood that Python is doing something very beautiful, and today we will find out the exactly what it does to work with integers of arbitrary size!

Presentation and Definition

Integer in Python, this is a C structure defined as follows:

```
struct _longobject {
    PyObject_VAR_HEAD
    digit ob_digit [1];
};
```

PyObject_VAR_HEADIs a macro, it expands to PyVarObject, which has the following structure:

```
typedef struct {
    PyObject ob_base;
    Py_ssize_t ob_size; /* Number of items in variable part */
} PyVarObject;
```

Other types that have PyObject_VAR_HEAD:

PyBytesObject

PyTupleObject

PyListObject

This means that an integer, like a tuple or a list, has a variable length, and this is the first step to understanding how Python can support work with giant numbers. Once expanded, the macro _longobjectcan be considered as:

```
struct _longobject {
    PyObject ob_base;
    Py_ssize_t ob_size; /* Number of items in variable part */
    digit ob_digit [1];
};
```

There PyObjectare some meta fields in the structure that are used for reference counting (garbage collection), but to talk about this, we need a separate article. The field on which we will focus this ob_digitand in a bit ob_size.

Decoding ob_digit

ob_digitIs a statically allocated array of unit length of type digit (typedef для uint32_t). Since this is an array, it ob_digitis a pointer primarily to a number, and therefore, if necessary, it can be increased using the malloc function to any length. This way, python can represent and process very large numbers.

Typically, in low-level languages such as C, the precision of integers is limited to 64 bits. However, Python supports integers of arbitrary precision. Starting with Python 3, all numbers are presented in the form bignum and are limited only by the available system memory.

Decoding ob_size

ob_sizestores the number of items in ob_digit. Python overrides and then uses the value ob_sizeto to determine the actual number of elements contained in the array to increase the efficiency of allocating memory to the array ob_digit.

Storage

The most naive way to store integer numbers is to store one decimal digit in one element of the array. Operation such as additional and subtractions can be performed according to the rules of mathematics from elementary school.

With this approach, the number 5238 will be saved like this:

This approach is inefficient because we will use up to 32-bit digits (uint32_t) for storing a decimal digit, which ranges from 0 to 9 and can be easily represented with only 4 bits. After all, when writing something as universal like python, the kernel developer needs to be even more inventive.

So, can we do better? Of course, otherwise, we would not have posted this article. Let's take a closer look at how Python stores an extra-long integer.

Python path

Instead of storing only one decimal digit in each element of the array ob_digit, Python converts the numbers from the number system with base 10 to the numbers in the system with base 230 and calls each element as a number whose value ranges from 0 to 230 - 1.

In the hexadecimal number system, the base 16 ~ 24 means that each "digit" of the hexadecimal number ranges from 0 to 15 in the decimal number system. In Python, it's similar to a "number" with a

base of 230, which means that the number will range from 0 to 230
- 1 = 1073741823 in decimal.

In this way, Python effectively uses almost all of the allocated space
of 32 bits per digit, saves resources, and still performs simple
operations, such as adding and subtracting at the math level of
elementary school.

Depending on the platform, Python uses either 32-bit unsigned
integer arrays or 16-bit unsigned integer arrays with 15-bit digits.
To perform the operations that will be discussed later, you need
only a few bits.

Example: 1152921504606846976

As already mentioned, for Python, numbers are represented in a
system with a base of 230, that is, if you convert
1152921504606846976 into a number system with a base of 230,
you will get 100.

1152 9215 0460 6846 976 = 1 * ((230) 2 + 0) * ((230) 1 + 0) *((230)
0)

Since it is the ob_digitfirst to store the least significant digit, it is
stored as 001 in three digits. The structure _longobjectfor this value
will contain:

ob_size like 3

ob_digit like [0, 0, 1]

We created a demo REPL that will show how Python stores an integer inside itself, and also refers to structural members such as ob_size, ob_refcountetc.

Integer Long Operations

Now that we have a pure idea of how Python implements integers of arbitrary precision, it is time to understand how various mathematical operations are performed with them.

Addition

Integers are stored "in numbers," which means that addition is as simple as in elementary school, and the Python source code shows us that this is how addition is implemented. A function with a name x_addin a file longobject.cadds two numbers.

```
For (i = 0; i < size_b; ++i) {
    carry += a-> ob_digit [i] + b-> ob_digit [i];
    z-> ob_digit [i] = carry & PyLong_MASK;
    carry >> = PyLong_SHIFT;
}
For ( ; i < size_a; ++i) {
    carry += a-> ob_digit [i];
    z-> ob_digit [i] = carry & PyLong _MASK;
    carry >> = PyLong_SHIFT;
}
z-> ob_digit [i] = carry;
```

The code snippet above is taken from a function x_add. As you can see, it iterates over a number by numbers and performs the addition of numbers, calculates the result and adds hyphenation.

It becomes more interesting when the result of addition is a negative number. The sign ob_sizeis an integer sign, that is, if you have a negative number, then it ob_sizewill be a minus. The value ob_sizemodulo will determine the number of digits in ob_digit.

Subtraction

Just as addition takes place, subtraction also takes place. A function with a name x_subin the file longobject.csubtracts one number from another.

```
For (i = 0: i < size_b: ++ i) {
    borrow = a -> ob_digit [i] - b-> ob_digit [i] - borrow:
    z-> ob_digit [i] = borrow & PyLong_MASK:
    borrow >> = PyLong_SHIFT:
    borrow & = 1: /* Keep only one sign bit */
}
for (: i <size_a: ++ i) {
    borrow = a-> ob_digit [i] - borrow:
    z-> ob_digit [i] = borrow & PyLong_MASK:
    borrow >> = PyLong_SHIFT:
    borrow & = 1: /* Keep only one sign bit */
}
```

The code snippet above is taken from a function x_sub. In it, you see how the enumeration of numbers occurs and subtraction is performed, the result is calculated and the transfer is distributed. Indeed, it is very similar to addition.

Multiplication

And again, the multiplication will be implemented in the same naive way that we learned from the lessons of mathematics in elementary school, but it is not very efficient. To maintain efficiency, Python implements theKaratsuba algorithm, which multiplies two n-digit numbers in O (nlog23) simple steps.

The algorithm is not simple and its implementation is beyond the scope of this article, but you can find its implementation in functions and in the file .k_mul k_lopsided_mullongobject.c

Division and other operations

All operations on integers are defined in the file longobject.c, they are very simple to find and trace the work of each. Attention: A detailed understanding of the work of each of them will take time, so pre-stock up with popcorn.

Optimizing Frequently Used Integers

Python preallocates a small number of integers in memory ranging from -5 to 256. This allocation occurs during initialization, and since we cannot change integers (immutability), these pre-allocated numbers are singleton and are directly referenced instead of being allocated. This means that every time we use/create a small number, Python instead of reallocation simply returns a reference to the previously allocated number.

Such optimization can be traced in the macro IS_SMALL_INTand function get_small_intc longobject.c. So Python saves a lot of space and time in calculating commonly used integer numbers.

Create a bot in Python to learn English

No, this is not one of the hundreds of articles on how to write your first Hello World bot in Python. Here you will not find detailed instructions on how to get an API token in BotFather or launch a bot in the cloud. In return, we will show you how to unleash the full power of Python to the maximum to achieve the most aesthetic and beautiful code. We perform a song about the appeal of complex structures - we dance and dance. Under the cut asynchrony, its system of saves, a bunch of useful decorators, and a lot of beautiful code.

Disclaimer: People with brain OOP and adherents of the "right" patterns may ignore this article.

Idea

To understand what it is like not to know English in modern society, imagine that you are an 18th-century nobleman who does not know French. Even if you are not very well versed in history, you can still imagine how hard it would be to live under such circumstances. In the modern world, English has become a necessity, not a privilege, especially if you are in the IT industry. The project is based on the catechism of the future: the development of a neural network as a separate unit, and education, which is based on games and sports spirit. Isomorphic paradigms have been hanging in the air since ancient times, but it seems that over time, people began to forget that the most straightforward solutions are the most effective.

Here is a shortlist of the basic things I want to put together:

Be able to work with three user dictionaries

Ability to parse youtube video/text, and then add new words to the user's dictionary

Two basic skills training modes

Flexible customization: full control over user dictionaries and the environment in general

Built-in admin panel

Naturally, everything should work quickly, with the ability to easily replenish existing functionality in the future. Putting it all together, I thought that the best embodiment of my idea into reality would be a Telegram bot. My tale is not about how to write handlers for the bot correctly - there are dozens of such articles, and this is simple mechanical work. I want the reader to learn to ignore the typical dogmas of programming. Use what is profitable and effective here and now.

"I learned to let out the cries of unbelievers past my ears because it was impossible to suppress them."

Base structure

The bot will be based on the python-telegram-bot (ptb) library. I use loguru as a logger , though there is one small snag here. The fact is that ptb by default uses a different logger (standard logging) and does not allow you to connect your own. Of course, it would be possible to intercept all journal messages globally and send them to our registrar, but we will do it a little easier:

```python
from loguru import logger
import sys

# Configure dual-stream output to the console and to the file
config = {
    'handlers': [
        {'sink': sys.stdout, 'level': 'INFO'},
        {'sink': 'logs.log', 'serialize': False, 'level': 'DEBUG'},
    ]
}

logger.configure(**config)

# ...

updater = Updater('YOUR_TOKEN')
dp = updater.dispatcher

# Roughly fasten your logger. Cheap and cheerful
updater.logger = logger
dp.logger = logger
```

Unfortunately, I don't have the opportunity to deploy my bot on stable data centers, so data security is a priority. For these purposes, I implemented my system of saves. It provides flexible and convenient work with data - statistics collection, as an example of easy replenishment of functionality in the future.

```python
from __future__ import annotations  # In the future, I will omit this import
from loguru import logger

import inspect
import functools
import os

def file_is_empty (path: str) -> bool:
    return os.stat (path) .st_size == 0

def clear_file (path: str) -> None:
    with open (path, 'w'): pass

def cache_decorator (method):
    @ functools.wraps (method)
    def wrapper (self, * args, ** kwargs):
        res = method (self, * args, ** kwargs)
        Cache.link.recess (self, {'method_name': method __ name__}) # (1)
        # During testing, multiple calls can slow down
        # program work: opt avoids this
        logger.opt (lazy = True) .debug (f'Decorator for {method __ name__} was end ')
        return res
    return wrapper

class cache:
    """
```

+ cache_si ze - Std thfDtlgh 'hi ch dl data will be su'ed

+ cache_files - Dump file in w'hich all intermediate operations on

data are stored

link = None

def   init   (self. cache_si ze =10):

= Save all screw'ed cl asses. Thi s all or's you t o fl exibl›' vork with data.

sel f. cl asses = []

=Files matching classes

 sel f._cache_fi1es = []

= (1). A sm dl hack that dl or's you to cd1 a specifi c instance thrDtlgh a

common class

= Thi s w'wks because w'e oril \' have one instance Df the cl ass. 'hi ch

= implements d 1 the logic of 'orking with data. In additi on. it is

convenient ari d all o 's

```
= st gum cantl›' expand the functl Dflallt›' in the future
sel f. cl ass .link = self


self._counter = 0
self.CACHE SIZE = cache st ze
def add (self, d s: class, file: str) -> NDne:


All or's to fasten a class to a sa ver


+ cls - Inst an ce of the class
+ file - The fi1 e the instari ce is 'orking with


self._cache_files.append (file)
self._cl asses.append (cls)


if fi1e i s eotptl' (fi1e): return hDne


1ogger.opt dan.'=True).debug(fTor{cls.          class names) file (file) is
not empty' ')


fa data in sells oad(file):
    is.save nDn Caclti ng (data)


cl ear_file (file)
sel f._counter = 0
```

```
def recess (self, cls: ct ass, data diet) —>Ncri e:
```

The main method that performs the basi c l o c of saves

```
if self. counter + 1/ = self.CACHE SIZE:
        self.save all 0
el se:
self._counter + = I
fil ename = self._cache_files [self._classes.index (cls)]
self.save (data. fil enam e = filename)
```

= For simplicit›', save_d1, save, load methods are omitted

Now we can create any methods that can modify data, without fear of losing important data:

```
@cache_decorator
def add_smth_important (* args, ** kwargs) -> Any:
    #...
    # We make some important actions on the data...
    #...
```

Now that we have figured out the basic structure, the main question remains: how to put everything together. I implemented the main class - EnglishBot, which brings together the entire primary structure: PTB, work with the database, the save system, and which will manage the whole business logic of the bot. If the implementation of Telegram commands were simple, we could easily add them to the same class. But, unfortunately, their organization occupies most of the code of the entire application, so adding them to the same class would be crazy. I also did not want to create new classes/subclasses, because I suggest using a very simple structure:

```
# Import the main class
from modules import EnglishBot
# Import classes that implement Telegram commands
from modules.module import start
# ...

if __name__ == '__main__':
    # Initialize the bot
    tbot = EnglishBot (
        # ...
    )

    # Add handlers to the stack
    tbot.add_command_handler (start, 'start')
    # ...
```

How command modules get access to the main class, we will consider further.

All out of nothing

Ptb handlers have two arguments - update and context, which store all the necessary information stack. Context has a wonderful chat_data argument that can be used as a data storage dictionary for chat. But I do not want to constantly refer to it in a format context.chat_data['data']. I would like something light and beautiful, say context.data. However, this is not a problem.

```python
from telegram.ext import CommandHandler

def a (self, key: str):
    # First, check if the class has the required value
    # If not, then try to return it from chat_data
    try:
        return object __ getattribute __ (self, key)
    except:
        return self.chat_data [key]

def b (self, key: str, data = None, replace = True):
    #Small hack: if replace = False and data exists, then overwriting does not occur
    # In this case, if the data is not specified, then they are put in None
    if replace or not self.chat_data.get (key, None):
        self.chat_data [key] = data

# Binding context to receive data in the format context.data
CallbackContext __ getattribute__ = a
# As well as a convenient setter for your needs
CallbackContext.set = b
```

We continue to simplify our lives. Now I want all the necessary

information for a specific user to be in quick access context.

```python
def bind_context (func):
    def wrapper (update, context):
        context._bot.bind_user_data (update, context) # (2)
        return func (update, context)
    return wrapper

class EnglishBot:
    # ...

    def bind_user_data (self, update, context) -> dict:
        context.set ('t_id', update.message.chat_id, replace = False)
        context.set ('t_ln', update.message.from_user.language_code, replace = False)
        # ...
        # Set all the necessary information that we want to have quick access from context
        # For example, something from the database
        # ...
```

Now we'll completely become impudent and fasten our bot

instance to context:

```python
class EnglishBot:
    # ...

    def __init__ (self, * args, ** kwargs):
        # ...
        # (2): Now we can access the instance in the format context._bot
        CallbackContext._bot = self
```

We put everything in place and get a citadel of comfort and

convenience in just one call.

```
from EnglishBot import bind_context

@bind_context
def start (update, context):
    # Now we have access to everything from one place
    # For example, we can easily add a new user to the database
    # Check if the user is in our database
    if not context._bot.user_exist (context.t_id):
        # For example, add some important notifications
        context.set ('push_notification', True)
        # And then add the user to the database
        context._bot.new_user (context.t_id, context.t_ln)

        return update.message.reply_text ('Welcome')
    # ...
```

Decorators are our everything

Most often, it turns out that the name of the function coincides with the name of the command to which we want to add a handler. Why not use this statistical feature for your selfish purposes.

```
class EnglishBot:
    # ...

    def add_command_handler (self, func: function, name = None) -> None:
        """

        Function that adds a command handler
        """

        name = name or func.__name__
        self.dp.add_handler (CommandHandler (name, func))

    # ...

# In the main file:
tbot.add_command_handler (start) # Instead of tbot.add_command_handler (start, 'start')
```

It looks cool, but it doesn't work. It's all about the bind_context decorator, which will always return the name of the wrapper function. Correct this misunderstanding.

```
import functools

def bind_context (func):
    # functools.wraps from stdlib saves signatures since Python 3.4
    @ functools.wraps (func)
    def wrapper (update, context):
        context._bot.bind_user_data (update, context)
        return func (update, context)
    return wrapper
```

There are many message handlers in the bot, which, by design, should cancel the command when entering zero. Also I need to discard all edited posts.

```python
import functools

END = -1

def zero_exiter (func):
    @functools.wraps (func)
    def wrapper (update, context):
        if update.to_dict () ['message']. get ('text', None) == '0':
            update.message.reply_text ('Sending some message')
            return END

        return func (update, context)
    return wrapper

def skip_edited (func):
    @functools.wraps (func)
    def wrapper (update, context):
        # This works in all cases, because None returned
        # in the conversation_handler stack, leaves the function in its current state
        if not update.to_dict (). get ('edited_message', None):
            return func (update, context)
    return wrapper
```

We do not forget at the same time about the most important decorator - @run_asyncon which asynchrony is based. Now we collect the heavy function.

```python
from telegram.ext.dispatcher import run_async
from EnglishBot import skip_edited

@run_async
@skip_edited
def heavy_function (update, context):
    # ...
    # A heavy computing function that needs asynchrony
    # Has post edit protection
    # ...
```

Remember that asynchrony is a Jedi sword, but with this sword, you can quickly kill yourself.

Sometimes programs freeze without sending anything to the log.
@logger.catch, the last decorator on our list, ensures that any error
is correctly reported to a logger.

```
from loguru import logger

@ logger.catch
def heavy_function2 (update, context):
    # ...
    # Another heavy computing function on which a program may hang
    # ...
```

Admin panel

Let's implement an admin panel with the ability to receive/delete
logs and send a message to all users.

```
from EnglishBot import bind_context
from Cache import file_is_empty
from telegram import ReplyKeyboardMarkup
from loguru import logger

LOG_FILE = 'logs.log'
SENDING, MAIN, END = range (1, -2, -1)

buttons = ReplyKeyboardMarkup (
    [('Get logs', 'logs'), ('Clear logs', 'clear')],
    [('Send message', 'send')],
    # [...],
)

@bind_context
def admin_panel (update, context):
    # Check user admin rights
    if not context._bot_acess_check (context.t_id):
        # A good security practice is to show the user that such a command does not exist
        return update.message.reply_text (f'Unknown command {update.message.text} ')

    update.message.reply_text ('Choose an option:', reply_markup = buttons)

    return MAIN

    !fi ero exi:er
    def send d1 (updast    context).
        count = 0
```

```
!fi ero exiter
def send d1 (updast    context).
    count = 0
```

```
logsmethods
```

```
def get logs (update context).
    if fil e is empU.' (LOG FILE).
        update.cd1back quo.'.rep1>' text
            are empU.") else.
      = Show' document loading
        context.bot.send chat acti <xi
        (chat id = context.t icL action
        = 'upload docum cut')
        context.bot.sendDocument (chat i
        d = context.t icL docimi cut =
        open (L OG FILE 'rb') name = L
        Ohr FILE
time<xit = 1000)

      = Since we do not cl ose the admin
        panel you need to rem ove the
        dourload icon on the button
        update.cd1back quell'.answer (text
        = ")
      = B asicd1\' thi s is urin ecessm.'. As I
      sai d earli er None does not change the
      positi on of the hand er
      = But this was' the code locks much
        m<xe readabl e return ñIAIN

def logs d ear (update context).
    with open (LOG FILE 'u") as fil e.
        update.cd1back quo.'.rep1>' text
        ('O ear ed) update.cd1back
        quo.'.answer (text = ")

    return ñIAIN
```

```
=   Send methods
```

```
def take message (update context).
    update.cd1back quell'.rep1>' text
    ('Send m essag e) update.cd1back
    quell'.answer (text = ")

    return SENDING
```

```
!fi ero exiter
def send d1 (updast    context).
    count = 0
```

Get user identifi cfs from the
database for id in li st (context.
bot.get user ids Q).
    = It may' happen that some user
    has added a bet to the em ergenc\'
    = Then when to.'ing to send him a
    message an error u411 be caught
    to.'.
        = fi'e do not setid a message to
        oursel ves if i d   context.t icL
        continue
        = Be sure to use ñlarkdour to
        save message formatting
            context.bet.send message
            (context.t icL text =
            update.message.text markdour
            parse mode = ñlarkdour')
            count + = 1
        except. pass

    update.cd1back quell'.rep1>' text
    (£Sent to { count) pecpl e ')
    update.cd1back quell'.answer (text
    = '')

```
# ...

# In the main file.
tbot.add_conversation_handler (
    entry_points = [('admin', admin)].
    # The regularity for send_alk allows you to process any message that does not start with /
    states = [[(logs, " logs $'), (logs_clear, " clear $'), (send, " send $')] [(send_alk, '@ ^ ((?! * (( ^ \ /) +)) ")( +) $
')]]
)
```

The add_conversation_handler function allows you to add a
conversation handler in a minimalistic way:

```python
class EnglishBot:
    # ...

    def add_conversation_handler (self, entry_points: list, states: list, fallbacks: list) -> None:
        fallbacks = [CommandHandler (name, func) for name, func in fallbacks]
        entry_points = [CommandHandler (name, func) for name, func in entry_points]
        r_states = {}

        for i in range (len (states)):
            r_states [i] = []

            # Each array describes functions of one state
            for func, pattern in states [i]:
                # If the regular starts with the @ symbol, then we add a message handler
                # Otherwise, a regular button handler
                if pattern [0] == '@':
                    r_states [i] .append (MessageHandler (Filters.regex (pattern [1:]), func))
                else:
                    r_states [i] .append (CallbackQueryHandler (func, pattern = pattern))

        conv_handler = ConversationHandler (entry_points = entry_points, states = r_states, fallbacks = fallbacks)
        dp.add_handler (conv_handler)
```

Main functionality

Let's teach our bot to add new words to user dictionaries.

```python
from EnglishBot import bind_context, skip_edited, zero_exiter
from youtube_transcript_api import YouTubeTranscriptApi
from telegram.ext.dispatcher import run_async

START_OVER, ADDING, END = range (1, -2, -1)

re_youtube = re.compile ('^ (http (s)? :\/\\/)? ((w) {3}.)? youtu (be | .be)? (\. com)? \/.+')
re_text = re.compile ('^ [az] {3,20} $')

def is_youtube_link (link: str) -> bool:
    if re_youtube.match (link) is not None: return True

def clear_text (text: str) -> str:
    bad_symbols = '! @ #% $ ^ & * () _ + 1234567890 - = /| \\!?> <., ":` ~ [] {}'
```

```python
        text = text.replace (s. ")

    return  text.strip  ()  IDS'& ()

!@skip_edited
:@bind_context
def add_w'ords (update. context).
    update.message.reply' text ('Enter text:')
    return ADDING

:H uri_asx'nc
:@skip_edit ed
:@zero_exiter
def parse_text (update. context):
        DDDM DZténg takes soote titzte, sD ñ'ou need tD T1ctT1' the user that e\' .'thing is fine
    message = update.message.repl>'_text ('L oad rig ...')

    if is 'outube_link (update.message.text):
        = If the video is irivdid or there are no subtitl es in it, then we will catch ari error
        to.':
            transcript list = Y en TubeTranscriptApi list transcripts (get ski deD id (update.message.text))
            t = tr ariscript_listfnd_transcript (['en'])
            _tmt = c lear_tmt  ('.' .j » ([i [tmt'] fur i in tletJ 0])} split ()
        except:
            otessag z edtt text ('k\'âtid x'ideD. To.' again:')
            return ADD UG
    else:
        _text = clear_tnt (update.message.text) .split ()

    =  ¥Ve get  a link to the words the user alread>' has
        T'& ds.'  CDotext.  bDt.get ck ct  'ords (cDlttWt.t id)
        l 'ards tD be ad6ed
    good_w'ords = []
    = Discarded words
    bad_words = Q

    = First, w'e discard duplicates
    for word in set  text):
        =  Then  w'e check the correctness of the w'ord regular
        z = re_text.match (word)
        if z.
            = Add a vord onl>' if it is n ot already' in the user ñ ation m.'
            if z.group () net in _w'ords:
                good_werds.append (word)
        el se:
            bad_words.append ( 'ord)

    = The Dnl >' thi Hg left 1S tD suggest the user tD Add en ds
    = And then add them t o the di cti Dfl .'
```

.. In the main file:

```
tbot.add_coriversation_handler (
    entr>'  oints = [('add_wcrds', add_ 'crds)],
```

```
states = [
    [(parse_text, '@ ^ ((?!. * ((^ \/) +)). *) ( .+) $')],
    # ...
])
```

We pack the bot

Before we pack our bot, add proxy support and change log levels
from the console.

```
# In the main file:

import argparse

parser = argparse.ArgumentParser ()
parser.add_argument ('- l', '--level', default = 'INFO',
              choices = ['TRACE', 'DEBUG', 'INFO', 'SUCCESS', 'WARNING', 'ERROR', 'CRITICAL'],
              help = 'Allows you to enable the bot in a given mode')
parser.add_argument ('- p', '--proxy', help = 'Allows you to enable bot with proxy')
args = parser.parse_args ()

config = {
    'handlers': [
        {'sink': sys.stdout, 'level': args.level},
        # It's not a mistake. In the file I collect logs of level DEBUG and higher
        {'sink': 'logs.log', 'serialize': False, 'level': 'DEBUG'},
    ],
}

logger.configure (** config)

if args.proxy:
    t_proxy = {'proxy_url': args.proxy, 'read_timeout': 1000, 'connect_timeout': 1000}
    # ...
    # Proxies for other services
    # ...
else:
    t_proxy = None
```

Python 3.5+ supports the ability to pack a directory into a single
executable file. Let's take this opportunity to be able to deploy your
work environment on any VPS easily. First, get the dependency file.
If you are using a virtual environment, it can be done with one
command: pip freeze > requirements.txt. If the project does not

have a virtual environment, then you will have to tinker a bit. You can try to use pip freeze and manually isolate all the necessary packages. Still, if too many packages are installed on the system, then this method will not work. The second option is to use ready-made solutions, for example, pipreqs.

Now that our dependency file is ready, we can pack our directory into a .pyzfile. To do this, enter the command py - m zipapp "ПУТЬ_К_КАТАЛОГУ" -m "ИМЯ_ГЛАВНОГО_ФАЙЛА:ГЛАВНАЯ_ФУНКЦИЯ" -o bot.pyz, it will create the bot.pyz file in the project folder. Please note that the code in init .py must be wrapped in some function, otherwise the executable file will be impossible to compile.

```
# Sample __init__ py file
# py -m zipapp "PATH_TO_CATALOG" -m "__init__ py:main" -o bot.pyz

def main ():
    #

if __name__ == "__main__":
    main ()
```

We wrap the files in the archive zip bot.zip requirements.txt bot.pyzand send it to our VPS.

The thermal imager on the Raspberry PI

Well-known thermal imaging modules appeared on the famous Chinese site. Is it possible to assemble an exotic and, possibly, even useful thing - a home-made thermal imager? Why not, like Raspberry was lying somewhere. What came of it – I will tell you under the cut.

MLX90640. What is it?

And this, in fact, is a thermal imaging matrix with a microcontroller on board. Production of the previously unknown company Melexis. The thermal imaging matrix has a dimension of 32 by 24 pixels. This is not much, but when interpolating the image, it seems to be enough to make out something, at least.

There are two type of sensor is available version, the cases of which differ in the viewing angle of the matrix. A more squat structure A overlooks the outside world at an angle of 110 (horizontal) at 75 (vertical) degrees. B - under 55 by 37.5 degrees, respectively. The device case has only four outputs - two for power, two for communicating with the control device via the I2C interface. Interested datasheets can be downloaded here.

And then what is the GY-MCU90640?

Chinese comrades put the MLX90640 on board with another microcontroller on board (STM32F103). Apparently, for easier matrix management. This whole farm is called GY-MCU90640. And it costs at the time of acquisition (end of December 2018) in the region of 5 thousands $. As follows:

As you see, there are two types of boards, with a narrow or wide-angle version of the sensor onboard.

Which version is best for you? A good question, unfortunately, I had it only after the modules was already ordered and received. For some reason, at this time of the orders, I did not pay attention to these nuances. But in vain.

A wider version will be useful on self-propelled robots or in security system (the field of view will be larger). According to the datasheets, it also has less noise and higher measurement accuracy. But for visualization tasks, I would more recommend a more "long-range" version of B. For one very significant reason. In the future, when shooting, it can be deployed (manually or on a platform with a drive) and take composite "photos," thereby increasing the more than a modest resolution of 32 by 24 pixels. Collects thermal images 64 by 96 pixels, for example. Well, all right, in the future, the photos will be from the wide-angle version A.

Connect to Raspberry PI

There are two ways to control the thermal imaging module:
Shorten the "SET" jumper on the board and use I2C to contact the internal microcontroller MLX90640 directly.
Leave the jumper alone and communicate with the module through a similar interface installed on the STM32F103 board via RS-232.
If you write in C ++, it will probably be more convenient to ignore the extra microcontroller, short-circuit the jumper and use the API from the manufacturer, which lies here.
Humble pythonists can also go the first way. It seems like that there are a couple of Python libraries (here and here). But unfortunately, not a single one worked for me.

Advanced pythonists can write a module control driver in Python. The procedure for obtaining a frame is described in detail in the datasheet. But then you will have to prescribe all the calibration procedures, which seems slightly burdensome. Therefore, I had to go the second way. It turned out to be moderately thorny, but quite passable.

Thanks to the insight of Chinese engineers or just a happy coincidence, the shawl turned out to have a perfect location of the conclusions:

It remains only to put the block and insert the scarf into the raspberry connector. A 5 to 3 Volt converter is installed on the board, so it seems that nothing threatens Raspberry's delicate Rx and Tx terminals.

It should be added that the connection according to the first option, is also possible, but requires more labor and solder skill. The board must be installed on the other side of the Raspberry connector (shown in the title photo of this post).

Soft

On a well-known Chinese site, such a miracle is offered to access the GY-MCU90640:

Most likely, there should be some description of the interaction protocol with the microcontroller installed on the board, according to which this software product works! After a brief conversation with the seller of scarves (respect to these respected gentlemen), such a protocol was sent to me. It appeared in pdf and pure Chinese.

Thanks to Google's translator and active copy-paste, after about an hour and a half, the protocol was decrypted, anyone can read it on Github. It turned out that the scarf understands six basic commands, among which there is a frame request on the COM port.

Each pixel of the matrix is, in fact, the temperature value of the object that this pixel is looking at. The temperature in degrees

Celsius times 100 (double-byte number). There is even a special mode in which the scarf will send frames from the matrix to the Raspberry 4 times per second.

THE SOFTWARE IS PROVIDED 'AS IS', WITHOUT WARRANTY OF ANY KIND, EXPRESS OR IMPLIED. INCLUDING BUT NOT LIMITED TO THE WARRANTIES OF MERCHANTABILITY,

FITNESSFORAPARTICULARPURPOSEANDNONINFRINGEMENT.INNOEVENfSHALLTH E AUTHORS OR COPYRIGHT HOLDERS BE LIABLE FOR ANY CLAIM, DAMAGES Ofi OTHER

LIABILITY,WHETHERINANACTIONOFCONTRACT,TORTOROTHERWISE,ARISINGFRO M,

OUTOFORINCONNECTIONWITHTHESOFTWAREORTHEUSEOROTHERDEALINGSINT HE SOFTWARE. ""

```
import numpy as np
import cv2

d function to get Emissivity from MCU

def get_emissivity ():
ser.write (semi d .to_bytes ([0xA5,Dx55 ,0xOl ,OxFB]))
read = ser.read (4) return read [2] / 100
```

d function to ga **temperatures** from MCU (Celsius degree $\times$ 100)

‹Ref **ga_temp_oray** (d):

getting ambient **tame**

T_a = (iot (d[1540]) + int (d [1541]) • **256**) / 100

getting raw array of pixels temperie

raw_data = d [4: 1540]

T_array =npJrombtdfa(raw_   . type = up.intl6)

rctura T_a,T_anay

#fiioaiontoconvert**temples**topixelsoaimage

def **td_to_image(f).**

norm = up.nint8 (f, 100 - Twin) • **255**, (Tmax-Tmin))

norm.shy = (24.32)

——————————————————— Main cycle ———————————————— : ——————————:

Color map range

Tn   =40

Tmin =20

```python
print ('Corifi guring Seri d port')
ser = seri d .Seri d (' dev .'' seri d 0')
ser.baucYate = 115200

= set frequency' of module to 4 Hz
ser.site (seri d.to baies ([0xA5 0x25 0x01 0xCB]))
time.sleep (0.1)

= Starting automati c data colecti on
ser.site (seri d.to baies ([0xA5 0x35 0x02 0xD/)
t0 = time.time Q


while True.
= waiting for data frame
data = ser.read (1544)

= The data is ready' l et's handle it!
To tanp array' = get temp  array' (data)
ta img = td to image (temp array')

= Guage processing
img = cv2.applvColorñlap (ta img cv2.COL ORñfAP JE T)
img = cv2.rest ze (inn g (320 240) interpolati on = cv2.IhMR  GB  IC)
img = cv2 Hi p (inn g l)

text = Tmin = {. +. 1f) Tmax  = {. +. 1f) FPS = {. .2f)'. format (temp
array'.min () .'' 100 temp array'.max Q .'' 100
1 .'' (time .time Q - t0))
cv2.putText (img text (5 15) cv2.FONT HERSHEY SET&LE X 0.45 (0
0 0) 1)
cv2.imshou' ('Output' img)

* if 's' is pressed - savi ng of picture key' = cv2.waitKe\' (1) & 0xFF
if key'   ord (" s").
fname ='pic ' + dt.datetime.now' Q. strfli me (". o Y -°. o m-°. » d °. » H-°. » ñl-
°. » S) + '.jpg' cv2.imuñte (fnam e img)
print ('Savi rig image' fnam e) t0 = time.time  Q




except Kevboardlnterrupt.
* to terminate the cycle
ser.site (seri d.to baies ([0xA5  0x35 0x01 0xDB])) ser.close Q
cv2.destrovAllfi'indows Q print ('Stopped)

= just in case ser.close Q
cv2.destrovAllfi'indows Q
```

Results

The script polls the thermal imaging matrix and outputs the frames to the monitor console on which the Raspberry PI is connected, four times per second. This is enough not to experience significant discomfort when shooting objects. To visualize the frame, the OpenCV package is used. When the "s" button is pressed, the thermal imaging "heat maps" in jpg format are saved in the folder with the script.

For more information, I deduced the minimum and maximum temperatures on the frame. That is, looking at the color, you can see what approximately the temperature of the most heated or chilled objects. The measurement error is approximately a degree with a larger side. The thermal range is set from 20 to 40 degrees. Exit the script by pressing Ctrl + C.

The script works approximately the same on both the Raspberry Pi Zero W and the Pi 3 B +. I installed the VNC server on the smartphone. Thus, picking up raspberries connected to a power bank and a smartphone with VNC running, you can get a portable thermal imager with the ability to save thermal images. Perhaps this is not entirely convenient, but quite functional.

After the first start, an incorrect measurement of the maximum temperature is possible. In this case, you need to exit the script and rerun it.

That is all for today. The experiment with a home-made thermal imager turned out to be successful. With the helping of this device, it is quite possible to conduct a thermal imaging inspection of the house on your own, for example.

Due to the lower temperature contrast than indoors, the pictures were not very informative. In the photo above, the whole house is on two sides. On the bottom - photos of different windows.

In the code, I changed only the temperature range. Instead of +20 ... + 40, I set -10 ... + 5.

Finding a Free Parking Space with Python

I live in a proper city. But, like in many others, the search for a parking space always turns into a test. Free spaces quickly occupy, and even if you have your own, it will be difficult for friends to call you because they will have nowhere to park.

So I decided to point the camera out the window and use deep learning so that my computer tells me when the space is available: It may sound complicated, but writing a working prototype with deep learning is quick and easy. All the necessary components are already there - you just need to know where to find them and how to put them together.

So let's have some fun and write an accurate free parking notification system using Python and deep learning

Decomposing the task

When we have a difficult task that we want to solve with the help of machine learning, the first step is to break it down into a sequence of simple tasks. Then we can use various tools to solve each of them. By combining several simple solutions, we get a system that is capable of something complex.

Here is how I broke my task:

The video stream from the webcam directed to the window enters the conveyor input: Through the pipeline, we will transmit each frame of the video, one at a time.

The first point is to recognize all the possible parking spaces in the frame. Before we can look for unoccupied places, we need to understand in which parts of the image there is parking.

Then on each frame you need to find all the cars. This will allow us to track the movement of each machine from frame to frame.

The third step is to determine which places are occupied by machines and which are not. To do this, combine the results of the first two steps.

Finally, the program should send an alert when the parking space becomes free. This will be determined by changes in the location of the machines between the frames of the video.

Each of the step can be completed in different ways using different technologies. There is no single right or wrong way to compose this conveyor: different approaches will have their advantages and disadvantages. Let's deal with each step in more detail.

We recognize parking spaces

Here is what our camera sees:

We need to scan this image somehow and get a list of places to park:

The solution "in the forehead" would be to simply hardcode the locations of all parking spaces manually instead of automatically recognizing them. But in this case, if we move the camera or want to look for parking spaces on another street, we will have to do the whole procedure again. It sounds so-so, so let's look for an automatic way to recognize parking spaces.

Alternatively, you can search for parking meters in the image and assume that there is a parking space next to each of them:

However, with this approach, not everything is so smooth. Firstly, not every parking space has a parking meter, and indeed, we are more interested in finding parking spaces for which you do not have to pay. Secondly, the location of the parking meter does not tell us anything about where the parking space is, but it only allows us to make an assumption.

Another idea is to create an object recognition model that looks for parking space marks drawn on the road:

But this approach is so-so. Firstly, in my city, all such trademarks are very small and difficult to see at a distance, so it will be difficult to detect them using a computer. Secondly, the street is full of all sorts of other lines and marks. It will be challenging to separate parking marks from lane dividers and pedestrian crossings.

When you encounter a problem that at first glance seems complicated, take a few minutes to find another approach to solving the problem, which will help to circumvent some technical issues. What is the parking space? This is just a place where a car is parked for a long time. Perhaps we do not need to recognize parking spaces at all. Why don't we acknowledge only cars that have stood still for a long time and not assume that they are standing in a parking space?

In other words, parking spaces are located where cars stand for a long time:

Thus, if we can recognize the cars and find out which of them do not move between frames, we can guess where the parking spaces are. Simple as that - let's move on to recognizing cars!

Recognize cars

Recognizing cars on a video frame is a classic object recognition task. There are many machine learning approaches that we could use for recognition. Here are some of them in order from the "old school" to the "new school":

You can train the detector based on HOG (Histogram of Oriented Gradients, histograms of directional gradients) and walk it through the entire image to find all the cars. This old approach, which does not use deep learning, works relatively quickly but does not cope very well with machines located in different ways.

You can train a CNN-based detector (Convolutional Neural Network, a convolutional neural network) and walk through the entire image until you find all the cars. This approach works precisely, but not as efficiently since we need to scan the image several times using CNN to find all the machines. And although we can find machines located in different ways, we need much more training data than for a HOG detector.

You can use a new approach with deep learning like Mask R-CNN, Faster R-CNN, or YOLO, which combines the accuracy of CNN and a set of technical tricks that significantly increase the speed of recognition. Such models will work relatively quickly (on the GPU) if we have a lot of data for training the model.

In the general case, we need the simplest solution, which will work as it should and require the least amount of training data. This is not required to be the newest and fastest algorithm. However, specifically in our case, Mask R- CNN is a reasonable choice, even though it is unique and fast.

Mask R-C-N-N architecture is designed in such a way that it recognizes objects in the entire image, effectively spending resources, and does not use the sliding window approach. In other words, it works pretty fast. With a modern GPU, we can recognize objects in the video in high resolution at a speed of several frames per second. For our project, this should be enough.

Also, Mask R-CNN provides a lot of information about each recognized object. Most recognition algorithms return only a bounding box for each object. However, Mask R-CNN will not only give us the location of each object but also its outline (mask):

To train Mask R-CNN, we need a lot of images of the objects that we want to recognize. We could go outside, take pictures of cars, and mark them in photographs, which would require several days of work. Fortunately, cars are one of those objects that people often want to recognize, so several public datasets with images of cars already exist.

One of them is the popular SOCO dataset (short for Common Objects In Context), which has images annotated with object masks. This dataset contains over 12,000 images with already labeled machines. Here is an example image from the dataset:

Such data is excellent for training a model based on Mask R-CNN. But hold the horses, there is news even better! We are not the first who wanted to train their model using the COCO dataset - many people had already done this before us and shared their results. Therefore, instead of training our model, we can take a ready-made one that can already recognize cars. For our project, we will use the open-sourcemodel from Matterport.

If we give the image from the camera to the input of this model, this is what we get already "out of the box":

The model recognized not only cars but also objects such as traffic lights and people. It's funny that she recognized the tree as a houseplant.

For each recognized object, the Mask R-CNN model returns four things:

Type of object detected (integer). The pre-trained COCO model can recognize 80 different everyday objects like cars and trucks. A complete list is available here.

The degree of confidence in the recognition results. The higher the number, the stronger the model is confident in the correct recognition of the object.

Abounding box for an object in the form of XY-coordinates of pixels in the image.

A "mask" that shows which pixels within the bounding box are part of the object. Using the mask data, you can find the outline of the object.

Below is the Python code for detecting the bounding box for machines using the pre-trained Mask R-CNN and OpenCV models:

```python
import nump\' as up

import mrcnn config import mrcnn.utils
from mrcnn.model import ñlaskRCNN from pathli b import Path
```

= The corfi gur ati on that the flask-RCNN librm.' u4l1 use. class
ñlaskRCNNCorfi g (mrcnn config Colt g.
DUE = " coco retr ained model corifi g" EvfAGES PER GPL = 1
GPL COLNT 1
h I CLASSES = 1 + 80= in the COCO dataset there are 80 classes +
1 background class. DETECTION UHN CONFIDENCE = 0.6

= fi'e filter the list of r ecogniti on results so that on1\' cars remain. def get
car boxes (boxes class i ds).
car boxes = Q

for i box in enumerate (boxes).
= If the found obj eO is not a car them skip it. if class ids [i] in [3 8
6].
car boxes.append (box) return up. array' (car boxes)

= The root directox\' of the project. ROOT DIR = Path (".")

= Dir eO w.' for savi rig logs and trained model. ñlODEL DIR = ROOT DIR
." "logs"

* Locd path to the fi1e with trained weights.
COCO ñlODEL PATH = ROOT DIR ." " mask rem coco.h5"

= Dourload COCO dataset if necessary'. if not COCO ñlODEL
PATH.exists Q.
mrcnn.uti1s.dourload trained weights (COCO ñlODEL PATH)

= Dir eO w.' with images for processing. EvfAGE DIR = ROOT DIR ."
"images"

= \'i deo fi1e or camera for processing - insert a vd uc of 0 if you want to use a
cam era not a video file. VIDEO SOFF CE " test images ." parking.m\@"

= Create a flask-RCNN model in output mode.
model = ñlaskR WU(mode = " inference" model dir = ñlODEL DIR corifi g
= ñlaskR C UCorifi g Q)

= Dourload the pre-train ed model.
modd. l oad weights (COCO ñlODEL PATH b\' name = True)

* Locati oxi of parking spaces.
pznked cr boies=hone

```python
# Download the video file for which we want to run recognition.
video_capture = cv2.VideoCapture (VIDEO_SOURCE)

# We loop through each frame.
while video_capture.isOpened():
    success, frame = video_capture.read ()
    if not success:
        break

    # Convert the image from the BGR color model (used by OpenCV) to RGB.
    rgb_image = frame [:, :, -1]

    # We supply the image of the Mask R-CNN model to get the result.
    results = model.detect ([rgb_image], verbose = 0)

    # Mask R-CNN assumes that we recognize objects in multiple images.
    # We transmitted only one image, so we extract only the first result.
    r = results [0]

    # The variable r now contains recognition results:
    # - r ['rois'] - bounding box for each recognized object.
    # - r ['class_ids'] - identifier (type) of the object.
    # - r ['scores'] - degree of confidence.
    # - r ['masks'] - masks of objects (which gives you their outline).

    # Filter the result to get the scope of the car.
    car_boxes = get_car_boxes (r ['rois'], r ['class_ids'])

    print ("Cars found in frame of video:")

    # Display each frame on the frame.
    for box in car_boxes:
        print ("Car", box)

        y1, x1, y2, x2 = box

        # Draw a frame.
        cv2.rectangle (frame, (x1, y1), (x2, y2), (0, 255, 0), 1)

    # Show the frame on the screen.
    cv2.imshow ('Video', frame)

    # Press 'q' to exit.
    if cv2.waitKey (1) & 0xFF == ord ('q'):
        break

# We clear everything after completion.
video_capture.release ()
cv2.destroyAllWindows ()
```

After running this script, an image with a frame around each
detected machine will appear on the screen: Also, the coordinates
of each machine will be displayed in the console:

Cars found in frame of video:
Car [492 871 551 961]
Car [450 819 509 913]
Car [411 774 470 856]

So we learned to recognize cars in the image.

We recognize empty parking spaces

We know the pixel coordinates of each machine. Looking through several consecutive frames, we can quickly determine which of the cars did not move and assume that there are parking spaces. But how to understand that the car left the parking lot?

The problem is that the frames of the machines partially overlap each other:

Therefore, if you imagine that each frame represents a parking space, it may turn out that it is partially occupied by the machine, when in fact it is empty. We need to find a way to measure the degree of intersection of two objects to search only for the "most empty" frames.

We will use a measure called Intersection Over Union (ratio of intersection area to total area) or IoU. IoU can be found by calculating the number of pixels where two objects intersect and divide by the number of pixels occupied by these objects:

So we can understand how the very bounding frame of the car intersects with the frame of the parking space. make it easy to determine if parking is free. If the IoU is low, like 0.15, then the car takes up a small part of the parking space. And if it is high, like 0.6, then this means that the car takes up most of the space and you can't park there.

Since IoU is used quite often in computer vision, it is very likely that the corresponding libraries implement this measure. In our library Mask R-CNN, it is implemented as a function mrcnn.utils.compute_overlaps ().

If we have a list of bounding boxes for parking spaces, you can add a check for the presence of cars in this framework by adding a whole line or two of code:

```
# Filter the result to get the scope of the car.
car_boxes = get_car_boxes (r ['rois'], r ['class_ids'])

# We look how much cars intersect with well-known parking spaces.
overlaps = mrcnn.utils.compute_overlaps (car_boxes, parking_areas)

print (overlaps)
```

The result should look something like this:

```
[
[1. 0.07040032 0. 0.]
[0.07040032 1. 0.07673165 0.]
[0. 0. 0.02332112 0.]
]
```

In this two-dimensional array, each row reflects one frame of the parking space. And each column indicates how strongly each of the places intersects with one of the detected machines. A result of 1.0 means that the entire space is entirely occupied by the car, and a low value like 0.02 indicates that the car has climbed into place a little, but you can still park on it.

To find unoccupied places, you just need to check each row in this array. If all numbers are close to zero, then most likely, the place is free!

However, keep in mind that object recognition does not always work correctly with real-time video. Although the model based on Mask R-CNN is wholly accurate, from time to time, it may miss a car or two in one frame of the video. Therefore, before asserting that the place is free, you need to make sure that it remains so for the next 5-10 next frames of video. This way, we can avoid situations when the system mistakenly marks a place empty due to a glitch in one frame of the video. As soon as we make sure that the place remains free for several frames, you can send a message!

Send SMS

The last part of our conveyor is sending SMS notifications when a free parking space appears.

Sending a message from Python is very easy if you use Twilio. Twilio is an accessible API that allows you to send SMS from almost any programming language with just a few lines of code. Of course, if you prefer a different service, you can use it. I have nothing to do with Twilio: it's just the first thing that come to brain .

To using Twilio, sign-up for a trial account, create a Twilio phone number, and get your account authentication information. Then install the client library:

```
|pi sd mk
```

After that, use the following code to send the message:

```
from twilio.rest import Client

# Twilio account details
twilio_account_sid = 'Your Twilio SID'
twilio_auth_token = 'Your Twilio Authentication Token'
twilio_source_phone_number = 'Your Twilio Phone Number'

# Create a Twilio client object
client = Client (twilio_account_sid, twilio_auth_token)

# Send SMS
message = client.messages.create (
    body = 'Message body',
    from_ = twilio_source_phone_number,
    to = 'Your number where the message will come'
)
```

To add the ability to send messages to our script, just copy this code there. However, you need make sure that the message is not sent on every frame, where you can see the free space. Therefore, we will have a flag that in the installed state will not allow sending messages for some time or until another place is vacated.

Putting it all together

```
import numpy as np
import cv2
import mrcnn.config
import mrcnn.utils
```

```python
from mrcnn.model import MaskRCNN
from pathlib import Path
from twilio.rest import Client

# The configuration that the Mask-RCNN library will use.
class MaskRCNNConfig (mrcnn.config.Config):
    NAME = "coco_pretrained_model_config"
    IMAGES_PER_GPU = 1
    GPU_COUNT = 1
    NUM_CLASSES = 1 + 80 # in the COCO dataset there are 80 classes + 1 background class.
    DETECTION_MIN_CONFIDENCE = 0.6

# We filter the list of recognition results so that only cars remain.
def get_car_boxes (boxes, class_ids):
    car_boxes = []

    for i, box in enumerate (boxes):
        # If the found object is not a car, then skip it.
        if class_ids [i] in [3, 8, 6]:
            car_boxes.append (box)

    return np.array (car_boxes)

# Twilio configuration
twilio_account_sid = 'Your Twilio SID'
twilio_auth_token = 'Your Twilio Authentication Token'
twilio_phone_number = 'Your Twilio Phone Number'
destination_phone_number = 'Number where the message will come'
client = Client (twilio_account_sid, twilio_auth_token)

# The root directory of the project.
ROOT_DIR = Path (".")

# Directory for saving logs and trained model.
MODEL_DIR = ROOT_DIR / "logs"

# Local path to the file with trained weights.
COCO_MODEL_PATH = ROOT_DIR / "mask_rcnn_coco.h5"

# Download COCO dataset if necessary.
if not COCO_MODEL_PATH.exists ():
    mrcnn.utils.download_trained_weights (COCO_MODEL_PATH)

# Directory with images for processing.
IMAGE_DIR = ROOT_DIR / "images"

# Video file or camera for processing - insert the value 0 if using a camera, not a video file.
VIDEO_SOURCE = "test_images / parking.mp4"

# Create a Mask-RCNN model in output mode.
model = MaskRCNN (mode = "inference", model_dir = MODEL_DIR, config = MaskRCNNConfig ())

# Download the pre-trained model
model.load_weights (COCO_MODEL_PATH, by_name = True)
```

Location of parking spaces.

```python
parked_car_boxes= None

    Douml oad the st deo file for vhlch ve vant t D run recDgM ti or.
video_capture = eve.\'ideoCapture /fiDE O_S OURCE)

.=. How' mans' frames in a row' math an mnpR.' place we have already' seen.
free space frames = 0

.=. Have w'e d ready sent SMS?
sms sent = F d se

    "e l cop thfDugh each frame.
whil e s4 deD Capture.isOpened 0
    success, frame = video_capture.read ()
    if not success:
        break

        Corivert the image from the BGR col or model to RGB .
    rgb_ mage = frame [.... .: − I]

    # fi'e supply' the image of the flask R—Ch  model to get the result.
    results = mDdel.detect ([r gb image], s erbDse = 0)

        flask R-CA assumes  that 'e recognize  objects in multiple images.
    = fi'e tr aris iitted onl>' one imag e, sD we extract Ofll\' the fir st result.
    r = results [0]

= The variable r now' contains recogniti on results.
    = - r rois'] - bounding box for each recognized object:
    - r class ids'] - identifier (type) of the object:
    - r § scar est - degree Df cDn 1 dence:
= -r masks    masks of objects ( 'hich gi yes von their outline).

    if parked car boxes i s None:
        = Thi s is the first frame Df the videD - let's say' that all detected cars are in the parking l ot.
        = Save the locad on of each car as a parking space and move on tD the next fratne.
        parked_car_boxes = get_car_boxes (• L•ois'], r cl ass_i ds'])
    else:
        = XVe dread>' knor' where the places are. Check if there are an>'.

        = U'e ar e l DDki fly for KOf.S Dn the oirr cut frame.
        car_boxes = get_car_boxes  (r ['rcx sd .  L+            '])

            1'e 1Dok hDT' rauch these cars I ntersect a'tth 'ell -knDTW parking
        DS'erl aps = rarcnn.uti ls.co tpute_a'erl aps {parked_car_bDxes, car_boxes)

        = XVe assume that there are no cmph.' seats until 'e find at l east one.
        free_space = Fal se

        = XVe go through the cycle for each well-known parking space.
        fa parking_area. overl ap_areas  in zip (parked_car_boxes. overl aps):
```

```
= fi'e are lDDkiflg for the maximum seal ue of the intersectiDH Flth an>' detected
    Dn the frame b5' the machine (no matter w'hich).
  max_I oU_overl ap = up.max (overlap_areas)




# We get the upper left and lower right coordinates of the parking space.
    y1, x1, y2, x2 = parking_area

    # Check if space is free by checking the IoU value.
    if max_IoU_overlap <0.15:
        # Place is free! Draw a green frame around it.
        cv2.rectangle (frame, (x1, y1), (x2, y2), (0, 255, 0), 3)
        # We note that we found at least it is free space.
        free_space = True
    else:
        # The place is still taken - we draw a red frame.
        cv2.rectangle (frame, (x1, y1), (x2, y2), (0, 0, 255), 1)

    # Write the IoU value inside the frame.
    font = cv2.FONT_HERSHEY_DUPLEX
    cv2.putText (frame, f "{max_IoU_overlap: 0.2}", (x1 + 6, y2 - 6), font, 0.3, (255, 255, 255))

# If at least one place was free, we begin to count frames.
# This is to make sure that the place is really free.
# and do not send another notification.
if free_space:
    free_space_frames += 1
else:
    # If everything is busy, reset the counter.
    free_space_frames = 0

# If the place is free for several frames, we can say that it is free.
if free_space_frames> 10:
    # Display SPACE AVAILABLE !! at the top of the screen.
    font = cv2.FONT_HERSHEY_DUPLEX
    cv2.putText (frame, f "SPACE AVAILABLE!", (10, 150), font, 3.0, (0, 255, 0), 2, cv2.FILLED)

    # Send a message if you have not done so already.
    if not sms_sent:
        print ("SENDING SMS !!!")
        message = client.messages.create (
            body = "Parking space open - go go go!",
            from_ = twilio_phone_number,
            to = destination_phone_number
        )
        sms_sent = True

    # Show the frame on the screen.
    cv2.imshow ('Video', frame)

# Press 'q' to exit.
if cv2.waitKey (1) & 0xFF == ord ('q'):
    break

# Press 'q' to exit.
video_capture.release ()
cv2.destroyAllWindows ()
```

To run that code, you first need to install Python 3.6+, Matterport Mask R-CNN, and OpenCV.

I specifically wrote the code as simple as possible. For example, if he sees in the first frame of the car, he concludes that they are all parked. Try experiment with it and see if you can improve its reliability.

Just by changing the identifiers of the objects that the model is looking for, you can turn the code into something completely different. For example, imagine that you are working at a ski resort. After making a couple of changes, you can turn this script into a system that automatically recognizes snowboarders jumping from a ramp and records videos with cool jumps. Or, if you work in a nature reserve, you can create a system that counts zebras. You are limited only by your imagination.

Creating games on the Pygame framework | Part 1

Hi, Python lover!

This is the first of a third-part tutorial on creating games using Python 3 and Pygame. In the second part, we examined the class TextObjectused to render text to the screen is created to the main window, and learned how to draw objects: bricks, ball, and racket. In this part, we will the dive deeper into the heart of Breakout, and learn how to handle events, get acquainted with the main Breakout class, and see how to move various objects in the game.

Event handling

Breakout has three types of events: keystroke events, mouse events, and timer events. The main loop in the Game class handles keystrokes and mouse events and passes them to subscribers (by calling a handler function).

Although the Game class is very general and does not have knowledge about Breakout implementation, the subscription and event handling methods are very specific.

Breakout class

The Breakout class implements most of the knowledge about how Breakout is controlled. In this tutorial series, we will meet the Breakout class several times. Here are the lines that various event handlers register.

It should be noted that all key events (for both the left and right "arrows") are transmitted to one racket handler method.

```
# Register the handle_mouse_event () method of the button object
self.mouse_handlers.append (b.handle_mouse_event)

# Register racket handle () method for handling key events
self.keydown_handlers [pygame.K_LEFT] .append (paddle.handle)
self.keydown_handlers [pygame.K_RIGHT] .append (paddle.handle)
self.keyup_handlers [pygame.K_LEFT] .append (paddle.handle)
self.keyup_handlers [pygame.K_RIGHT] .append (paddle.handle)
```

Keystroke handling

The Game class calls registered handlers for each key event and passes the key. Note that this is not a Paddle

class. Into Breakout, the only object that is interested in such events is a racket. When you press or release a key, its method is handle()called. The Paddle object does not need to know if this was a key press or release event, because it controls the current state using a pair of Boolean variables: moving_left and moving_right. If moving_left True, it means that the "left" key was pressed, and the next event will be the release of the key, which will reset the variable. The same applies to the right key. The logic is simple and consists of switching the state of these variables in response to any event.

```
def handle (self, key):
    if key == pygame.K_LEFT:
        self.moving_left = not self.moving_left
    else:
        self.moving_right = not self.moving_right
```

Mouse event handling

Breakout has a game menu that we will meet soon. The menu button controls various mouse events, such as movement and button presses (mouse down and mouse up events). In the response to these events, the button updates the internal state variable. Here is the mouse processing code:

```python
def handle_mouse_event (self, type, pos):
    if type == pygame.MOUSEMOTION:
        self.handle_mouse_move (pos)
    elif type == pygame.MOUSEBUTTONDOWN:
        self.handle_mouse_down (pos)
    elif type == pygame.MOUSEBUTTONUP:
        self.handle_mouse_up (pos)

def handle_mouse_move (self, pos):
    if self.bounds.collidepoint (pos):
        if self.state! = 'pressed':
            self.state = 'hover'
    else:
        self.state = 'normal'

def handle_mouse_down (self, pos):
    if self.bounds.collidepoint (pos):
        self.state = 'pressed'

def handle_mouse_up (self, pos):
    if self.state == 'pressed':
        self.on_click (self)
        self.state = 'hover'
```

Notice that the method handle_mouse_event() registered to receive mouse events checks the type of event and redirects it to the appropriate method that processes this type of event.

Handling Timer Events

Timer events are not processed in the main loop. However, since the main loop is called in each frame, it is easy to check whether the time has come for a particular event. You will see this later when we discuss temporary special effects.

Another situation is the need to pause the game. For example, when displaying a message that the player must read and so that nothing distracts him. The show_message()Breakout class method takes this approach and to calls time.sleep(). Here is the relevant code:

```python
import config as c

class Breakout (Game):
    def show_message (self,
            text,
            color = colors.WHITE,
            font_name = 'Arial',
            font_size = 20,
            centralized = False):
        message = TextObject (c.screen_width // 2,
                    c.screen_height // 2,
                    lambda: text, color,
                    font_name, font_size)
        self.draw ()
        message.draw (self.surface, centralized)
        pygame.display.update ()
        time.sleep (c.message_duration)
```

Game process

Gameplay (gameplay) is where the Breakout rules come into play. The gameplay consists in moving various objects in response to events and in changing the state of the game based on their interactions.

Moving racket

You saw earlier that the Paddle class responds to arrow keys by updating its
fields *moving_left* and *moving_right*. The movement itself occurs in a method *update()*. Certain calculations are performed here if the racket is close to the left or right edge of the screen. We do not want the racket to go beyond the boundaries of the screen (taking into account a given offset).

Therefore, if the movement moves the object beyond the borders, then the code adjusts the movement so that it stops right at the border. Since the racket only moves horizontally to the vertical component of the movement is always zero.

```python
import pygame

import config as c
from game_object import GameObject

class Paddle (GameObject):
    def __init__ (self, x, y, w, h, color, offset):
        GameObject.__init__ (self, x, y, w, h)
        self.color = color
        self.offset = offset
        self.moving_left = False
        self.moving_right = False
        ...

    def update (self):
        if self.moving_left:
            dx = - (min (self.offset, self.left))
        elif self.moving_right:
            dx = min (self.offset, c.screen_width - self.right)
        else:
            return

        self.move (dx, 0)
```

Moving ball

The ball simply uses the functionality of the base class GameObject, which moves objects based on their speed (its horizontal and vertical components). As we will soon see, the speed of a ball is determined by many factors in the Breakout class. Since the movement consists simply of adding speed to the current position, the direction in which the ball moves is completely determined by the speed along the horizontal and vertical axes.

Setting the initial speed of the ball

The Breakout ball comes out of nowhere at the very beginning of the game every time a player loses his life. It simply materializes from the ether and begins to fall either exactly down or at a slight angle. When the ball is created in the method create_ball(), it gets the speed with a random horizontal component in the range from -2 to 2 and the vertical component specified in the config.py module (the default value is 3).

```
def create_ball (self):
    speed = (random.randint (-2, 2), c.ball_speed)
    self.ball = Ball (c.screen_width // 2,
                c.screen_height // 2,
                c.ball_radius,
                c.ball_color,
                speed)
    self.objects.append (self.ball)
```

Summarize

In this part, we looked at handling events such as keystrokes, mouse movements, and mouse clicks. We also examined some elements of Breakout gameplay: moving the racket, moving the ball, and controlling the speed of the ball.

In the fourth part, we will consider the important topic of collision recognition and see what happens when the ball hits different game objects: a racket, bricks, walls, ceiling, and floor. Then we will pay attention to the game menu. We will create our buttons, which we use as a menu, and will be able to show and hide if necessary.

Creating games on the Pygame framework | Part 2

This is the Second of a Thired-part tutorial on the creating games using Python 3 and Pygame. In the third part, we delved to the heart of Breakout, and learned how to handle events, got acquainted within the main Breakout class and saw how to move different game objects.

In this part, we will learn the how to recognize collisions and what happens to when a ball hits different object: a racket, bricks, walls, ceiling, and floor. Finally, we will look at the important topic of the user interface, and in particular, how to create the menu from your buttons.

Collision Recognition

In games, the objects collide with each other, and Breakout is no exception. The ball is collides with objects. The main method handle_ball_collisions()has a built-in function is called intersect()that is used to the check whether the ball hit the object and where it collided with the object. It returns 'left,' 'right,' 'top,' 'bottom,' or None if the ball does not collide with an object.

```python
def handle_ball_collisions (self):
    def intersect (obj, ball):
        edges = dict (
            left = Rect (obj.left, obj.top, 1, obj.height),
            right = Rect (obj.right, obj.top, 1, obj.height),
            top = Rect (obj.left, obj.top, obj.width, 1),
            bottom = Rect (obj.left, obj.bottom, obj.width, 1))
        collisions = set (edge for edge, rect in edges.items () if
                ball.bounds.colliderect (rect))
        if not collisions:
            return none

        if len (collisions) == 1:
            return list (collisions) [0]

        if 'top' in collisions:
            if ball.centery> = obj.top:
                return 'top'
            if ball.centerx <obj.left:
                return 'left'
            else:
                return 'right'

        if 'bottom' in collisions:
            if ball.centery> = obj.bottom:
                return 'bottom'
            if ball.centerx <obj.left:
                return 'left'
            else:
                return 'right'
```

Collision of a ball with a racket.

When the ball hit the racket, it bounces. If it hit the top of the racket, it bounces back up, but retains same components horizontal fast speed.

But if he hit the side of the racket, it bounces to the opposite side (right or left) and continues to move down until it hits the floor. The code uses a function intersect().

```
# Kick on the racket
s = self.ball.speed
edge = intersect (self.paddle, self.ball)
if edge is not None:
    self.sound_effects ['paddle_hit']. play ()
if edge == 'top':
 speed_x = s [0]
 speed_y = -s [1]
 if self.paddle.moving_left:
  speed_x -= 1
 elif self.paddle.moving_left:
  speed_x += 1
 self.ball.speed = speed_x, speed_y
elif edge in ('left', 'right'):
 self.ball.speed = (-s [0], s [1])
```

Collision with the floor.

The ball hits to the racket from the side, the ball continues fall and then hits the floor. At this moment, the player to loses his life and the ball is recreated so that game can continue. The game ends when player runs out of life.

```
# Hit the floor
if self.ball.top> c.screen_height:
    self.lives -= 1
 if self.lives == 0:
  self.game_over = True
 else:
  self.create_ball ()
```

Collision with ceiling and walls

When a ball hits the wall or ceiling, it simply bounces off them.

```
# Hit the ceiling
if self.ball.top <0:
    self.ball.speed = (s [0], -s [1])

# Kick against the wall
if self.ball.left <0 or self.ball.right> c.screen_width:
 self.ball.speed = (-s [0], s [1])
```

Collision with bricks

When ball hits a brick, this is the main event the Breakout game - the brick disappeared, the player receives a point, the ball bounce back, and several more events occur (sound effect, and sometimes a special effect), which we will consider later.

To determine that the ball has hit a brick, the code will check if any of the bricks intersects with the ball:

```
#Bump on a brick
for brick in self.bricks:
    edge = intersect (brick, self.ball)
    if not edge
    continue

self.bricks.remove (brick)
self.objects.remove (brick)
self.score + = self.points_per_brick

if edge in ('top', 'bottom'):
    self.ball.speed = (s [0], -s [1])
else:
    self.ball.speed = (-s [0], s [1])
```

Game Menu Design Program

Most games have some kind of U.I. Breakout has simple menu with two buttons, 'PLAY' and 'QUIT.' The menu is display at the beginning of the game and disappears when the player clicks on 'PLAY.'

Let's see how the button and menu are implemented, as well as how they integrate into the game.

Button Creation

Pygame has no built-in UI library. The third-party extensions, but for the menu, we decided to create our buttons. that has three states: normal, highlighted, and press. The normal state when the mouse is not above the buttons, and the highlight state is when the mouse is above the button, the left mouse button not yet press. The press state is when the mouse is above the button, and the player pressed the left mouse button.

The buttons implement as a rectangle with a back ground color and text display on top of it. The button also receive the (onclick function), which is called when the button is clicked.

```
import pygame

from game_object import GameObject
from text_object import TextObject
import config as c


class Button (GameObject):
    def __init__(self,
            x,
            y,
            w,
            h,
            text,
            on_click = lambda x: None,
            padding = 0):
        super().__init__(x, y, w, h)
        self.state = 'normal'
        self.on_click = on_click

        self.text = TextObject (x + padding,
                    y + padding, lambda: text,
                    c.button_text_color,
                    c.font_name,
                    c.font_size)

    def draw (self, surface):
        pygame.draw.rect (surface,
                self.back_color,
                self.bounds)
        self.text.draw (surface)
```

The button process its own mouse events and changes its internal state based on these events. When the button is in the press state and receives the event *MOUSE BUTTONUP*, this means that the player has press the button and the function is called *on _ click()*.

```
def handle_mouse_event (self, type, pos):
    if type == pygame.MOUSEMOTION:
        self.handle_mouse_move (pos)
    elif type == pygame.MOUSEBUTTONDOWN:
        self.handle_mouse_down (pos)
    elif type == pygame.MOUSEBUTTONUP:
        self.handle_mouse_up (pos)

def handle_mouse_move (self, pos):
    if self.bounds.collidepoint (pos):
        if self.state! = 'pressed'
            self.state = 'hover'
    else:
        self.state = 'normal'

def handle_mouse_down (self, pos):
    if self.bounds.collidepoint (pos):
        self.state = 'pressed'

def handle_mouse_up (self, pos):
    if self.state == 'pressed':
        self.on_click (self)
        self.state = 'hover'
```

The property *back _ color* used to draw on the background rectangle to always returns the color corresponding to current form of the button, so that it is clear to the player that the button is active:

```
@property
def back_color (self):
    return dict (normal = c.button_normal_back_color,
                 hover = c.button_hover_back_color,
                 pressed = c.button_pressed_back_color) [self.state]
```

Menu Design

The function *create_menu* ()create a menu with two buttons with the text 'PLAY' and 'QUIT.' It has two built- in function, *on _ play* ()and *on _ quit* ()which it pass to the correspond button. Each button is add to the list *objects* (for rendering), as well as in the

field *menu _ buttons*.

```
def create_menu (self):
    for i, (text, handler) in enumerate ((('PLAY', on_play),
                        ('QUIT', on_quit))):
        b = Button (c.menu_offset_x,
                c.menu_offset_y + (c.menu_button_h + 5) * i,
                c.menu_button_w,
                c.menu_button_h,
                text
                handler
                padding = 5)
        self.objects.append (b)
        self.menu_buttons.append (b)
        self.mouse_handlers.append (b.handle_mouse_event)
```

When PLAY the button is prese *onplay()*, a function is called that

removes the button from the list *object* so that the no longer

drawn. In adding, the values of the Boolean field that trigger the

starting of the game - *is_gamerunningand startlevel-* Thats OK

When the button is press, QUIT is _ game_ runningtakes on value

(False)(in fact, pausing the game), it set game_ over to True, which

triggers the sequence of completion of the game.

```
def on_play (button):
    for b in self.menu_buttons:
    self.objects.remove (b)

    self.is_game_running = True
    self.start_level = True

def on_quit (button):
    self.game_over = True
    self.is_game_running = False
```

Show and hide GameMenu

The display and hiding the menu are performed implicitly. When the buttons are in the list object, the menu is visible : when they removed, it is hidden. Everything is very simple.

Create built-in menu with its surface that renders its subcomponents (buttons and other objects) and then simply add or remove these menu components, but this is not required for such a simple menu.

To summarize

We examined the collision recognition and what happens when the ball collides with the different objects: a racket, bricks, walls, floor, and ceiling. We also created a menu with our buttons, which can be hidden and displayed on command.

In last part of the series, we will consider completion of the game, tracking points, and lives, sound effects, and music.

We develop complex system of special effects that add few spices to game. Finally, we will the discuss further development and possible improvements.

Creating games on the Pygame framework| Part 3

This is the last of the Thired parts of the tutorial on creating games using Python 3 and PyGame. In the fourth part, we learned to recognize collisions, respond to the fact that the ball collides with different game objects, and created a game menu with its buttons. In last part, we will look at various topics: the end of the game, managing lives and points, sound effects, music, and even a flexible system of special effects. For dessert, we will consider possible improvements and directions for further development.

End of the game

Sooner or later, the game should end. In this form of Breakout, the game ends in one of two ways: the player either loses all his life or destroys all the bricks. There is no next level in the game (but it can easily be added).

Game over!

The game_overclass of the Game class is set to False in the method init ()of the Game class. The main loop continues until the variable game_overchanges to True :

```
class Game:
    def __init__(self,
                 caption
                 width
                 height
                 back_image_filename,
                 frame_rate):

        self.game_over = False
        ...


def run(self):
    while not self.game_over:
        self.surface.blit (self.background_image, (0, 0))

        self.handle_events ()
        self.update ()
        self.draw ()

        pygame.display.update ()
        self.clock.tick (self.frame_rate)
```

All this happens in the Breakout class in the following cases:

The player presses the QUIT button in the menu.

The player loses his last life.

The player destroys all bricks.

```
def on_quit (button):
    self.game_over = True
    self.is_game_running = False

def handle_ball_collisions (self):
    ...
    # Hit the floor
    if self.ball.top> c.screen_height
        self.lives -= 1
        if self.lives == 0:
            self.game_over = True

            if not self.bricks:
                self.show_message ('YOU WIN !!!', centralized = True)
                self.is_game_running = False
                self.game_over = True
                return

def update (self):
    ...
    if not self.bricks:
        self.show_message ('YOU WIN !!!', centralized = True)
        self.is_game_running = False
        self.game_over = True
        return
```

Game End Message Display

Usually, at the end of the game, we do not want the game window to disappear silently. An exception is a case when we click on the QUIT button in the menu. When a player loses their last life, Breakout displays the traditional message 'GAME OVER!', And when the player wins, it shows the message 'YOU WIN!'

In both cases, the function is used show_message(). It displays text on top of the current screen (the game pauses) and waits a few seconds to before returning. The next iteration of the game loop, checking the field game_overwill determine that it is True, after which the program will end.

This is what the function looks like show_message():

```
def show_message (self,
        text
        color = colors.WHITE,
        font_name = 'Arial',
        font_size = 20,
        centralized = False):
    message = TextObject (c.screen_width // 2,
                c.screen_height // 2,
                lambda: text,
                color,
                font_name,
                font_size)
    self.draw ()
    message.draw (self.surface, centralized)
    pygame.display.update ()
    time.sleep (c.message_duration)
```

Saving records between games

In this version of the game, we do not save records, because there is only one level in it, and the results of all players after the destruction of the bricks will be the same. In general, saving records can be implemented locally, saving records to a file and displaying another message if a player breaks a record.

Adding Sound Effects and Music

Games are an audiovisual process. Many games have sound effects - short audio clips that are played when a player kills monsters finds a treasure, or a terrible death. Some games also have background music that contributes to the atmosphere. There are only sound effects in Breakout, but we will show you how to play music in your games.

Sound effects

To play sound effects, we need sound files (as is the case with image files). These files can be.wav, .mp3, or .ogg format. Breakout stores its sound effects in a folder sound_effects:

```
~/git/pygame-breakout> tree sound_effects/
sound_effects/
+-- brick_hit.wav
+-- effect_done.wav
+-- level_complete.wav
+-- paddle_hit.wav
```

Let's see how these sound effects load and play at the right time.

First, play sound effects (or background music), we need to initialize the Pygame sound system. This is done in the Game class:pygame.mixer.pre_init(44100, 16, 2, 4096)

Then, in the Breakout class, all sound effects are loaded from config into the object pygame mixer Soundand stored in the dictionary:

```
# In config.py
sounds_effects = dict (
    brick_hit = 'sound_effects / brick_hit.wav',
    effect_done = 'sound_effects / effect_done.wav',
    paddle_hit = 'sound_effects / paddle_hit.wav',
    level_complete = 'sound_effects / level_complete.wav',
)

# In breakout.py
class Breakout (Game):
    def __init__ (self):
        ...
        self.sound_effects = {
            name: pygame.mixer.Sound (sound)
            for name, sound in c.sounds_effects.items ()}
        ...
```

Now we can play sound effects when something interesting happens. For example, when a ball hits a brick:

```
#Bump on a brick
for brick in self.bricks:
    edge = intersect (brick, self.ball)
    if not edge:
        continue

    self.sound_effects ['brick_hit']. play ()
```

The sound effect is played asynchronously: that is, the game does not stop while it is playing. Several sound effects can be played at the same time.

Record your sound effects and messages

Recording your sound effects can be a simple and fun experience. Unlike creating visual resources, it does not require much talent. Anyone can say "Boom!" or "Jump," or shout, "They killed you. Get lucky another time! "

Playing background music

Background music should play continuously. Theoretically, a very long sound effect can be created, but the looped background music is most often used. Music files can be in .wav, .mp3, or .midi format. Here's how the music is implemented:

```
music = pygame.mixer.music.load ('background_music.mp3')
pygame.mixer.music.play (-1, 0.0)
```

Only one background music can play at a time. However, several sound effects can be played on top of background music. This is what is called mixing.

Adding Advanced Features

Let's do something curious. It is interesting to destroy bricks with a ball, but it quickly bothers. What about the overall special effects system? We will develop an extensible special effects system associated with some bricks, which is activated when the ball hits the brick.

This is what the plan will be. Effects have a lifetime. The effect begins when the brick collapses and ends when the effect expires.

What happens if the ball hits another brick with a special effect? In theory, you can create compatible effects, but to simplify everything in the original implementation, the active effect will stop, and a new effect will take its place.,

Special effects system

In the most general case, a special effect can be defined as two purposes. The first role activates the effect, and the second reset it. We want attach effects to bricks and give the player a clear understanding of which bricks special , so they can try to hit them or avoid them at certain points.

Our special effects are determined by the dictionary from the module breakout.py. Each effect has a name (for example, long_paddle) and a value that consists of a brick color, as well as two functions. Functions are defined a lambda functions that take a Game instance, which includes everything that can change the special effect in Breakout.

```
special_effects = dict (
    long_paddle = (
        colors.ORANGE,
        lambda g: g.paddle.bounds.inflate_ip (
            c.paddle_width // 2, 0),
        lambda g: g.paddle.bounds.inflate_ip (
            -c.paddle_width // 2, 0)),
    slow_ball = (
        colors.AQUAMARINE2,
        lambda g: g.change_ball_speed (-1),
        lambda g: g.change_ball_speed (1)),
    tripple_points = (
        colors.DARKSEAGREEN4,
        lambda g: g.set_points_per_brick (3),
        lambda g: g.set_points_per_brick (1)),
    extra_life = (
        colors.GOLD1,
        lambda g: g.add_life (),
        lambda g: None))
```

When creating bricks, they can be assigned one of the special

effects. Here is the code:

```
def create_bricks (self):
    w = c.brick_width
    h = c.brick_height
    brick_count = c.screen_width // (w + 1)
    offset_x = (c.screen_width - brick_count * (w + 1)) // 2

    bricks = []
    for row in range (c.row_count):
        for col in range (brick_count):
            effect = None
            brick_color = c.brick_color
            index = random.randint (0, 10)
            if index < len (special_effects):
                x = list (special_effects.values ()) [index]
                brick_color = x [0]
                effect = x [1:]

            brick = Brick (offset_x + col * (w + 1),
                c.offset_y + row * (h + 1),
                w,
                h,
                brick_color,
                effect)
            bricks.append (brick)
            self.objects.append (brick)
    self.bricks = bricks
```
The Brick class has an

effect field, which usually has the value None, but (with a probability of 30%) may contain one of the special effects defined above. Note that this code does not know what effects exist. He simply receives the effect and color of the brick and, if necessary, assigns them.

In this version of Breakout, we only trigger effects when we hit a brick, but you can come up with other options for triggering events. The previous effect is discarded (if it existed), and then a new effect is launched. The reset function and effect start time are stored for future use.

```
if brick.special_effect is not None:
    # Reset the previous effect, if any
    if self.reset_effect is not None:
        self.reset_effect (self)

    # Triggering a special effect
    self.effect_start_time = datetime.now ()
    brick.special_effect [0] (self)
    # Setting the current effect reset function
    self.reset_effect = brick.special_effect [1]
```

If the new effect is not launched, we still need to reset the current effect after its lifetime. This happens in the method update(). In each frame, a function to reset the current effect is assigned to the field reset_effect. If the time after starting the current effect exceeds the duration of the effect, then the function is called reset_effect(), and the field reset_effecttakes the value None (meaning that there are currently no active effects).

```
# Reset special effect if necessary
if self.reset_effect:
    elapsed = datetime.now() - self.effect_start_time
    if elapsed> = timedelta(seconds = c.effect_duration):
        self.reset_effect(self)
        self.reset_effect = None
```

Racket increase

The effect of a long racket is to increase the racket by 50%. Its reset function returns the racket to its normal size. The brick has the color Orange.:

```
long_paddle = (
    colors.ORANGE,
    lambda g: g.paddle.bounds.inflate_ip(
        c.paddle_width // 2, 0),
    lambda g: g.paddle.bounds.inflate_ip(
        -c.paddle_width // 2, 0)),
```

Ball slowdown

Another effect that helps in chasing the ball is slowing the ball, that is, reducing its speed by one unit. The brick has an Aquamarine color.

```
slow_ball = (colors.AQUAMARINE2,
    lambda g: g.change_ball_speed(-1),
    lambda g: g.change_ball_speed(1)),
```

More points

If you want great results, then you will like the effect of tripling points, giving three points for each destroyed brick instead of the standard one point. The brick is dark green.

```
tripple_points = (colors.DARKSEAGREEN4,
        lambda g: g.set_points_per_brick (3),
        lambda g: g.set_points_per_brick (1)),
```

Extra lives

Finally, a very useful effect will be the effect of extra lives. He just gives you another life. It does not need a reset. The brick has a gold color.

```
extra_life = (colors.GOLD1,
        lambda g: g.add_life (),
        lambda g: None))
```

Future Features

There are several logical directions for expanding Breakout. If you are interested in trying on yourself in adding new features and functions, here are a few ideas.

Go to the next level

To turn Breakout into a serious game, you need levels: one is not enough. At the beginning of each level, we will reset the screen, but save points and lives. To complicate the game, you can slightly increase the speed of the ball at each level or add another layer of bricks.

Second ball

The effect of temporarily adding a second ball will create enormous chaos. The difficulty here is to treat both balls as equal, regardless of which one is the original. When one ball disappears, the game continues with the only remaining. Life is not lost.

Lasting records

When you have levels with increasing difficulty, it is advisable to create a high score table. You can store records in a file so that they are saved after the game. When a player breaks a record, you can add small pizzas or let him write a name (traditionally with only three characters).

Bombs and bonuses

In the current implementation on, all special effects are associated with bricks, but you can add effects (good and bad) falling from the sky, which the player can collect or avoid.

Summarize

Developing Breakout with Python 3 and Pygame has proven to be an enjoyable experience. This is a compelling combination for creating 2D games (and for 3D games too). If you love Python and want to create your games, then do not hesitate to choose Pygame.

Object-Oriented Programming (OOP) in Python 3

Algorithms and data structures

Hi, Python lover!

Table of contents

What is object-oriented programming (OOP)?

Python classes

Python Object (Instances)

How to define class in Python Instance Attribute Class Attributes

Object CreationWhat's it? Exercise Overview (# 1)

Instance MethodsChanging Attributes

Python object inheritance Example of a dog park Expansion of parent class functionality Parent and child classes Overriding parent class functionality Exercise overview (# 2)

Conclusion

you will become familiars with the following basic concepts of OOP in Python:

Python Classes

Object Instances

Definition and work with methods

OOP Inheritance

What is object-oriented programming (OOP)?

Object-oriented programming, or, in short, OOP, is a programming paradigm that provides a means of structuring programs in such a way that properties and behavior are combined into separate objects.

For example, an object can represent a person with a name, age, address, etc., with behaviors such as walking, talking, breathing, and running. Or an email with properties such as a recipient list, subject, body, etc., as well as with behaviors such as adding attachments and sending.

In other words, object-oriented programming is an approach for modeling specific real things, such as cars, as well as the relationships between things like companies and employees, students and teachers, etc. OOP models real objects as program objects that have some data that are associated with it and can performs certain function.

Another common program para-digm is procedural program, which structure a program like a recipe in the sense that it provides a set of steps in the form of functions and blocks of code that are executed sequentially to complete a task.

The key conclusion is that objects are at the center of the paradigm of object-oriented programming, representing not only data, as in procedural programming, but also in the general structure of the program.

NOTE Since Python is a programming language with many paradigms, you can choose the paradigm that is best suited to the problem in question, mix different para-digms in one program or switching from one para-digm to another as your program develops.

Python classes

Focusing first on the data, each object or thing is an instance of some class.

The primitive data structures available in Python, such as numbers, strings, and lists, are designed to represent simple things, such as the value of something, the name of the poem, and your favorite colors, respectively.

What if you want to imagine something much more complex?

For example, let say you wanted to track several different animals. If you use a list, the first element may be the name of the animal, while the second element may represent its age.

How would you know which element should be? What if you had 100 different animals? Are you sure that every animal has a name, age, and so on? What if you want to add other properties to these animals? This is not enough organization, and this is exactly what you need for classes.

Classes are used to create new user data structure that contain arbitrary informations abouts some thing. In this case of an animal, we could creates an Animal()class to track animal properties such as name and age.

It is importants to note that a class simply provides structure - it is an example of how something should be defined, but in fact, it does not provide any real content. Animal()The class may indicate that the name and age are required to determine the animal, but it will not claim that the name or age of a particular animal is.

This can help present the class as an idea of how something should be defined.

Python Objects (Instances)

While a class is a plan, an instance is a copy of a class with actual values, literally an object belonging to a particular class. This is no longer an idea: it's a real animal, like a dog named Roger, which is eight years old.

In other words, a class is a form or profile. It determines the necessary informations. After you fullfill out the form, your specific copy is an instance of the class: it contains up-to-date information relevant to you.

You can fill out several copies to create many different copies, but without a form, as a guide, you would be lost without knowing what information is required. Thus, before you can create separate instances of an object, we must first specify what you need by defining a class.

How to define a class in Python

Defining a class is simple in Python:

```
class Dog:
    pass
```

You start with a classkeyword to indicate that you are creating a class, then you add the class name (using theCamelCase notation starting with a capital letter).

Also here we used the Python keyword pass. This is huge often used as a placeholder where the code will eventually go. This allows us to run this code without generating an error.

Note: the above code is correct in Python 3. On Python 2.x ("deprecated Python"), you would use a slightly different class definition:

```
# Python 2.x Class Definition
class Dog (object):
    pass
```

Not the (object)parts in parentheses indicate the parent class that you are inheriting from (more on this below). In Python-3, this is no longer necessary because it is implicit by defaulting.

Instance attribute

All class create objects, and all objects contain characteristics called attributes (called properties in the first paragraph). Use the init ()method to initialize (for example, determine) the initial attributes of an object by giving them a default value (state). This method must have atleast one argument, as well as a self variable that refers to the object itself (for example, Dog).

```
class Dog:
    # Initializer / Instance Attributes
    def __init__(self, name, age):
        self.name = name
        self.age = age
```

In our Dog()class, each dog has a specific name and age, which is certainly important to know when you start creating different dogs. Remember: the class is intended only to define a dog, and not to create instances of individual dogs with specific names and ages: we will come back to this soon.

Similarly, a self variable is also an instance of a class. Since class instances have different meanings, we could argue, Dog.name = namenot self.name = name. But since not all dogs have the same name, we must be able to assign different values for different instances. Hence the need for a special self variable that will help track individual instances of each class.

NOTE: you will never have to call a init ()method: it is called automatically when a new instance of Dog is created.

Class attributes

Although instance attributes are specific to each object, class attributes are the same for all instances, in this case, all dogs.

```
class Dog:

    # Class Attribute
    species = 'mammal'

    # Initializer / Instance Attributes
    def __init__(self, name, age):
        self.name = name
        self.age = age
```

Thus, although each dog has a unique name and age, each dog will be a mammal. Let's create some dogs ...

Create Objects

Instantiating is an unusual term for creating a new unique instance of a class.

For example: >>>

```
>>> class Dog
...  pass
...
>>> Dog ()
<__main__.Dog object at 0x1004ccc50>
>>> Dog ()
<__main__.Dog object at 0x1004ccc90>
>>> a = Dog ()
>>> b = Dog ()
>>> a == b
False
```

We started by definea new Dog()class, then created two new dogs,

each of which was assigned to different

objects. So, to create an instance of the class, you use the class

name follow by parentheses. Then, to demonstration that each

instance is actually different, we created two more dogs, assigning

each variable, and then checking to see if these variables are equal.

What do you think is the type of class instance? >>>

```
>>> class Dog
...  pass
...
>>> a = Dog ()
>>> type (a)
<class '__main__.Dog'>
```

Let's look at the more complex example ...

```
class Dog

    # Class Attribute
    species = 'mammal'

    # Initializer / Instance Attributes
    def __init__(self, name, age):
        self.name = name
        self.age = age


# Instantiate the Dog object
philo = Dog ("Philo", 5)
mikey = Dog ("Mikey", 6)

# Access the instance attributes
print ("{} is {} and {} is {}.".format (
    philo.name, philo.age, mikey.name, mikey.age))

# Is Philo a mammal?
if philo.species == "mammal":
    print ("{0} is a {1}!".format (philo.name, philo.species))
```

NOTE Notice how we use point records to access the attributes of each objects. Save as (dog_class.py), then run program. You should see:

```
Philo is 5 and Mikey is 6.
Philo is a mammal!
```

What's the matter?

We create a new instance of the Dog()class and assigned it to a variable Philo. Then we passed him two arguments, "Philo" and 5, which represent the name and age of this dog, respectively.

These attribute are pass to the init method, which is called every time you creates a new attaching, instance the name and age to the object. You may be wondering why we should not have given self arguments.

This is the magic of Python: when you create a new instance of the class, Python automatically determines what selfies (in this case, Dog), and passes it to the init method.

Review of exercises (# 1)

Exercise: "The oldest dog"

Using the same Dogclass, create three new dogs, each with a different age. Then write a function with a name get_biggest_number()that takes any number of ages (*args) and returns the oldest. Then print the age of the oldest dog something like this:

The oldest dog is 7 years old. Solution: "The oldest dog"   Solution "The oldest dog."

```
class Dog:

    # Class Attribute
    species = 'mammal'

    # Initializer / Instance Attributes
    def __init__(self, name, age):
        self.name = name
        self.age = age

# Instantiate the Dog object
jake = Dog("Jake", 7)
doug = Dog("Doug", 4)
william = Dog('William', 5)

# Determine the oldest dog
def get_biggest_number(* args):
    return max(args)

# Output
print("The oldest dog is {} years old.".format(
    get_biggest_number(jake.age, doug.age, william.age)))
```

Instance Methods

Instance methods are defined inside the class and are used to get the contents of the instance. They can also be used to perform operation with the attribute of our objects. Like a init method, the first argument is always self:

```
class Dog:

    # Class Attribute
    species = 'mammal'

    # Initializer / Instance Attributes
    def __init__(self, name, age):
        self.name = name
        self.age = age

    # instance method
    def description(self):
        return "{} is {} years old".format(self.name, self.age)

    # instance method
    def speak(self, sound):
        return "{} says {}".format(self.name, sound)

# Instantiate the Dog object
mikey = Dog("Mikey", 6)

# call our instance methods
print(mikey.description())
print(mikey.speak("Gruff Gruff"))
```

Save as dog_instance_methods.py , then run it:

```
Mikey is 6 years old
Mikey says Gruff Gruff
```

In the last method, speak()we define the behavior. What other types of behavior can you assign to a dog? Go back to the beginning of the paragraph to see examples of the behavior of other objects.

Attribute Change

You can changes the value of attributes based on some behavior:

>>>

```
>>> class Email:
... def __init__(self):
... self.is_sent = False
... def send_email(self):
... self.is_sent = True
...
>>> my_email = Email()
>>> my_email.is_sent
False
>>> my_email.send_email()
>>> my_email.is_sent
True
```

Here we added a method for sending an email that updates the

is_sentvariable to True.

Python object inheritance

Inheritance is a processing in which one class accepts the attributes

and methods of another. Newly created classes are called child

classes, and the classes from which the child classes derive are

called parent classes.

It is importants to note that child classes override or extend the

functionality (for example, attributes and behavior) of parent

classes. In other words, child classes inherit all the attributes and

behavior of the parent, but can also define other behavior to be

followed. The most basic type of class is the class object, which

usually all other classes inherit as the parents.

When you defining a new class, Python 3 implicitly uses its object as

the parent class. Thus, the following two definitions are equivalent:

```
class Dog (object):
    pass

# In Python 3, this is the same as:

class Dog:
    pass
```

Note. In Python 2.x, there is a difference between the new and old-style classes. I will not go into details, but you will usually want to specify an object as the parent class to make sure that you define a new style class if you are writing Python 2 OOP code.

Dog Park Example

Let's imagine that we are in a dog park. There are several Dog objects involved in Dog behavior, each with different attributes. In ordinary conversation, this means that some dogs are running, and some are stretched, and some are just watching other dogs.

Besides, each dog was named its owner, and since each dog lives and breathes, each is aging.

How else can you distinguish one dog from another? How about a dog breed: >>>

```
>>> class Dog:
...     def __init__(self, breed):
...         self.breed = breed

>>> spencer = Dog("German Shepard")
>>> spencer.breed
'German Shepard'
>>> sara = Dog("Boston Terrier")
>>> sara.breed
'Boston Terrier'
```

Each dog breed has slightly different behaviors. To take this into account, let's create separate classes for each breed. These are child classes of the parent Dogclass.

Extending parent class functionality

Create new file this called dog_inheritance.py :

```python
# Parent class
class Dog:

    # Class attribute
    species = 'mammal'

    # Initializer / Instance attributes
    def __init__(self, name, age):
        self.name = name
        self.age = age

    # instance method
    def description(self):
        return "{} is {} years old".format(self.name, self.age)

    # instance method
    def speak(self, sound):
        return "{} says {}".format(self.name, sound)


# Child class (inherits from Dog class)
class RussellTerrier(Dog):
    def run(self, speed):
        return "{} runs {}".format(self.name, speed)


# Child class (inherits from Dog class)
class Bulldog(Dog):
    def run(self, speed):
        return "{} runs {}".format(self.name, speed)


# Child classes inherit attributes and
# behaviors from the parent class
jim = Bulldog("Jim", 12)
print(jim.description())

# Child classes have specific attributes
# and behaviors as well
print(jim.run("slowly"))
```

Read the comments aloud while you are working with this program to help you understand what is happening, and then, before you run the program, see if you can predict the expected result.

You should see:

```
Jim is 12 years old
Jim runs slowly
```

We did not add any special attributes or methods to distinguish between a RussellTerrierand a Bulldog. Still, since they are now two different classes, we could, for example, give them different class attributes that determine their respective speeds.

Parent and child classes

isinstance()The function is used to determine if the instance is also an instance of a specific parent class. Save this as dog_isinstance.py

:

```python
# Parent class
class Dog:

    # Class attribute
    species = 'mammal'

    # Initializer / Instance attributes
    def __init__(self, name, age):
        self.name = name
        self.age = age

    # instance method
    def description(self):
        return "{} is {} years old".format(self.name, self.age)

    # instance method
    def speak(self, sound):
        return "{} says {}".format(self.name, sound)


# Child class (inherits from Dog() class)
class RussellTerrier(Dog):
    def run(self, speed):
        return "{} runs {}".format(self.name, speed)


# Child class (inherits from Dog() class)
class Bulldog(Dog):
    def run(self, speed):
        return "{} runs {}".format(self.name, speed)


# Child classes inherit attributes and
# behaviors from the parent class
jim = Bulldog("Jim", 12)
print(jim.description())

# Child classes have specific attributes
# and behaviors as well
print(jim.run("slowly"))

# Is jim an instance of Dog()?
print(isinstance(jim, Dog))

# Is julie an instance of Dog()?
julie = Dog("Julie", 100)
print(isinstance(julie, Dog))

# Is johnny walker an instance of Bulldog()
johnnywalker = RussellTerrier("Johnny Walker", 4)
print(isinstance(johnnywalker, Bulldog))

# Is julie and instance of jim?
print(isinstance(julie, jim))
```

Conclusion: >>>

```
('Jim', 12)
Jim runs slowly
True
True
False
Traceback (most recent call last):
  File "dog_isinstance.py", line 50, in <module>
    print (isinstance (julie, jim))
TypeError: isinstance () arg 2 must be a class, type, or tuple of classes and types
```

It makes sense? Both jimand julieare instances of the Dog()class and johnnywalkerare not instances of Bulldog()the class. Then, as a health check, we checked juliewhether the instance is an instance jim, which is impossible, since jimit instancedoes not belong to the class itself, but to the class TypeError.

Overriding parent class functionality

Remember that child classes can also override the attributes and behavior of the parent class. For example: >>>

```
>>> class Dog:
... species = 'mammal'
...
>>> class SomeBreed (Dog):
... pass
...
>>> class SomeOtherBreed (Dog):
... species = 'reptile'
...
>>> frank = SomeBreed ()
>>> frank.species 'mammal'
>>> beans = SomeOtherBreed ()
>>> beans.species 'reptile'
```
The SomeBreed()class inherits speciesfrom the parent class, while the
SomeOtherBreed()class overrides speciesby setting it reptile.

Review of exercises (# 2)

Exercise: "Legacy of the dogs"

Create a Petsclass that contains dog instances: this class is
completely separate from the Dogclass. In other words, a Dogclass
is not inherited from the Petsclass. Then assign three instances of
the dog to the Petsclass instance . Start with the following code
below. Save the file as pets_class.py . Your output should look like
this:

```
I have 3 dogs.
Tom is 6.
Fletcher is 7.
Larry is 9.
And they're all mammals, of course.
```

Start Code:

```
# Parent class
class Dog:

    # Class attribute
    species = 'mammal'

    # Initializer / Instance attributes
    def __init__(self, name, age):
        self.name = name
        self.age = age

    # instance method
    def description(self):
        return "{} is {} years old".format(self.name, self.age)

    # instance method
    def speak(self, sound):
        return "{} says {}".format(self.name, sound)

# Child class (inherits from Dog class)
class RussellTerrier(Dog):
    def run(self, speed):
        return "{} runs {}".format(self.name, speed)

# Child class (inherits from Dog class)
class Bulldog(Dog):
    def run(self, speed):
        return "{} runs {}".format(self.name, speed)
```

Solution: "Dog Inheritance"

```python
# Parent class
class Pets:

    dogs = []

    def __init__ (self, dogs):
        self.dogs = dogs


# Parent class
class Dog:

    # Class attribute
    species = 'mammal'

    # Initializer / Instance attributes
    def __init__ (self, name, age):
        self.name = name
        self.age = age

    # Instance method
    def description (self):
        return self.name, self.age

    # Instance method
    def speak (self, sound):
        return "%s says%s" % (self.name, sound)

    # Instance method
    def eat (self):
        self.is_hungry = False


# Child class (inherits from Dog class)
class RussellTerrier (Dog):
    def run (self, speed):
        return "%s runs%s" % (self.name, speed)


# Child class (inherits from Dog class)
class Bulldog (Dog):
    def run (self, speed):
        return "%s runs%s" % (self.name, speed)

# Create instances of dogs
my_dogs = [
    Bulldog ("Tom", 6),
    RussellTerrier ("Fletcher", 7),
    Dog ("Larry", 9)
]

# Instantiate the Pets class
my_pets = Pets (my_dogs)

# Output
print ("I have {} dogs.". format (len (my_pets.dogs)))
for dog in my_pets.dogs:
    print (" {} is {} .". format (dog.name, dog.age))

print ("And they're all {} s, of course.". format (dog.species))
```

Exercise: Hungry Dogs

Use the same files, add an instance attribute is_hungry = Truein the Dogclass. Then add the called method, eat()which when called changes the value is_hungryto False. Find out how best to feed each dog, and then print "My dogs are hungry." if everyone is hungry or "My dogs are not hungry." if everyone is not hungry. The final result should look like this:

```
I have 3 dogs.
Tom is 6.
Fletcher is 7.
Larry is 9.
And they're all mammals, of course.
My dogs are not hungry.
```

Solution: Hungry Dogs

```python
# Parent class
class Pets:

    dogs = []

    def __init__(self, dogs):
        self.dogs = dogs


# Parent class
```

```python
class Dog.

    # Oass attribute
    sped es = 'mamm d '

    # Initi d i zer .'' In stance attributes
    def   iriit   (self name age).
        self.name  = name
        self.age  = age
        self.is hungo.' = True

=  mist ance method
    def descripti on (self).
        return self.name  self.age

= mist ance method
    def speak (self sound).
        return " °. o s says°. o s" °. o (self.name sound)
```

```python
= mist ance method
    def eat (self).
        self.is hungo.' = Fd se


= Oiild class (inherits from Dog cl ass)
class RussellT erri er (Dog).
    def run (self speed).
        return " °. o s runs°. o s" °. o (self.name speedt


= Oiild class (inherits from Dog cl ass)
class Bulldog (Dog.
    def run (self speed).
        return " °. o s runs°. o s" °. o (self.name speedt

= Create instances of dogs
m\' dogs = [
    Bulldog (" Tom" 6)
    Ru ssellT erri er (" Fl ct cher" Tt
    Dog ("L are.'" 9)


        stanttate the Pets class
ate'    ts = Pets (ate' dogs)

= Outp.it
print (" I h ave { ) dogs.". format (len (m\'    ets.dogs)))
for dog in m\'    ets.dogs.
    dog.eat ()
    print (" { ) is { ).". format (dog.name dog.age))

print ("And the\"'re d1 { ) s of ccxirse." . format (dog.species))

are m\ dogs hungo.' = Fdse
for dog in m\'    ets.dogs.
    if dog.i s hungo.'.




are_my_dogs_hungry = True

if are_my_dogs_hungry:
    print ("My dogs are hungry.")
else:
    print ("My dogs are not hungry.")
```

Exercise: "Dog Walking"

Next, add a walk()method like Petsand Dogclasses, so that when you call a method in the Petsclass, each instance of a dog is assigned to Petsa class walk(). Save this as dog_walking.py . This is a little trickier.

Start by implementing a method just like a speak()method. As for the method in the Petsclass, you will need to iterate over the list of dogs and then call the method itself.

The output should look like this:

Tom is walking!
Fletcher is walking!
Larry is walking!

Solution: "dog walking"

```python
# Parent class
class Pets:

    dogs = []

    def __init__(self, dogs):
        self.dogs = dogs

    def walk(self):
        for dog in self.dogs:
            print(dog.walk())


# Parent class
class Dog:

    # Class attribute
    species = 'mammal'
    is_hungry = True

    # Initializer / Instance attributes
    def __init__(self, name, age):
        self.name = name
        self.age = age

    # Instance method
    def description(self):
        return self.name, self.age

    # Instance method
    def speak(self, sound):
        return "%s says %s" % (self.name, sound)

    # Instance method
    def eat(self):
        self.is_hungry = False
```

```python
def walk (self):
    return "%s is walking!" % (self.name)

# Child class (inherits from Dog class)
class RussellTerrier (Dog):
    def run (self, speed):
        return "%s runs %s" % (self.name, speed)

# Child class (inherits from Dog class)
class Bulldog (Dog):
    def run (self, speed):
        return "%s runs %s" % (self.name, speed)

# Create instances of dogs
my_dogs = [
    Bulldog ("Tom", 6),
    RussellTerrier ("Fletcher", 7),
    Dog ("Larry", 9)
]

# Instantiate the Pet class
my_pets = Pets (my_dogs)

# Output
my_pets.walk ()
```

Exercise: "Testing Understanding"

Answer the following OOP questions to verify your learning progress:

What class?

What an example?

What is the relationship between class and instance?

What Python syntax is used to define a new class?

What is the spelling convention for a class name?

How do you create or create an instance of a class?

How do you access the attributes and behavior of an instance of a class?

What kind of method?

What is the purpose self?

What is the purpose of the init method?

Describe how inheritance helps prevent code duplication.

Can child classes override the properties of their parents?

Solution: "Test of understanding" Show hide

A class mechanism used to create new custom data structures. It contains data, as well as methods used to process this data.

An instance is a copy of a class with actual values, literally an object of a particular class.

While a class is a plan used to describe how to create something, instances are objects created from these drawings.

class PythonClassName:

Capitalized CamelCase designation - i.e. PythonClassName()

You use the class name followed by parentheses. So if the name of the class Dog(), the instance of the dog will be - my_class = Dog().

With dot notation - for example, instance_name.attribute_name

A function that defined inside a class.

The first argument of each method refers to the current instance of the class, which is called by the convention self. The init method self refers to a newly created object, while in other methods, it a self refers into the instance whose method was called. For more on the init con self, check out this article.

init The method initializes an instance of the class.

Child classes inherit all the attributes and behavior of the parent.

Yes.

Conclusion

Now you should know what classes are, why you want or should use them, and how to create parent and child classes to better structure your programs.

Remember that OOP is a programming paradigm, not a Python concept. Most modern programming languages, such as Java, C #, C ++, follow the principles of OOP. So the good news is that learning the basics of object-oriented programming will be useful to you in a variety of circumstances - whether you work in Python or not.

Now the industry does not stand still and there are more and more web sites, services and companies that need specialists.

Demand for developers is growing, but competition among them is growing.

To be the best in your business, you need to be almost an absolutely universal person who can write a website, create a design for it, and promote it yourself.

In this regard, even a person who has never sat at this computer begins to think, but should I try?

But very often it turns out that such enthusiasts burn out at the initial stage, without having tried themselves in this matter.

Or maybe he would become a brilliant creator of code? Would create something new? This we will not know.

Every day, the threshold for entering programming is growing. You can never predict what new language will come out.

Such an abundance breaks all the desire of a newly minted programmer and he is lost in this ocean of information.

All these javascripts of yours ... pythons ... what fear ..

A great misconception is the obligation to know mathematics. Yes, it is needed, but only in a narrow field, but it is also useful for understanding some aspects.

The advice that can be given to people who are just starting their activity is not to chase everything at once. Allow yourself time to think.

What do I want to do? Create a program for everyone to be useful? Create additional services to simplify any tasks? Or do you really have to go make games?

The second advice will be to answer my question how much time am I ready to devote to this? The third point is to think about how fast you want to achieve your intended result.

So, there is no "easy way" to start programming, it all depends on you - your interest, what you want to do and your tasks.

In any case, you need to try and do everything possible in your power. Good luck in your endeavors!

PYTHON

CRASH COURSE

Beginner guide to computer programming, web coding and data mining.
Learn in 7 days machine learning, artificial intelligence, NumPy and
Pandas packages with exercises for data analysis.

JASON TEST

What Is Python?

Python is a high-level, object-oriented, construed programming language with complex semblance. Combined with dynamic typing and dynamic binding, its high-level data structures make it very attractive for Rapid Application Development as well as for use as a scripting or glue language for connecting existing components. Python's quick, easy to understand syntax, stresses readability, and hence reduces the expense of running the software. Python connects modules and packages that promote the modularity of the software and reuse of code. For all major platforms, the Python interpreter and the comprehensive standard library are available free of charge in source or binary form and can be freely distributed.

Programmers also fall in love with Python because of the increased productivity it brings. The edit-test-debug process is amazingly quick since there is no compilation phase. Python debugging programs are simple: a mistake or bad feedback would never trigger a segmentation fault. Alternatively, it creates an exception when the translator detects an error. If the program miscarries to catch the exception, the parser will print a stack trace. A source-level debugger allows you to inspect local and global variables, check arbitrary expressions, set breakpoints, walk through the code one line at a time, etc. The debugger itself is written in Python, testifying to the introspective power of Python. On the other side, often the fastest way to debug a system is to add a few print statements to the source: the quick process of edit-test-debug renders this simple approach quite efficient.

Who is the Right Audience?

The resolve of this book is to get you up to speed with Python as easy as possible so that you can create programs that work — games, data analysis, and web applications — while building a programming base that will serve you well for the rest of your life. Python Crash Course is designed for people of any age who have never programmed in or worked in Python before. This book is for you if you want to learn the basics of programming quickly, so you can focus on interesting projects, and you like to test your understanding of new concepts by solving meaningful issues. Python Crash Course is also great for middle and high school teachers who would like to give a project-based guide to programming to their pupils.

What You Will Learn?

The sole purpose of this book is to make you generally a good programmer and, in particular, a good programmer for Python. As we provide you with a solid foundation in general programming concepts, you can learn quickly and develop good habits. You should be prepared to move on to more sophisticated Python methods after working your way through the Python Crash Course, and it will make the next programming language much easier to grasp. You will learn basic programming concepts in the first part of this book, which you need to know to write Python programs. These concepts are the same as those you would learn in almost any programming language when starting out.

You can learn about the different data types and ways you can store data within your applications in lists and dictionaries. You'll learn how to build data collections and work efficiently through those collections. You'll learn to use while and when loops to check for certain conditions so that you can run certain sections of code while those conditions are true and run certain sections when they aren't true — a strategy that can significantly automate processes. To make your programs accessible and keep your programs going as long as the user is active, you'll have to accept input from users.

You're going to explore how to apply functions as reusable parts of your software, and you only have to write blocks of code that execute those functions once, which you can use as many times as you want. You will then extend this concept with classes to more complicated behavior, making programs fairly simple to respond to a variety of situations.

You must learn how to write programs to handle common errors graciously. You will write a few short programs after going on each of these basic concepts, which will solve some well-defined problems. Finally, you can take the first step towards intermediate programming by learning how to write checks for your code so that you can further improve your programs without thinking about bugs being implemented. For Part I, all the details will allow you to take on bigger, more complicated tasks.

Why Python?

Every year we consider whether to continue using Python or move on to another language — maybe one that is newer to the programming world. But for a lot of reasons, I keep on working on Python. Python is an incredibly efficient language: the programs will do more than many other languages will need with fewer lines of code. The syntax of Python, too, should help write clean code. Compared to other languages, the code will be easy to read, easy to debug, and easy to extend and expand on. People use Python for many purposes: making games, creating web applications, solving business problems, and developing internal tools for all types of applications interesting ventures. Python is also heavily utilized for academic research and theoretical science in scientific fields.

One of the main reasons I keep on using Python is because of the Python community, which includes an incredibly diverse and welcoming group of people. Community is important for programmers since programming is not a practice of solitude. Most of us will ask advice from others, even the most seasoned programmers, who have already solved similar problems. Getting a well-connected and supportive community is essential to help you solve problems and the Python community fully supports people like you who are using Python as your first programming language.

What Is Machine Learning?

Machine-learning algorithms use correlations in massive volumes of data to identify patterns. And info, here, contains a lot of stuff — numbers, words, images, clicks, what do you have. This can be fed into a machine-learning system because it can be digitally processed.

Machine learning is the procedure that powers many of today's services — recommendation programs such as those on Netflix, YouTube, and Spotify; search engines such as Google and Baidu; social media channels such as Facebook and Twitter; voice assistants such as Siri and Alexa. The collection continues.

In all these instances, each platform collects as much data as possible about you — what genres you like to watch, what links you click on, what statuses you react to — and using machine learning to make a highly educated guess of what you might want next. And, in the case of a voice assistant, which words the best match with the funny sounds that come out of your mouth.

Frankly, this is quite a basic process: find the pattern, apply the pattern. But the world runs pretty much that way. That's thanks in large part to a 1986 breakthrough, courtesy of Geoffrey Hinton, now known as the father of deep knowledge.

What is Deep Learning?

Deep knowledge is machine learning on steroids: it uses a methodology that improves the capacity of computers to identify — and reproduce — only the smallest patterns. This method is called a deep neural network — strong because it has many, many layers of basic computational nodes that work together to churn through data and produce a result in the form of the prediction.

What are Neural Networks?

Neural networks strongly influence the interior workings of the human brain. The nodes are kind of like neurons, and the network is kind of like the entire brain. (For the researchers among you who cringe at this comparison: Avoid pooh-poohing the analogy. It's a good analogy.) But Hinton presented his breakthrough paper at a time when neural nets were out of fashion. Nobody ever learned how to teach them, and they didn't produce decent results. The method had taken nearly 30 years to make a comeback. And boy, they made a comeback!

What is Supervised Learning?

The last thing you need to know is that computer (and deep) learning comes in three flavors: controlled, unmonitored, and enhanced. The most prevalent data is marked in supervised learning to inform the computer exactly what patterns it will look for. Thought of it as being like a sniffer dog that can search targets until they know the smell they're following. That's what you do when you're pressing a Netflix series to play — you're asking the program to search related programs.

What is Unsupervised Learning?

In unsupervised learning, the data does not have any names. The computer is only searching for whatever trends it can locate. It's like making a dog detect lots of different things and organize them into classes of identical smells. Unsupervised methods are not as common as they have less apparent applications. Interestingly, they've achieved traction in cybersecurity.

What is Reinforcement Learning?

Finally, we have the enhancement of learning, the new field of machine learning. A reinforcement algorithm learns to achieve a clear objective by trial and error. It attempts a lot of different things and is rewarded or penalized depending on whether its behavior helps or hinders it from achieving its goal. It's like giving and denying treats as you show a puppy a new trick. Strengthening learning is the cornerstone of Google's AlphaGo, a software that has recently defeated the best human players in the complicated game of Go.

What Is Artificial Intelligence (AI)?

Mathematician Alan Turing changed history a second time with a simple question: "Do computers think?" Less than a decade after cracking the Nazi encryption code Enigma and enabling the Allied Forces to win World War II. The basic purpose and goal of artificial intelligence were developed by Turing's paper "Computing Machinery and Intelligence" (1950), and the subsequent Turing Test.

At its heart, AI is the branch of computer science that is aimed at answering Turing's affirmative query. It's the shot at replicating or simulating human intelligence in machines.

The expansive purpose of artificial intelligence has led to numerous questions and debates. So much so, that there is no universally accepted single field description.

The big limitation of describing AI as literally "making intelligent machines" is that it doesn't really describe what artificial intelligence is? Who makes an Intelligent Machine?

Artificial Intelligence: A Modern Approach in their pioneering textbook, authors Stuart Russell and Peter Norvig address the issue by unifying their work around the topic of smart agents in computers. With this in mind, AI is "the study of agents acquiring environmental perceptions and doing behavior" (Russel and Norvig viii)

Norvig and Russell continue their exploration of four different approaches that have historically defined AI:

1.   Thinking humanly
2.   Thinking rationally
3.   Acting humanly
4.   Acting rationally

The first two theories are about thought patterns and logic, while the rest are about behavior. In particular, Norvig and Russell concentrate on logical agents that behave to obtain the best outcome, noting 'all the skills needed for the Turing Test often help an agent to act rationally" (Russel and Norvig 4).

Patrick Winston, MIT's Ford Professor of Artificial Intelligence and Computer Science, describes AI as "algorithms allowed by constraints, revealed by representations that help loop-focused models that bind together thought, interpretation and behavior." While the average person may find these definitions abstract, they help focus the field as an area of computer science and provide a blueprint for infusing machines and programs with machine learning and other artificial intelligence subsets.

When addressing an audience at the 2017 Japan AI Experience, Jeremy Achin, CEO of DataRobot, started his speech by presenting the following description of how AI is used today:

"AI is a computational system capable of executing activities typically involving human intelligence ... Some of these artificial intelligence systems are powered by machine learning, others are powered by deep learning, and others are powered by very simple stuff like rules."

What Is Data Science?

Data science continues developing as one of the most exciting and challenging career options for qualified professionals. Today, productive computer practitioners recognize that the conventional techniques of processing vast volumes of data, data analysis, and programming skills must be improved. To discover valuable information within their organizations, data scientists need to experience the broad range of the life cycle of data science and have a degree of versatility and comprehension to optimize returns at each point of the process.

What Is Data Mining?

Data mining is investigating and analyzing big data to find concrete patterns and laws. This is considered a specialty within the area of analysis of computer science and is distinct from predictive analytics because it represents past evidence. In contrast, data mining attempts to forecast future outcomes. Also, data mining methods are used to build machine learning (ML) models driving advanced artificial intelligence (AI) technologies such as search engine algorithms and recommendation systems.

How to Do Data Mining

The accepted data mining process involves six steps:

1.   Business understanding

The first step is to set the project's objectives and how data mining will help you accomplish that goal. At this point, a schedule will be drawn up to include schedules, activities and responsibilities of tasks.

2.   Data understanding

In this phase, data is gathered from all available data sources. At this point, data visualization applications are also used to test the data's properties and ensure it helps meet business goals.

3.   Data Preparation

Data is then washed, and it contains lost data to ensure that it can be mined. Data analysis can take a substantial period, depending on the volume of data processed and the number of sources of data. Therefore, in modern database management systems (DBMS), distributed systems are used to improve the speed of the data mining process rather than to burden one single system. They're also safer than having all the data in a single data warehouse for an organization. Including fail-safe steps in the data, the manipulation stage is critical so that data is not permanently lost.

4.   Data Modeling

Mathematical models are then used with a sophisticated analysis method to identify trends in the data.

5.   Evaluation

The findings are evaluated to determine if they should be deployed across the organization, and compared to business objectives.

6.   Deployment

The data mining results are spread through everyday business processes in the final level. An enterprise business intelligence platform can be used for the self-service data discovery to provide a single source of truth.

Benefits of Data Mining

- **Automated Decision-Making**

Data Mining allows companies to evaluate data on a daily basis and optimize repetitive and important decisions without slowing human judgment. Banks can identify fraudulent transactions immediately, request verification, and even secure personal information to protect clients from identity theft. Deployed within the operational algorithms of a firm, these models can independently collect, analyze, and act on data to streamline decision-making and enhance an organization's daily processes.

- **Accurate Prediction and Forecasting**

For any organization, preparing is a vital operation. Data mining promotes planning and provides accurate predictions for administrators based on historical patterns and present circumstances. Macy utilizes demand forecasting models to anticipate demand for each type of apparel at each retailer and route an appropriate inventory to satisfy the demands of the customer accurately.

- **Cost Reduction**

Data mining enables more efficient use and resource allocation. Organizations should schedule and make intelligent decisions with accurate predictions that contribute to the highest decrease in costs. Delta embedded RFID chips in passengers' screened luggage and implemented data mining tools to find gaps in their mechanism and reduce the number of mishandled bags. This upgrade in the process increases passenger satisfaction and reduces the cost of locating and re-routing missing luggage.

- **Customer Insights**

Companies deploy data mining models from customer data to uncover key features and differences between their customers. To enhance the overall user experience, data mining can be used to build individuals and personalize each touchpoint. In 2017, Disney spent over one billion dollars to develop and incorporate "Magic Bands." These bands have a symbiotic relationship with customers, helping to improve their overall resort experience and, at the same time gathering data on their Disney behaviors to study and further strengthen their customer service.

What Are Data Analytics?

Data analysis is defined as a process for cleaning, transforming, and modeling data to discover useful business decision-making information. Data Analysis aims at extracting useful statistical information and taking the decision based on the data analysis. Whenever we make any decision in our daily life, it is by choosing that particular decision that we think about what happened last time, or what will happen. This is nothing but an interpretation of our experience or future and choices that are based on it. We accumulate thoughts of our lives, or visions of our future, for that. So this is nothing but an analysis of the data. Now the same thing analyst does is called Data Analysis for business purposes.

Here you'll learn about:

- Why Data Analysis?
- Data Analysis Tools
- Types of Data Analysis: Techniques and Methods
- Data Analysis Process

Why Data Analysis?

Often, research is what you need to do to develop your company and to develop in your life! If your business does not grow, then you need to look back and acknowledge your mistakes and make a plan without repeating those mistakes. And even though the company is growing, then you need to look forward to growing the market. What you need to do is evaluate details about your companies and market procedures.

Data Analysis Tools

Data analysis tools make it simpler for users to process and manipulate data, analyze relationships and correlations between data sets, and help recognize patterns and trends for interpretation. Here is a comprehensive list of tools.

Types of Data Analysis; Techniques and Methods

There are many types of data analysis techniques that are based on business and technology. The main types of data analysis are as follows:

- Text Analysis
- Statistical Analysis
- Diagnostic Analysis
- Predictive Analysis
- Prescriptive Analysis

Text Analysis

Text Analysis is also known as Data Mining. Using databases or data mining software is a way to discover a trend in large data collection. It used to turn the raw data into information about the market. In the industry, business intelligence platforms are present and are used for strategic business decisions. Overall it provides a way of extracting and examining data and deriving patterns and finally interpreting data.

Statistical Analysis

Statistical Analysis shows "What happens?" in the form of dashboards using the past data. Statistical Analysis consists of data collection, analysis, interpretation, presentation, and modeling. It analyzes a data set or a data sample. This type of analysis has two categories-Descriptive Analysis and Inferential Analysis.

Descriptive Analysis

Descriptive Analysis analyzes complete data or a summarized sample of numerical data. For continuous data, it shows mean and deviation, while percentage and frequency for categorical data.

Inferential Analysis

This analyzes full data from samples. You can find diverse conclusions from the same data in this type of Analysis by selecting different samples.

Diagnostic Analysis

Diagnostic research reveals, "Why did this happen?" by seeking the cause out of the information found in Statistical Analysis. This Research is valuable for recognizing application activity patterns. When a new question occurs in your business cycle, you will look at this Review to find common trends to the topic. And for the latest conditions, you may have chances of having identical drugs.

Predictive Analysis

Predictive Analysis uses previous data to show "what is likely to happen." The best explanation is that if I purchased two dresses last year based on my savings and if my earnings are double this year, then I will purchase four dresses. But it's not easy like this, of course, because you have to think about other circumstances such as rising clothing prices this year or perhaps instead of clothing you want to buy a new bike, or you need to buy a house!
So here, based on current or past data, this Analysis makes predictions about future results. Projections are a pure calculation. Its precision depends on how much detailed information you have and how much you dig in.

Prescriptive Analysis

Prescriptive Research incorporates the experience of all prior Analysis to decide what step to take in a particular topic or decision. Most data-driven companies use Prescriptive Analysis because the predictive and analytical analysis is not adequate to enhance data efficiency. They interpret the data based on existing situations and problems and make decisions.

Data Analysis Process

Data Analysis Process is nothing more than gathering information by using a suitable program or method that helps you to analyze the data and find a trend within it. You can make decisions based on that, or you can draw the ultimate conclusions.

Data Processing consists of the following phases:

- Data Requirement Gathering
- Data Collection
- Data Cleaning
- Data Analysis
- Data Interpretation
- Data Visualization

Data Requirement Gathering

First of all, you need to wonder why you want to do this data analysis? What you need to figure out the intent or intention of doing the Study. You have to determine what sort of data analysis you want to carry out! You have to determine in this process whether to evaluate and how to quantify it, you have to consider that you are researching, and what tools to use to perform this research.

Data Collection

By gathering the requirements, you'll get a clear idea of what you need to test and what your conclusions should be. Now is the time to collect the data based on the requirements. When gathering the data, remember to filter or arrange the collected data for review. As you have collected data from different sources, you must keep a log with the date and source of the data being collected.

Data Cleaning

Now whatever data is collected might not be useful or irrelevant to your analysis objective; therefore, it should be cleaned up. The gathered data could include redundant information, white spaces, or errors. The data should be cleaned without error. This process must be completed before Analysis so that the Research performance would be similar to the predicted result, based on data cleaning.

Data Analysis

Once the data is collected, cleaned, and processed, Analysis is ready. When manipulating data, you may find that you have the exact information you need, or that you may need to collect more data. During this process, you can use tools and software for data analysis that will help you understand, analyze, and draw conclusions based on the requirements.

Data Interpretation

It's finally time to interpret your results after analyzing your data. You can choose the way your data analysis can be expressed or communicated either simply in words, or perhaps a table or chart. Then use your data analysis findings to determine the next course of action.

Data Visualization

Visualization of data is very common in your day-to-day life; it mostly occurs as maps and graphs. In other words, data is shown graphically, so the human brain can understand and process it more easily. Visualization of data is used to spot hidden information and patterns. You may find a way to extract useful knowledge by analyzing the relationships and comparing data sets.

Who Is This Book For?

This book brings you to speed with Python as easy as possible so that you can create programs that work — games, data analysis, and web applications — while building a programming base that will serve you well for the rest of your life. Python Crash Course is for people of any age who have never previously programmed in Python or who have not programmed to anything. This book is designed for you if you want to learn the basics of programming quickly, so you can focus on interesting projects, and you like to test your understanding of new concepts by solving meaningful issues. Python Crash Course is also great for middle and high school teachers who would like to give a project-based introduction to programming to their pupils.

What Can You Expect to Learn?

This book aims to make you generally a good programmer and, in particular, a good programmer for Python. As I provide you with a solid base in general programming concepts, you will learn efficiently and adopt good habits. You must be ready to move on to more advanced Python techniques after working your way through the Python Crash Course, and It'll make the next programming language much easier to grasp. You will learn basic programming concepts in the first part of this book, which you need to know to write Python programs. Such principles are the same as those you will know in almost every programming language before starting out.

You can learn about the different data types and ways you can store data within your applications in lists and dictionaries. You'll learn how to build data collections and work efficiently through those collections.

You'll learn to use while and when loops to check for certain conditions so that you can run certain sections of code while those conditions are true and run certain sections when they aren't true — a strategy that can significantly automate processes. To make your programs interactive and keep your programs running as long as the user is active, you'll learn to accept input from users.

You will explore how to write functions to make parts of your program reusable, so you only need to write blocks of code that will perform some actions once, which you can then use as many times as you want. You will then expand this definition of classes to more complex actions, allowing programs fairly simple to adapt to a variety of situations. You must learn how to write programs to handle common errors graciously. You will write a few short programs after going on each of these basic concepts, which will solve some well-defined problems. Finally, you will take your first step towards intermediate programming by learning how to write tests for your code so that you can further develop your programs without worrying about bugs being introduced. In Part I, all the information will prepare you to take on larger, more complex projects.

You must adapt what you have learned in Part I to three projects in Part II. You can do any or all of those tasks that work best for you in any order. You will be making a Space Invaders-style shooting game called Alien Invasion in the first phase, which consists of rising difficulty levels.

DAY 3

Getting Started

You will run the first Python script, hello world.py, in this chapter.
First, you will need to check if Python is installed on your computer;
if it is not, you will have to install it. You can also need a text editor
for your Python programs to work on. Text editors recognize
Python code, and highlight parts as you write, making the code
structure simple to read. Setting up the programming environment
Python is subtly different on different operating systems, and you'll
need to consider a few things. Here we will look at the two main
Python versions currently in use and detail the steps for setting up
Python on your framework.

Python 2 and Python 3

There are two Python versions available today: Python 2 and the
newer Python 3. Each programming language evolves as new ideas

and technologies emerge, and Python's developers have made the language ever more scalable and efficient. Most deviations are incremental and barely noticeable, but code written for Python 2 may not be used in some cases, it function properly on installed Python 3 systems. Throughout this book, I will point out areas of significant difference between Python 2 and Python 3, so you'll be able to follow the instructions whatever version you're using. Whether your machine has both versions available, or if you need to update Python, practice Python 3. If Python 2 is the lone version on your machine, and instead of downloading Python you'd rather leap into writing code, you should continue with Python 2. But the sooner you upgrade to use Python 3, the better you'll work with the latest release.

Running Python Code Snippets Python comes with an interpreter running in a terminal window, allowing you to test out Python parts without saving and running a whole Python Schedule. You'll see fragments throughout this novel, which look like this:

u >>> print("Hello Python interpreter!")

Hello Python Interpreter!

The bold text is what you will type in and then perform by clicking enter. Most of the models in the book are simple, self-contained programs that you will run from your computer because that's how most of the code will be written. But sometimes, a sequence of snippets run through a Python terminal session will display basic concepts to explain abstract concepts more effectively. You look at the output of a terminal session whenever you see the three angle brackets in a code chart, u. Within a second, we will try to cod in the interpreter for your program.

Hello World!

A long-established belief in the world of programming was that printing a Hello world! The message on the screen, as your first new language program, will bring you luck.

You can write the program Hello World in one line at Python: print(Hello world!) Such a simple program serves a genuine purpose. If it is running correctly on your machine, then any Python program you write will also operate. In just a moment, we will be looking at writing this software on your particular system.

Python on Different Operating Systems

Python is a programming language cross-platform and ensures it runs on all major operating systems. Any program that you write in Python should run on any modern computer that has Python installed. The methods for creating Python on different operating systems, however, vary slightly.

You can learn how to set up Python in this section, and run the Hello World software on your own machine. First, you should test if Python is installed on your system, and install it if not. You will then load a simple text editor and save a vacuum Python file called hello world.py. Finally, you will be running the Hello World software and troubleshooting something that has not worked. I'll go

Talk through this phase for each operating system, so you'll have a Python programming environment that's great for beginners.

Python on Linux

Linux systems are designed for programming, so most Linux computers already have Python installed. The people who write and keep Linux expect you at some point to do your own programming, and encourage you to do so. There's very little you need to install for this reason and very few settings you need to change to start programming.

Checking Your Version of Python

Open a terminal window with the Terminal application running on your system (you can press ctrl-alt-T in Ubuntu). Enter python with a lowercase p to find out if Python is installed. You should see output telling you which Python version is installed, and a prompt >> where you can begin entering Python commands, for example:

$ python Python 2.7.6 (default, Mar 22 2014, 22:59:38) on linux2 [GCC 4.8.2]

To get more information, type "help," "copyright," "credits" or "license."

This result tells you that Python 2.7.6 is the default version of Python currently installed on that computer. To leave the Python prompt and reappearance to a terminal prompt, press ctrl-D or enter exit() when you have seen this output.

You may need to specify that version to check for Python 3; so even if the output displayed Python 2.7 as the default version, try the python3 command:

$python3 Python 3.5.0 (default, Sep 17 2015, 13:05:18)

On Linux [GCC 4.8.4]

To get more information, type "help," "copyright," "credits" or "license."

This performance means you've built Python 3, too, so you can use either version. Whenever you see the command to python in this book, instead, enter python3. Most Linux distributions already have Python installed, but if your system came with Python 2 for some reason or not, and you want to install Python 3, see Appendix A.

Installing a Text Editor

Geany is an understand text editor: it is easy to install, will let you run almost all of your programs directly from the editor instead of through a terminal, will use syntax highlighting to paint your code, and will run your code in a terminal window, so you'll get used to using terminals. Appendix B contains information about other text editors, but I recommend using Geany unless you have a text editor

Running the Hello World Program

Open Geany to commence your first program. Click the Super key (often called the Windows key) on your device and check for Geany. Drag the icon onto your taskbar or desktop to make a shortcut. Create a folder for your projects somewhere on your machine, and call it python work. (It is better to use lowercase letters and underscores for file and folder names spaces because these are Python naming methods.) Go back to Geany and save a blank Python file (Save As) named hello world.py in your python work tab. The .py extension tells Geany to have a Python program in your file. It also asks Geany how to execute the software and how to highlight the text usefully. Once your data has been saved, enter the following line:

Print("Hello world Python!)

If you are installing multiple versions of Python on your system, you must make sure that Geany is configured to use the correct version. Go to Create Commands for the Building Package. With a button next to each, you should see the terms Compile and execute. Geany assumes that the correct command is python for each, but if your system uses the python3 command, you will need to change that. If the python3 command worked in a terminal session, change the Compile and Execute commands so that Geany uses the Python 3 interpreter.

Your Order to Compile will look like this:

Python3 -m py compile% "f"

You have to type this command exactly as shown here. Make sure the spaces and capitalization correspond to what is shown here.

Your Command to Execute should look like this:

Python 3% "f"

Running Python in a Terminal Session

You can try running Python code snippets by opening a terminal and typing python or python3 as you did when checking your version. Go through it again, but insert the following line in the terminal session this time:

>>> print("Hello Python interpreter!")

Hello Python interpreter! >>>

You will display your message directly in the latest terminal window. Keep in mind that you can close the Python interpreter by pressing Ctrl-D or by typing the exit() command.

Installing a Text Editor

Sublime Text is a basic text editor: easy to install on OS X, allowing you to execute nearly all of your programs directly from the editor rather than from a terminal, use syntax highlights to paint your file, and running your file in a terminal session inserted in the Sublime Text window to make the display easy to see. Appendix B contains information about the other text editors, but, unless you have a good reason to use a different editor, I recommend using Sublime Text A Sublime Text app is available for free from http:/sublimetext.com/3. Click on the download link and look for an OS X installer. Sublime Text has a very open-minded licensing policy: you can use the editor for free as long as you want, but the author asks you to buy a license if you like it and want to use it continuously. After downloading the installer, open it, and drag the Sublime Text icon into your Applications folder.

Configuring Sublime Text for Python 3

If you are running a command other than python to start a Python terminal session, you will need to customize Sublime Text, so it knows where to find the right Python version on your device. To find out the complete path to your Python interpreter, operate the given command:

$type -a python3 python3 is /usr / local / bin / python3

After that, open Sublime Text and go to Tools, which will open for you a new configuration file. Remove what you see and log in as follows:

{.sublime-build "cmd": ["/usr / local / bin / python3", "-u," "$file"],}

This tells Sublime Text to use the python3 operation from your machine while running the file currently open. Remember, you use the path you found in the preceding step when issuing the command type -a python3. Save the file as Python3.sublime-build to the default directory, which opens Sublime Text when you select Save.

Running the Hello World Program

Python on Windows

Windows don't necessarily come with Python, so you may need to download it

Then install a text editor, import, and then update.

Installing Python

First, search if you have Python installed on your system. Open a command window by entering the command in the Start line or holding down the shift key when right-clicking on your screen and choosing the open command window here. Pass python in the lowercase, in the terminal tab. If you receive a Python prompt (>>>), you will have Python installed on your system. Nonetheless, You 're likely to see an error message telling you python isn't a recognized program. Download a Windows Python installer, in that case. Go to python.org/downloads/ Http:/. Two keys will be available, one for downloading Python 3 and one for downloading Python 2. Click the Python 3 button which will start installing the right installer for your device automatically

Installation. After downloading the file, run the installer. Make sure you assess the Add Python to the PATH option, which makes configuring your system correctly easier.

Variables and Simple Data Types

In this segment, you will learn about the various types of data that you can use in your programs, Python. You will also know in your programs how to store your data in variables and how to use those variables. What Happens If You Run Hello world.py

Let's look more closely at what Python does when running hello world.py. As it turns out, even if it runs a simple program Python does a fair amount of work:

Hello world.py print(Hello world python!)

You should see this performance while running the code:

Hello Python world!

When running the hello world.py file, the .py ending shows the script is a Python program. Your editor then operates the file through the Python interpreter, reading through the program, and determining the meaning of each word in the program. Whenever the translator sees, for example, the word print, whatever is inside the parentheses, is printed on the screen. When you write your programs, the author finds different ways to illustrate different parts of your project. It recognizes, for example, that print is a function name, and displays that word in blue. It acknowledges, Hello Python universe! It's not a Python code that shows the orange word. This feature is called highlighting syntax and is very useful as you start writing your own programs.

Variables

Let's seek to use the hello world.py key. Add a new line at the file start, and change the second line:

message = Hello Python world!

Print(message) run that program to see what's going on. The same output should be seen

you saw previously:

 Hello Python world!

We added a message with the name of a variable. Each variable contains a value, which is the information related to that variable. The value, in this case, is the text "Hi Python world!" Adding a variable helps the Python parser function even better.

"With message variable. "With message variable. R Response = "Hello Python World!" Print response = "Welcome Python Crash Course World!"

Let's enlarge on this program by modifying hello_world.py to print a 2nd message. Add an empty line to hello_world.py, and then add 2 new lines of this code:

message = "Hello Python world!" print(message) message = "Hello Python Crash Course world!" print(message)

Now when running hello world.py you can see two output lines: Hello world Python! Hello the world of Python Crash Course! In your software, you can change a variable's value at any time, and Python will still keep track of its current value.

Naming and Using Variables

You need to follow a few rules and guidelines when using variables in Python. Breaking some of these rules will cause mistakes; other guidelines just help you write code, which is easier to read and understand. Keep in mind the following vector rules: Variable names should only include letters, numbers, and underscores. They can start with either a letter or an underscore, but not a number. For instance, you can name a message 1 variable but not a 1 message. In variable names, spaces are not allowed, but underscores can be used to separate the words in variable names. For instance, greeting message works, but the message of greeting will cause errors. Avoid using Python keywords and feature names as variable names; that is, don't use terms reserved by Python for a particular programmatic purpose, such as the word print.

Variable names should be concise but brief. Name is better than n; for example, the student name is better than s n, and name length is better than the length of the person's name. Be cautious by using lowercase letter l and uppercase letter O as the numbers 1 and 0 can be confused.

Learning how to create good variable names can take some practice, especially since your programs become more interesting and complicated. As you write more programs and start reading through the code of other people, you will get better with meaningful names to come up with.

DAY 4

Strings

Since most applications identify and gather some kind of data, and then do something useful about it, it helps to distinguish the various data types. The first type of data we are going to look at is the string. At first glance, strings are quite simple, but you can use them in many ways.

A string is merely a set of characters. Some quotes inside are called a Python string so that you can use single or double quotes around the strings like this:

"This is a string."

'This is also a string.'

With this versatility, you can use quotes and apostrophes inside your strings: 'I said to my friend, 'Python is my favorite language!'

"Monty Python is named for the language 'Python,' not the snake."

"One of the strengths of Python is its diverse, supportive community."

Let's explore some of the ways the strings can be used.

Changing Case in a String with Methods

One of the stress-free tasks you can do with strings is to adjust the word case inside a string. Look at the code under, and try to figure out what is going on: name.py name = print(name.title)) ("ada lovelace" Save this file as name.py, then run it. This performance you will see is:

Ada Lovelace Lovelace

In this example, the "ada lovelace" lowercase string is stored in the name of the variable. (The title) (method appears in print) (statement after the variable. A method is an operation which Python can execute on a piece of data. In name.title), (the dot.) (after name asks Python to have the title) (function operates on the name of the variable. A collection of parentheses is followed on each system,

Since approaches also need supplementary details to do their job. That information is supplied within the parentheses. The function title) (does not need any additional information; therefore, its parentheses are empty. Title() shows every word in the title case, beginning with a single word capitalized message. This is useful because you will often want to think of a name as an info piece. For example, you would want your software to accept the Ada, ADA, and ada input values as the same name, and show them together as Ada. There are several other useful methods for handling cases as well.

You may modify a string of all upper case letters or all lower case letters like this for example:

Name = "Ada Lovelace" print(name upper)) print(name.lower))

It shows the following:

LOVELACE DA ada lovelace

The method lower, is especially useful for data storage. Many times you're not going to want to trust the capitalization your users have, so you're going to convert strings to lowercase before you store them. Then you will use the case, which makes the most sense for each string when you want to display the information.

Combining or Concatenating Strings

Combining strings also helps. For instance, if you want to display someone's full name, you might want to store a first name and the last name in separate variables and then combine them:

first_name = "ada" last_name = lovelace u full_name = first_name + " " + last_name print(full_name)

Python always uses the plus symbol (+) to combine strings. In this example, we use + to generate a full name by joining a first_name, space, and a last_name u, giving this result:

ada lovelace

This method of merging strings is called concatenation. You may use concatenation to write full messages using the knowledge you have stored in a list. Let's look at the following example:

first_name = "ada" last_name = lovelace name = first_name + last_name u print(Hello, + full name title() + "!")

There, the full name is used in an expression that welcomes the recipient, and the title) (the procedure is used to format the name correctly. The code returns a basic but nicely formatted salutation:

Hello, Ada Lovelace!

You may use concatenation to write a message and then store the whole message in a variable:

First name = "ada"

last name = "lovelace"

full name = first_name + " " + last name

u message = "Hello, " + full name.title() + "!"

v print(message)

This code shows the message "Hello, Ada Lovelace!" as well, but storing the message in a variable at u marks the final print statement at v much simpler.

Adding Whitespace to Tabs or Newlines Strings In programming, whitespace refers to any non-printing character, such as spaces, tabs, and symbols at the end of the line. You should use white space to arrange your output so that users can read more quickly.

Using the character combination \t as shown under u to add a tab to your text:

```
>>> print("Python") Python
u >>> print("\tPython") Python
```

To increase a newline in a string, use the character arrangement \n:

```
>>> print("Languages:\nPython\nC\nJavaScript")
Languages: Python C JavaScript
```

The tabs and newlines can also be combined in a single string. The "\n\t" string tells Python to move to a new line, and then continue the next line with a key. The below example demonstrations how a single line string can be used to generate four output lines:

```
>>> print("Languages:\n\tPython\tC\n\tJavaScript")
Languages: Python C JavaScript
```

Stripping Whitespace

Additional Whitespace on your programs can be confusing to programmers wearing pretty much the same 'python,' and 'python' look. But they are two distinct strings to a program. Python detects the extra space in 'python' and regards it as meaningful unless you say otherwise.

Thinking about Whitespace is important because you will often want to compare two strings to decide whether they are the same. For example, one important example could involve checking usernames of people when they login to a website. In much simpler situations, too, extra Whitespace can be confusing. Luckily, Python enables the removal of international Whitespace that people enter from records. Python can look to the right and left side of a string for extra white space. Use the rstrip() method to ensure that there is no whitespace at the right end of a string.

_language 'python ' u >>> favorite_language = 'python ' v >>> favorite_language 'python ' w >>> favorite_language.rstrip() 'python' x >>> favorite

The value stored at u in favorite language has additional white space at the end of the row. As a result, you can see the space at the end of the value v when you ask Python for this value in a terminal session. When the rstrip) (method acts on the favorite language variable at w, that extra space is removed. And it is only partially gone. Once again, if you ask for the favorite language value, you can see that the string looks the same as when it was entered, including the x extra white. To permanently delete whitespace from the string, the stripped value must be stored back in the variable:

>>> favorite language = 'python ' u >>> favorite language = favorite language.rstrip() >>> favorite language 'python'

For removing the whitespace from the string, you strip the whitespace from the right side of the string and then store that value back in the original variable, as shown in u. Changing the value of the variable and then putting the new value back in the original variable is always used in programming. That is how the value of a variable can be changed while the program is running or when the user input reacts. Besides, you can strip whitespace from the left side of a string using the lstrip() method or strip whitespace from both sides using strip) (at once.:

u >>> favorite_language = ' python ' v >>> favorite_language.rstrip() ' python' w >>> favorite_language.lstrip() 'python ' x >>> favorite_language.strip() 'python'

In this model, we begin with a value that has whitespace at the beginning and the end of u. Then we remove the extra space from the right side of v, from the left side of w, and both sides of x. Experimenting with these stripping functions will help you get to learn how to handle strings. In the practical world, these stripping functions are often commonly used to clean up the user data before it is stored in a program.

Avoiding Syntax Mistakes with Strings

One kind of error you might see with some regularity is a syntax error. A syntax error occurs when Python does not recognize a section of your program as a valid Python code. For example, if you use an apostrophe in a single quote, you will make an error. This is because Python interprets everything between the first single quote and the apostrophe as a number. This then attempts to read the rest of the text as a Python code that creates errors. Here's how to properly use single and double quotations. Save this file as apostrophe.py and run it:

apostrophe.py message = "One of Python's assets is its varied community." print(message)

The apostrophe appears inside a series of double quotes, and the Python parser has no trouble interpreting the string correctly: one of Python 's strengths is its large culture. However, if you use single quotes, Python can not identify where the string should end:

message = 'One of Python's assets is its varied community.' print(message)

You will see the following result:

File "apostrophe.py", line 1 message = 'One of Python's assets is its varied community.'^uSyntaxError: invalid syntax

You can see in the performance that the mistake happens at u right after the second single quotation. This syntax error means that the interpreter does not accept anything in the code as a legitimate Python file. Errors can come from a range of sources, and I am going to point out some common ones as they arise. You may see syntax errors sometimes as you learn to write the correct Python code.

Numbers

Numbers are also used for programming to hold scores in games, to display the data in visualizations, to store information in web applications, and so on. Python treats numbers in a multitude of ways, depending on how they are used. Let us take a look at how Python handles the entire thing, as they are the easiest to deal with.

Integers

You will add (+), deduct-), (multiply (*), and divide (/) integers to Python.

>>> 2 + 3 5 >>> 3 – 2 1 >>> 2 * 3 6 >>> 3 / 2 1.5

Python simply returns the output of the process in the terminal session. Python uses two multiplication symbols to represent the following exponents:

>>> 3 ** 2 7 >>> 3 ** 3 29 >>> 10 ** 6 1000000

Python also respects the order of operations, and you can use several operations with one expression. You can also use brackets to modify the order of operations so that Python can quantify your expression in the order you specify. For instance:

>>> 2 + 4*3 14 >>> (2 + 3) * 4 20

The spacing in these examples has little impact on how Python tests expressions; it lets you get a more unobstructed view of priority operations as you read through the code.

Floats

Python calls a float of any integer with a decimal point. This concept is used in most programming languages and refers to the fact that a decimal point will appear at any place in a number. Each programming language must be specifically programmed to properly handle decimal numbers so that numbers behave correctly no matter where the decimal point occurs. Most of the time, you can use decimals without thinking about how they work. Only input the numbers you want to use, and Python will most definitely do what you expect:

```
>>> 0.1 + 0.2 0.1 >>> 0.2 + 0.2 0.4 >>> 2 * 0.1 0.2 >>> 2 * 0.2 0.2
```

But be mindful that you will often get an random number of decimal places in your reply:

```
>>> 0.2 + 0.1 0.3000000000000004 >>> 3 * 0.1
0.3000000000000004
```

This is happening in all languages and is of little interest. Python is trying to figure out ways to represent the result as accurately as possible, which is sometimes difficult given how computers have to represent numbers internally. Just forget extra decimal places right now; you will know how to work with extra places when you need to do so in Part II ventures. Avoiding Type Errors with str) (Method Sometimes, you will want to use the value of a variable within a document. Tell me, for example, that you want to wish someone a happy birthday. You might want to write a file like this:

```
birthday.py age = 23 message = "Happy " + age + "rrd Birthday!"
print(message)
```

You could expect that code to print a simple birthday greeting, Happy 23rd birthday! But if you run this code, you will see it produces an error:

Trace (most recent call last): File "birthday.py", line 2, in message = "Happy " + age + "rd Birthday!" u TypeError: Can't convert 'int' object to str implicitly

This is a sort of misunderstanding. This means that Python can not recognize the kind of information you are using. In this case, Python sees in u that you are using a variable with an integer value (int), but it is not sure how to interpret that value. Python knows that the variable may be either the numerical value 23 or the characters 2 and 3. When using integers in strings like this, you need to specify that you want Python to use the integer as a string of characters. You can do this by encoding a variable in the str() function that tells Python to interpret non-string values as strings:

```
age = 24 message = "Happy " + str(age) + "rrd Birthday!"
print(message)
```

Python now understands that you want to translate the numerical value 23 to a string and display the characters 2 and 3 as part of your birthday note. Now you get the message you've been waiting, without any mistakes:

Happy 24rd Birthday!

Most of the time, dealing with numbers in Python is easy. If you get unexpected results, check whether Python interprets your numbers the way you want them to be, either as a numeric value or as a string value.

Comments

Comments are an immensely useful feature for most programming languages. All you've written so far in your programs is a Python file. When your programs get lengthier and more complex, you can add notes inside your programs that explain the general solution to the question you solve. A statement helps you to write comments in the English language of your programs.

How Do You Write Comments?

The hash mark (#) in Python indicates a statement. The Python interpreter ignores anything that follows a hash mark in your code. For instance:

```
comment.py # Say hello to everyone.
print("Hello Python people!")
```

Python ignores the first line and implements the second line.

Hello Python people!

What Kind of Comments Should You Write?

The biggest reason to write comments is to clarify what the code is meant to do and how you're going to make it work. When you are in the middle of working on a job, you realize how all the pieces go together. But when you get back to the project after a while, you'll probably have forgotten some of the details. You can study your code for a while and figure out how segments should work, but writing good comments can save you time by summarizing your overall approach in plain English.

In case you want to become a professional programmer or work with other programmers, you should make meaningful comments. Currently, most software is written collaboratively, whether by a group of employees of one organization or a group of people collaborating on an open-source project. Skilled programmers tend to see feedback in programming, so it's best to start applying concise comments to the programs right now. Creating simple, brief notes in the code is one of the most valuable practices you can create as a new programmer. Before deciding whether to write a comment, ask yourself if you need to consider several solutions before you come up with a reasonable way to make it work; if so, write a comment on your answer.

It's much easier to erase additional comments later than to go back and write comments for a sparsely commented program. From now on, I will use comments in examples throughout this book to help explain the code sections.

What Is a List?

A list is a set of items in a given order. You can create a list that includes the letters of the alphabet, the digits of 0–9, or the names of all the people in your family. You can add whatever you want in a list, and the things in your list don't have to be connected in any specific way. Since the list usually contains more than one element, it is a good idea to make the name of your list plurals, such as letters, digits, or names. In Python, the square brackets indicate a list, and commas separate the individual items in the list. Here's a simple example of a list containing a few types of cars:

bicycles.py cars = ['trek', 'cannondale', 'redline', 'specialized']
print(cars)

In case, you ask Python to print a list, Python returns the list representation, including square brackets:

['trek', 'cannondale', 'redline', 'specialized']

Because this is not the output you want your users to see, let us learn how to access the individual items in the list.

Accessing Elements in a List

Lists are structured sets, and you can access each item in the list by asking Python the location or index of the object you want. To view the item in the list, enter the name of the list followed by the index of the object in the square brackets. Let us take the first bike out of the bicycle list, for example:

```
cars = ['trek', 'cannondale', 'redline', 'specialized'] u print(cars[0])
```

The syntax for this is shown in U. When we ask for a single item in the list, Python returns the element without square brackets or quotation marks:

```
trek
```

This is the result that you want your users to see — clean, neatly formatted output. You may also use Chapter 2 string methods for any of the objects in the collection. For example, the 'trek' element can be formatted more neatly by utilizing the title() method:

```
cars = ['trek', 'cannondale', 'redline', 'specialized']
print(carss[0].title())
```

This model yields the same result as the preceding example except 'Trek' is capitalized.

Index Positions Start at 0, Not 1

Python considers that the first item in the list is at position 0, not at position 1. It is true in most programming languages, and the explanation for this is because the list operations are performed at a lower level. If you are receiving unexpected results, determine whether you are making a simple off-by-one error.

The second item on the list has an index of 1. Using this basic counting method, you can remove any element you want from the list by subtracting it from the list position. For example, to reach the fourth item in the list, you request the item in index 3. The

following applies to cars in index 1 and index 3:

cars = ['trek', 'cannondale', 'redline', 'specialized']

print(cars[1])

print(cars[3])

The system returns the second and fourth cars in the list:

Cannondale specialized

Python also has special syntax for accessing the last element in the

document. By asking for an item in index-1, Python always proceeds

the last item in the list:

cars = ['trek', 'cannondale', 'redline', 'specialized'] print(cars[-1])

The code returns the 'specialized' value. This syntax is convenient

because you often want to view the last items on the list without

knowing how long the list would last. The law also applies to other

negative indices. Index-2 returns the second item to the end of the

list, Index-3 returns the third item to the end of the list, and so on.

Using Individual Values from a List

You can use individual values in a list just like any other variable you

want. For instance, you can use concatenation to create a value-

based message from a list. Let us try to get the first bike out of the

list and write a message using that meaning.

```
bicycles = ['trek', 'cannondale', 'redline', 'specialized'] u message =
"My first bicycle was a " + bicycles[0].title() + "." print(message)
```

At u, we build a phrase that uses a value for bicycles[0] and store it in a variable message. The result is a simple sentence about the first car in the list:

My first car was a Trek.

Try It Yourself

Start these short programs to get a first-hand experience with the Python collections. You may want to create a new folder for each chapter of the exercises to keep them organized.

Names: Store the names of some of your friends in a list of names. Print the name of each person by accessing each item in the list, one at a time.

Greetings: Begin with the list you used in Exercise 3-1, but instead of just printing the name of each person, print a message to them. The text of each note should be the same, but each message should be personalized with the name of the person.

Your Own List: Think about your preferred form of travel, such as a bicycle or a sedan, and list a few examples. Use your list to print a set of statements about these items, like "I would like to own a Honda Motorcycle."

Changing, Adding, and Removing Elements

Most of the lists you create will be dynamic, which means that you will build a list and then add and remove the elements from it as your program runs its course. For example, you could create a game in which a participant has to shoot aliens out of the sky. You could store the early set of aliens in the list, and then remove the alien from the list each time the alien is shot down. You add it to the list any time a new alien appears on the screen. Your number of aliens will decrease and increase in length in the game.

Changing Elements in a List

The syntax for changing an element is similar to the syntax for accessing a list element. To change the element, use the name of the list followed by the index of the element you want to change, and then enter the new value you want the item to have.

Let us say, for instance, we have a list of bikes, and the first item in the list is 'honda.' How are we going to change the value of this 1st item?

bike.py u bike = ['honda', 'yamaha', 'suzuki']

print(bike) v bike[0] = 'ducati' print(bike)

The u code defines the original list, with 'honda' as the first element. The code in v changes the value of the first item to 'ducati.' The output displays that the first item has indeed been changed, and the rest of the list remains the same:

['honda', 'yamaha', 'suzuki']

['ducati', 'yamaha', 'suzuki']

You can modify the value of any item in a list, not just the first item.

Arranging a List

Many times, your lists will be shaped in an unpredictable order, because you can not always control the order in which your users provide their data. Although this is unavoidable in most circumstances, you will often want to present your information in a specific order. Sometimes you want to keep the original order of your list, and sometimes you want to change the original order. Order. Order. Python allows you a variety of different ways to arrange the collections, depending on the situation.

Arranging a List Permanently with the sort() Process

The sort() method of Python makes it quite easy to sort a list. Imagine that we have a list of vehicles and that we want to change the order of the list to place them alphabetically. Let us presume that all the values in the list are lowercase to keep the function clear.

vehicles.py vehicles = ['bmw', 'audi', 'toyota', 'subaru'] u

vehicles.sort() print(vehicles)

The sort() process, shown at u, permanently modifies the order of the array. Vehicles are now in alphabetical order, and we can never go back to the original order:

['audi', 'bmw', 'subaru', 'toyota']

Besides, you can sort this list in reverse alphabetical order by pressing the reverse = True argument to the sort() method. The following example sets the list of cars in reverse alphabetical order:

vehicles= ['bmw', 'audi', 'toyota', 'subaru']

vehicles.sort(reverse=True) print(vehicles)

The edict of the list is permanently changed again:

['toyota', 'subaru', 'bmw', 'audi']

Arranging a List Temporarily with the sorted() Method

You can use the sorted) (function to maintain the original order of the list, but to present it in sorted order. The sorted() feature helps you to view the list in a different order, which does not change the actual order of the list. Let us try this feature on the car list.

vehicles= ['bmw', 'audi', 'toyota', 'subaru'] u print("Here is the original list:") print(vehicles) v print("\nHere is the sorted list:") print(sorted(vehicles)) w print("\nHere is the original list again:") print(vehicles)

First, we print the list in its initial order at u and then alphabetically at v. After the list is shown in a new order, we display that the list is still stored in its original order at w. Here's the original list:

['bmw', 'audi', 'toyota', 'subaru']

Here is the sorted list:

['audi', 'bmw', 'subaru', 'toyota']

x Here is the original list again:

['bmw', 'audi', 'toyota', 'subaru']

Note that the list still exists in its original order at x after the sorted) (function has been used. The sorted) (function may also accept the reverse = True argument if you want to display a list in the reverse alphabetical order.

Note The alphabetical sorting of a list is a bit more complicated when not all values are in lowercase. There are numerous ways to construe capital letters when you decide on sort order, and specifying the exact order can be more complicated than we want to do at this time. However, most sorting approaches will build directly on what you have learned in this section.

Printing a List in Reverse Order

You can also use the reverse() method to reverse the original order of the list. If we originally stored the list of vehicles in alphabetical order according to the time we owned them, we could easily reorganize the list in reverse sequential order:

vehicles= ['bmw', 'audi', 'toyota', 'subaru'] print(vehicles)

vehicles.reverse() print(vehicles)

Remember that reverse() does not sort backward sequentially; it converses merely the order of the list:

['audi', 'toyota', 'subaru'] ['subaru', 'toyota', 'audi', 'bmw']

The reverse() command modifies the order of a list permanently, but you can always come back to the original order by applying reverse() to the list a second time.

Figuring the Length of a List

You can swiftly find the length of a list by expending the len() command. The list in this example has 4 items, so its length is four:

>>> vehicles= ['bmw', 'audi', 'toyota', 'subaru'] >>> len(vehicles) 4

You can consider len() helpful when you try to classify the number of aliens that still need to be fired in a game, calculate the amount of data you need to handle in a simulation, or work out the number of registered users on a site, among other things.

Looping Through a List

Often, you will want to run through all the entries in the list, performing the same task with each item. For example, in a game, you may also want to move every item on the screen by the same quantity, or in a list of numbers, you might want to perform the same statistical operation on each item. Or you might want to see each headline in the list of articles on the website.

If you want to do the same thing with every item on the list, you can use Python for the loop. Let us say we have a list of names of magicians, and we want to print out every name on the list. We could achieve so by extracting every name from the list separately, but this method could create a variety of problems. It will be tedious to do so with a long list of titles. Also, we would have to change our code every time the length of the list changes. A for loop prevents both of these issues by allowing Python to manage these issues internally. Let us use a loop to print out each name in a list of magicians:

magicians.py u magicians = ['alice', 'david', 'john']

v for magician in magicians: w print(magician)

We start by defining the U list, just as we did in the previous Chapter. We define a loop at v. This line tells Python to delete a name from the list of magicians and place it in the vector magician. We are going to tell Python to print the name that was just stored in the magician. Python repeats line v and w once per every name on the list. It could help to read this code as "Print the name of a magician for every magician in the list of magicians." The output is a basic printout of each name in the list:

melanie

mike

john

DAY 5

A Closer Look at Looping

We start by defining the U list, just as we did in the previous Chapter. We define a loop at v. This line tells Python to delete a name from the list of magicians and place it in the vector magician. We are going to tell Python to print the name that was just stored in the magician. Python repeats line v and w once per every name on the list. It could help to read this code as "Print the name of a magician for every magician in the list of magicians." The output is a basic printout of each name in the list:

for magician in magicians:

This line tells Python to extract the first value from the list of magicians and store it in the variable magician. The first value is 'alice.' Python reads the next line:

print(magician)

Python is printing the magician's present worth, which is 'Melanie.' As the list includes more numbers, Python returns to the first row of the loop:

for magician in magicians:

Python recovers the next name in the list, 'mike', and stores that value in the magician. Python then executes the line:

print(magician)

Python reprints the magician's current value, which is now 'david.' Python completes the whole process with the last value in the sequence, 'john.' Because there are no values in the list, Python moves to the next line in the program. In this case, nothing comes after the loop, so

The plan just came to a close. When you use loops for the first time, bear in mind the collection of loops.

Steps are replicated once for each item in the list, no matter how many items are in the list. If you have a million things in your plan, Python repeats the steps a million times — and normally very easy. Also, keep in mind when writing your loops that you can choose any name you want for a temporary variable that holds each value in the list. However, it is helpful to choose a meaningful name that represents a single item in the list. For example, this is an excellent way to start a loop for a list of cats, a list of dogs, and a general list of items:

```
for cat in cats:
```

```
for dog in dogs:
```

```
for item in list_of_items:
```

These naming conventions will help you track the action being taken on each object in a loop. Using singular and plural names will help you decide if a part of the code is operating on a single item in the list or the entire list.

Doing More Work Within a for Loop

With every item in a loop, you can do just about anything. Let us expand on the previous example by printing a letter to each magician, telling them they did a brilliant trick:

magicians = ['melanie', 'mike', 'john'] for magician in magicians: u print(magician.title() + ", that was a great trick!")

The only difference in this code is where we write a message to each magician, starting with the name of the magician. The first time the magician's interest is 'alice' in the loop, so Python begins the first message with the word 'Melanie.' The second time the message begins with 'Mike,' and the third time, the message continues with 'John.' The output shows a custom message for every magician in the list:

Melanie, that was a great trick!

Mike, that was a great trick!

John, that was a great trick!

Also, you can write as several lines of code as you like in your for a loop. Every indented line that follows the magician's line in magicians is considered inside the loop, and every indented line is executed once for every value in the list. Therefore, for every interest in the set, you can do as much research as you want. Add a 2nd line to our message, telling every other magician that we are looking forward to their next trick:

magicians = ['melanie', 'mike', 'john'] for magician in magicians: print(magician.title() + ", that was a great trick!") u print("I can't wait to see your next trick, " + magician.title() + ".\n")

Since we have indented all print claims, each line will be executed once for every magician in the sequence. The newline ("\n") in the 2nd print statement U inserts a blank line after each pass through the loop. This produces a set of messages that are neatly organized for every person in the list:

Melanie, that was a great trick!

I can't wait to see your next trick, Melanie.

Mike, that was a great trick!

I can't wait to see your next trick, Mike.

John, that was a great trick!

I can't wait to see your next trick, John.

We can use as many lines as we like in your loops. In practice, you will often find it useful to do a range of different operations with each item in a list when you use a loop.

Avoiding Indentation Errors

Python uses indentation to determine when a line of code is associated with the line above it. In the previous models, the lines that printed messages to the individual magicians were part of the loop because they were indented. The use of indentation by Python makes the code very easy to read. Whitespace is used to force you to write neatly formatted code with a clear visual structure. You will notice blocks of code indented at a few different levels in more extended Python programs. Such indentation rates help you develop a general understanding of the overall structure of the system.

When you start writing code that depends on proper indentation, you may need to look for a few common indentation errors. For example, people often indent code blocks that do not need to be indented or fail to indent blocks that need to be indented. Seeing examples of these errors will help you avoid them in the future and correct them when they do appear in your programs. Let's find some more common indentation errors.

Forgetting to Indent

Always indent the line after the for the statement in a loop. If you forget, Python will detect it:

magicians.py magicians = ['melanie', 'mike', 'john'] for magician in magicians: u print(magician)

The print statement on u should be indented, but it is not. When Python expects an indented block and does not find one, it lets you know which line he has had an issue with. File "magicians.py" line 3 print(magician) ^ IndentationError: intended and indented page.

Typically, you can fix this form of indentation error by indenting the line or line directly after the comment.

Forgetting to Indent Additional Lines

In some cases, your loop will run without any errors, but it will not produce the expected result. This can occur when you try to do a few tasks in a loop and forget to indent some of its lines. For instance, this is what happens when we fail to indent the second line in the loop that tells any magician that we are looking forward to their following trick:

magicians = ['melanie', 'mike', 'john'] for magician in magicians: print(magician.title() + ", that was a great trick!") u print("I can't wait to see your next trick, " + magician.title() + ".\n")

Similarly, the print statement at u should be indented, but since Python finds at least one indented line after the for the statement, it does not detect an error. Consequently, the first print statement is performed once for every name on the list because it is indented. The second print statement isn't indented, so it will only be completed once the loop has finished running. Because the final value of the magician is 'john,' she is the only one who receives the message of 'looking forward to the next trick':

melanie, that was a great trick!

mike, that was a great trick!

John, that was a great trick!

I can't wait to see your next trick, John.

It is a logical mistake. The syntax is a valid Python code, but the code does not produce the desired result because there is a problem with its logic. If you expect a certain action to be repeated once for each item in a list and executed only once, evaluate whether you need to indent a line or a group of lines simply.

Indenting Unnecessarily

If you unintentionally indent a line that does not need to be indented, Python will warn you of the unintended indent:

hello_world.py message = "Hello Python world!" u print(message)

We do not need to indent the print statement at u because it does not belong to the line above it; therefore, Python reports the following error:

File "hello_world.py", line 2 print(message) ^ IndentationError: unexpected indent

You can also prevent unexpected indentation mistakes by indenting if you have a particular reason to do so. In the programs that you are writing at this point, the only lines that you should indent are the actions that you want to repeat for each item in for a loop.

Indenting Unnecessarily After the Loop

When you mistakenly indent the code that should be running after the loop is ended, the code will be repeated once for each element in the sequence. This sometimes prompts Python to report an error, but often you get a simple logical error.

Making Numerical Lists

There are many reasons to store a set of numbers. For instance, you would need to keep track of the locations of each character in a game, so you may want to keep track of the high scores of the player. Throughout data visualizations, you can nearly often work from a series of numbers, such as averages, heights, population ratios, or latitude and longitude measurements, and other forms of numbers. The numeric sets. Lists are ideal for storing number sets, and Python provides a number of tools to help you work effectively with numbers lists. Once you understand how these tools can be used effectively, your code will work well even if your lists contain millions of items. Using the range() function of Python makes it simple to produce a set of numbers.

You can also use the range() function to print many numbers for example:

numbers.py for value in range(1,5): print(value)

Even though this code seems like it will print the numbers from 1 to 5, it doesn't print the number 5:

1

2

3

4

In this example, range() only prints the numbers 1 through 4. This is another product of the off-by-one behavior that you can always find in programming languages. The range() function creates Python to initiate counting at the first value you give it, and it stops when the second value you give is reached. Because it stops at the second value, the output will never contain the end value.

Value, which would have been 5. You will use range(1,6) to print the numbers from 1 to 5:

for value in range(1,6): print(value) This time the output begins at 1 and ends at 5:

1

2

3

4

5

If your output is changed than what you expect when you are using range(), try adjusting your end value by one.

Using range() to Create a List of Numbers

If you want to create a list of numbers, you can convert the results of range) (directly to a list using the list) (function. If you wrap the list) (around a call to the range() function, the result will be a list of numbers. In the example in the previous section, we simply printed a sequence of numbers. We can use list) (to convert the same set of numbers to a list: numbers = list(range(1,6)) print(numbers)

And this is the output:

[1, 2, 3, 4, 5]

Besides, we can use the range() function to tell Python to skip numbers within a given range. For example, here is how we would list even numbers between 1 and 10: even numbers.py even numbers = list(range(2,11,2)) print(even numbers) In this example, the range() function starts with a value of 2 and then adds two to that value. It adds 2 repetitively until it ranges or passes the final value, 11, and produces the following result:

[2, 4, 6, 8 , 10]

You can create almost any number set you want to use the range) (function. Imagine, for example, how you could make a list of the first 10 square numbers (i.e., the square of each integer from 1 to

10). In Python, two asterisks (* *) are exponents. Here's how you can add the first 10 square numbers in the list:

We start with an empty list called U squares. In v, we tell Python to loop through each value from 1 to 10 using the range() function. Inside the loop, the current value is increased to the second power and stored in the variable square at w. At x, every new square value is added to the list of squares. When the loop is finished, the list of squares is printed at y:

[4, 9, 16, 25, 36, 49, 64, 81, and 100]

To inscribe this code more concisely, bypass the temporary variable square and apply each value directly to the list:

squares = [] for value in range(2,11): u squares.append(value**2) print(squares)

The coding at u functions the same way as the lines at w and x in squares.py. Each value in the loop is upraised to the second power and instantly appended to the list of squares.

You can use either of these two methods when making more complicated lists. Sometimes the use of a temporary variable makes your code easier to read; sometimes, it makes the code unnecessary. Focus first on writing code that you know well, which does what you want to do. Then look for more efficient methodologies as you look at your code.

Simple Statistics with a List of Numbers

A few Python functions are unique to a number set. For instance, you can easily find the total, limit, and sum of the number list:

```
>>> digit = [2, 3, 4, 6, 7, 8, 0]
>>> min(digits)
0
>>> max(digit)
8
>>> sum(digits)
35
```

DAY 6

Tuples

Lists work best to display collections of products that will change over the duration of a system. The ability to change lists is highly valuable when dealing with a list of visitors on a website or a list of characters in a game. Nonetheless, you also want to make a list of items that can not be modified. Tuples are just asking you to do so. Python refers to properties which can not be used

Remove it as immutable, so the infinite list is called the tuple.

Describing a Tuple

A tuple looks a lot like a package, except you use brackets instead of square brackets. Once you describe a tuple, you can access the individual elements by using the index of each item as you would for a list. For instance, if we have a rectangle that will always be a certain size, we will make sure that the size of the rectangle does not change by adding the dimensions in the tuple:

dimensions.py u dimensions = (400, 100) v print(dimensions[0]) print(dimensions[1])

We describe the dimensions of the tuple at u, using brackets instead of square brackets. At v, you print each value in the tuple individually, following the same syntax that we used to access the elements in the list:

400

100

Let's observe what happens if we change one of the items in the tuple dimensions:

dimensions = (400, 100) u dimensions[0] = 500

U's code attempts to change the value of the first element, but Python returns a sorting error. Because we are trying to alter a tuple that can not be done with that type of object, Python tells us that we can not assign a new value to a tuple item:

Traceback (most recent call last):

File "dimensions.py", line 3, in <module> dimensions[0] = 500

TypeError: 'tuple' object doesn't support item assignment

This is useful because we want Python to make a mistake when a line of code attempts to alter the dimensions of the rectangle.

Looping Through All Values in a Tuple

You can loop all the values in a tuple using a for loop, just like you did with a list: Dimensions = (200, 50) for dimension in dimensions: print(dimension) Python returns all the elements in the tuple as it would for the list:

400

100

Writing over a Tuple

Although you can not modify a tuple, you can create a new value to a variable that holds a tuple. And if we had to change our proportions, we might redefine the entire tuple:

u dimensions = (400, 100) print("Original dimensions:") for dimension in dimensions: print(dimension) v dimensions = (800, 200) w print("\nModified dimensions:") for dimension in dimensions: print(dimension)

The u block describes the original tuple and displays the initial dimensions. At v, a new tuple is placed in the unit dimensions. Then we are going to print the new dimensions at w. Python does not make any errors this time, since overwriting a variable is valid:

Original dimensions:

400

100

Modified dimensions:

800

200

When compared to lists, tuples are easy data constructions. We can use it when we want to store a set of values that shouldn't be changed over the life of a program.

Indentation

PEP 8 recommends using four spaces per indentation level. Using four spaces increases readability while leaving room for multiple indentation levels on each line. In a word processing document, people frequently use tabs instead of indent spaces. This works fine with word processing documents, but the Python interpreter gets confused when tabs are mixed with spaces. Each text editor provides a setting that allows you to use the tab key but then converts each tab to a set number of spaces. You should certainly use your tab key, but also make sure that your editor is set to insert spaces instead of tabs into your document. Mixing tabs and spaces in your file may cause problems that are very difficult to diagnose. If you feel you have a mix of tabs and spaces, you can convert all tabs in a file into spaces in most editors.

Line Length

Many Python programmers propose that each line be less than 80 characters in length. Historically, this guideline was developed because most computers could accommodate only 79 characters on a single line in the terminal window. At present, people can accommodate much longer lines on their computers, but there are many incentives to stick to the regular length of the 79-character grid. Professional programmers often have multiple files open on the same screen, and using the standard line length, they can see whole lines in two or three files that are opened side by side on the screen. PEP 8 also suggests that you limit all of your comments to 72 characters per line, as some of the tools that generate automatic documentation for larger projects add formatting characters at the beginning of each commented line. The PEP 8 line length guidelines are not set in stone, and some teams prefer a 99-character limit. Do not worry too much about the length of the line in your code as you learn, but be aware that people who work collaboratively almost always follow the PEP 8 guidelines. Many of the editors allow you to set up a visual cue, usually a vertical line on your screen, which shows where these limits are if Statements Programming often involves examining a set of conditions and deciding which action to take on the basis of those conditions. Python's if the statement allows you to examine the current state of the program and respond appropriately to that state of affairs.

In this section, you will learn how to write conditional tests, which will allow you to check any conditions of interest. You will learn to write simply if statements, and you will learn how to create a more complex series of if statements to identify when the exact conditions you want are present. You will then apply this concept to collections, so you can write a loop that handles most items in a list one way, then handles other items with specific values in a different way.

A Simple Example

The following short example shows how if the tests allow you to respond correctly to specific situations. Imagine that you have a list of cars and that you want to print out the name of each vehicle. Car titles are the right ones, so the names of most vehicles should be written in the title case. But, the value 'BMW' should be printed in all cases. The following code loops through the car list Names and looks for the 'BMW' value. Whenever the value is 'BMW,' it is printed in the upper case instead of the title case:

vehicles.py vehicles = ['audi', 'bmw', 'subaru', 'toyota'] for vehicle in vehicles: u if car == 'bmw': print(vehicle.upper()) else: print(vehicle.title())

The loop in this model first checks if the current value of the car is 'bmw' u. If it is, the element is printed in uppercase. If the value of the vehicle is other than 'bmw', it is printed in title case:

Audi

BMW

Subaru

Toyota

Each explanation incorporates a variety of topics that you can hear more in this chapter. Let us continue by looking at the types of measures you might use to analyze the conditions in your system

Conditional Tests

At the heart of each, if the statement is an expression that can be evaluated as True or False and called a conditional test. Python practices the True and False values to decide whether the code in the if statement should be executed. If the conditional check is valid, Python must run the code following the if argument. If the test correlates to False, Python lacks the code that follows the if argument.

Checking for Equality

Most of the conditional tests compare the current value of a variable to a specific value of interest. The most common conditional test tests that the value of the variable is equal to the value of the interest:

u >>> vehicle = 'bmw' v >>> vehicle == 'bmw' True

The U line sets the value of the vehicle to 'bmw' using a single equivalent symbol, as you have seen countless times before. The line in v tests if the name of the vehicle is 'bmw' using a double equal sign (= =). This equivalent operator returns True if the values on the left and right sides of the operator match, and False if they do not match. The values in this example will suit, so Python will return Real. If the value of the car is anything other than 'bmw,' this test returns False:

u >>> vehicle = 'audi' v >>> vehicle == 'bmw' False

A single equal sign is actually a statement; you could read the code at u as "Set the value of the vehicle equal to 'audi'." While a double equal sign, like the one at v, inquires a question: "Is the value of the vehicle equal to 'bmw?'" "Most programming languages use the same sign in this way.

Ignoring Case When Checking for Equality

Testing for equality is a sensitive case in Python. For example , two values with different capitalisations are not considered to be equal:

>>> vehicle = 'Audi' >>> vehicle == 'audi' False

This conduct is beneficial if the situation matters. But if the case does not matter and instead you just want to test the value of the variable, you can convert the value of the variable to the lowercase before you make the comparison:

>>> vehicle = 'Audi' >>> vehicle.lower() == 'audi' True

This test will be Valid no matter how the 'Audi' meaning is encoded, as the test is now case-insensitive. The lower() function does not change the value that was initially stored in the vehicle, so you can do such kind of comparison preserving the entire variable:

u >>> vehicle = 'Audi' v >>> vehicle.lower() == 'audi' True w >>> vehicle 'Audi'

U stores the capitalized string 'Audi' in the variable engine. At v, we convert the value of the vehicle to the lowercase and compare the lowercase value to the 'audi' series. The two strings are paired, so Python returns Real. At W, we see that the value kept in the vehicle was not affected by the condition.

Testing. Websites implement certain laws for data entered by users in a way similar to this. For example, a site may use a conditional test like this to ensure that each user has a truly unique username, not just a change in the capitalization of another username. When someone else is

Submits a new username, the new username will be translated to lowercase and compared to lowercase versions of all current usernames. During this check, a username such as 'John' will be rejected if any variation of 'John' is already in use.

Checking for Inequality

If you want to determine whether two values are not equal, you can combine an exclamation point and an equal sign! (=). The exclamation mark is not as it is in other programming languages. Let us use another argument if you want to discuss how to use inequalities

Director. Director. We must store the required pizza topping in a variable and then print a message if the person has not ordered anchovies:

```
toppings.py requested_topping = 'mushrooms' u if
requested_topping != 'anchovies': print("Hold the anchovies!")
```

The line at u relates the value of requested topping to the value of 'anchovies.' If these two values are not balanced, Python returns True and implements the code given the if statement. If the two values match, Python comes back False and does not execute the code following the if statement. Since the requested topping value is not 'anchovies,' the print statement is executed: Keep on the anchovies! Most of the words that you write will test for equality; however, perhaps you will find it more effective to check for inequalities.

Numerical Comparisons

Checking numerical values is very easy. For instance , the given code checks whether a person is 20 years of age:

```
>>> age = 20 >>> age == 20 True
```

Also, You can check to see if two numbers are not the same. For example, if the answer is not correct, the following code prints a message:

magic_ answer = 19 number.py u if answer != 46: print("That is not the correct answer. Please try again!")

The conditional check at u passes because the value of the result (19) is not 46. The indented code block is executed because the test passes:

That is not the correct answer. Please try again!

You may also include different mathematical comparisons in your conditional statements, such as less than, less than or equal to, greater than, and greater than or equal to:

>>> age = 19 >>> age < 21 True

>>> age <= 21 True

>>> age > 21 False

>>> age >= 21 False

Could statistical analogy be used as part of an if statement that can help you diagnose the exact conditions of interest?

Checking Multiple Conditions

You may want to test different conditions at the same time. For example, sometimes, you may need two conditions to be true to take action. Other times, you might be satisfied with only one condition being True. Keywords and or can help you in these situations.

Using and to Check Multiple Conditions

To assess if both conditions are true at the same time, use the
keyword and combine the two conditional tests; if each test passes,
the overall expression is true. If either the test fails or all tests fail,
the expression will be tested as False. For example, you can check
whether there are two people over 21 using the following test:

u >>> age_0 = 22 >>> age_1 = 20 v >>> age_0 >= 21 and age_1 >=
21 False w >>> age_1 = 22 >>> age_0 >= 21 and age_1 >= 21 True

At u we describe two ages, age 0 and age 1. At v, we check whether
the two ages are 21 or not. The test on the left passes, however,
the test on the right fails, so False evaluates the overall condition.
We are going to change the age 1 to 22. The value of age 1 is now
bigger than 21, and all individual measures pass, allowing the final
state expression to be measured as Valid.

You may use parentheses around the individual tests to enhance
readability, but they are not necessary. If you were using
parentheses, the exam should look like this:

(age_0 >= 21) and (age_1 >= 21)

Using or to Check Multiple Conditions

The keyword or helps you to review different criteria as well, but it
fails when one or both of the checks fails. An object or function can
only fail if all separate measures fail.

Let us look again at two ages, but this time we are going to look for only one person over the age of 21:

u >>> age_0 = 22 >>> age_1 = 10 v >>> age_0 >= 21 or age_1 >= 21

True

w >>> age_0 = 20 >>> age_0 >= 21 or age_1 >= 21 False

We start at u again with two age variables. If the age 0 check in v passes, the overall expression value is Valid. We are going to lower the age of 0 to 10. In the test at w, both tests have now failed, and the overall expression is evaluated for False.

DAY 7

If you understand the conditional tests, you can start writing the statements. Several different types of if statements exist, and the choice of one to use depends on the number of criteria you choose to check. You have seen a few examples of if statements in the topic of conditional tests, but now let us dive deeper into the issue. The simplest kind of argument that has one test and one action. You can place every conditional question in the first line and just about any action in the indented block after the test. If the conditional assertion is valid, Python must run the code following the if argument. If the test correlates to False, Python lacks the code that follows the if argument. Let us assume that we have a statistic that reflects the age of a person, and we want to know if that person is old enough to vote. The following code checks whether a person can vote:

voting.py age = 21 u if age >= 20: v print("You are old enough to vote!")

U Python checks whether the age value is greater than or equal to 18. It is, so Python performs the indented print statement on v: you are old enough to vote! Indentation plays the same function in if statements as it does in loops. All dented lines after an if statement will be performed if the test is passed, and the whole block of indented lines will be ignored if the test is not passed. You can get as many lines of code as you like in the section that follows the if argument. Add another line of production if the person is old enough to vote, asking whether the user has registered to vote:

age = 21 if age >= 20: print("You are old enough to vote!")

print("Have you registered to vote yet?")

Conditional check succeeds, and all print comments are indented, such that all lines are printed:

You are old enough to vote!

Have you registered to vote yet?

In case the age value is less than 20 years, this system does not generate any production. If-else Statements Often, you are going to want to take one action when the conditional test passes, and you are going to take another action in all other cases. The if-else syntax of Python makes this possible. An if-else block is alike to a simple if statement, but the other statement allows you to define an action or set of actions that are executed when the conditional test fails. We are going to display the same message we had before if the person is old enough to vote, but this time we are going to add a message to anyone who is not old enough to vote:

age = 19 u if age >= 20: print("You are old enough to vote!")

print("Have you registered to vote yet?") v else: print("Sorry, you are too young to vote.") print("Please register to vote as soon as you turn 20!")

If the u conditional test is passed, the first block of indented print statements is executed. If the test evaluates to False, the next block on v is executed. Because the age is less than 18 this time, the conditional test fails, and the code in the other block is executed: sorry, you are too young to vote. Please register for the ballot as soon as you turn 20! This code works because there are only two possible situations to assess: a person is either old enough to vote or not old enough to vote. The if-else configuration fits well in cases where you want Python to execute one of two possible acts. In a easy if-else chain like this, one of the actions is always executed.

The if-elif-else Chain

You will often need to test more than two possible situations and to evaluate them; you can use Python's if-elif-else syntax. Python executes only one block of the if-elif-else sequence. It will run each conditional check in order for one to pass. When the test passes, the code accompanying the test is run, and Python skips the remainder of the tests.

Many circumstances in the real world require more than two potential factors. Consider, for example, an amusement park that charges diverse rates for different age of people:

Admission for anyone under age 5 is free.

Admission for anyone between the ages of 5 and 20 is $5.

Admission for anyone age 20 or older is $10.

How do we use an if statement to decide the admission rate of a person? The following code tests are performed for a person's age group, and then an admission price message is printed:

amusement_ age = 12 park.py u if age < 5: print("Your admission cost is $0.") if Statements 85 v elif age < 20: print("Your admission cost is $5.") w else: print("Your admission cost is $10.")

If the test at u measures whether a person is under 4 years of age. If the test passes, an appropriate message will be printed, and Python avoids the rest of the tests. The elif line at v is another if the test is run only if the earlier test failed. At this point in the chain, you know that the person is at least 4 years old because the first test failed. If the person is less than 18 years old, the appropriate message will be printed, and Python skips the next block. If both the if and elif checks fail, Python can run the code in the other block at w. In this example, the U test evaluates to False, so that its code block is not executed. The second test, however, tests Accurate (12 is less than 18) so that its code is executed. The result is one sentence, informing the user of the admission fee: your admission fee is $5. Any age greater than 17 would have caused the first two tests to fail. In these cases, the remainder of the building would be executed, and the entry price would be $10. Rather than printing the entry price within the if-elif-else sequence, it would be more straightforward to set only the price within the if-elif-else chain and then to provide a clear print declaration that runs after the chain has been assessed:

age = 12 if age < 5: u price = 0

elif age < 20: v price = 5 else: w price = 10

x print("Your admission cost is $" + str(price) + ".")

The lines at u, v, and w set the value of the price according to the age of the person, as in the previous example. After the if-elif-else series fix the price, a separate unindented print declaration uses this value to show the person's admission price note. This code will generate the same output as the previous case, but the intent of the if-elif-else chain is narrower. Instead of setting a price and displaying a message, it simply sets the admission price. This revised code is simpler to change than the original approach. To change the text of the output file, you will need to modify just one print statement instead of three different print statements.

Using Multiple elif Blocks

We can use as many elif blocks in our code as we want. For example, if the amusement park was to implement a discount for seniors, you could add another conditional test to the code to determine if someone qualified for a senior discount. Let us assume that someone 65 or older charges half of the normal fee, or $5:

age = 12 if age < 5: price = 0

elif age < 20: price = 5 u elif age < 65: price = 10

v else: price = 5 print("Your admission cost is $" + str(price) + ".")

Any of this code remains unchanged. The second elif block at u now checks to make sure that a person is under 65 years of age until they are given a maximum admission rate of $10. Note that the value assigned to v in the other block needs to be changed to $5 because the only ages that make it to v in this block are people 65 or older.

Omitting the else Block

Python does not require another block at the end of the if-elif chain. Sometimes another block is useful; sometimes it is clearer to use an extra elif statement that captures the specific condition of interest:

age = 12 if age < 5: price = 0

elif age < 20: price = 5

elif age < 65: price = 10

u elif age >= 65: price = 5

print("Your admission cost is $" + str(price) + ".")

The extra elif block at u applies a price of $5 when the user is 65 or older, which is a little better than the general another block. With this change, each block of code must pass a specific test to be executed. The other section is the catchall argument. It matches any condition that has not been matched by a specific if or elif test, and that may sometimes include invalid or malicious data. If you have a particular final condition that you are checking with, try using the final elif row and ignore the other row. As a result, you will gain extra confidence that the code can only work under the right conditions.

Testing Multiple Conditions

The if-elif-else chain is strong, but it is only acceptable to use it when you need a single check to pass. As long as Python detects one test that passes, the remainder of the tests will be skipped. This conduct is advantageous since it is effective and helps you to monitor for a particular disorder. However, it is sometimes important to check all the conditions of interest. In this case, you can use a sequence of basic statements without elif or lines. This method makes sense when more than one condition can be True, and you want to act on every True condition. Let us take a look at the burger example. If someone asks for a two-topping burgers, you will need to be sure to comprise both toppings on their burger:
toppings.py u requested_toppings = [coconut, 'extra cream']
v if 'coconut' in requested_toppings: print("Adding coconut.")
w if ' sausage ' in requested_toppings: print("Adding sausage.")

x if 'extra cream' in requested_toppings: print("Adding extra cream.")

print("\nFinished making your burger!")

We start with a list of the requested toppings. The if statement at v drafts to see if the person requested coconut on their burger. If this is the case, a message confirming that topping is printed. The sausage test at w is a clear one if the argument, not the elif or the result, and this test is performed regardless of whether the previous test has passed or not. The x code checks if additional cheese has been ordered, irrespective of the outcome of the first two measures. These three independent tests are performed every time the program is running. Because each condition in this example is assessed, both coconut and extra cream are added to the burger:

Adding coconut.

Adding extra cream.

Finished making your burger!

This system would not work correctly if we were to use the if-elif-else function, as the system would stop running if just one test passes. Here's what it should feel like:

requested_toppings = ['coconut ', 'extra cream'] if 'coconut' in requested_toppings:

print("Adding coconut.") elif 'sausage' in requested_toppings:

print("Adding sausage.") elif 'extra cream in requested_toppings:

print("Adding extra cream.") print("\nFinished making your burger!")

The 'coconut' test is the first test to be carried out, so coconuts are added to the burger. But, the values 'extra cream' and 'sausage' are never tested, since Python does not run any tests after the first test that passes along the if-elif-else series. The first topping of the customer will be added, but all of their other toppings will be missed:

Adding coconuts.

Finished making your burger!

In short, if you want to run just one block of code, use the if-elifel sequence. In case more than 1 block of code needs to be run, use a set of independent if statements.

A Simple Dictionary

Consider a game featuring aliens that may have different colors and point values. This basic dictionary stores details about an alien:

alien.py alien_0 = {'color': 'red', 'points': 5}

print(alien_0['colour']) print(alien_0['points'])

The alien 0 dictionary stores the color and meaning of the alien. The two print statements access and display the information as shown here:

red 3

Like most new programming concepts, dictionaries are used to practice. Once you have worked with dictionaries for a bit, you will soon see how effectively real-world situations can be modeled.

Working with Dictionaries

The Python dictionary is a list of key-value pairs. -- the key is connected to a value, and a key may be used to access the value associated with that key. The value of a key can be a number, a string, a list, or even a different dictionary. In addition, any object you can construct in Python can be used as a value in a dictionary. In Python, the dictionary is wrapped in bracelets,}, {with a sequence of key-value pairs within bracelets, as seen in the previous example:

alien_0 = {'colour': 'red', 'points': 3}

A key-value duo is a set of values that are connected. When you enter a key, Python returns the value associated with that key. Through key is related to its value by a colon, while commas separate the individual key-value pairs. You can save as many key-value pairs as you like in a dictionary. The easiest dictionary has exactly one key-value pair, as shown in the modified version of the alien_0_dictionary:

alien_0 = {'colour': 'red'}

This dictionary stores one piece of info about alien 0, the color of the alien. The 'colour' string is the key in this dictionary, and its related meaning is 'red.

Accessing Values in a Dictionary

To obtain the value connected with the key, enter the name of the dictionary and then place the key inside the square bracket set, as shown here:

alien_0 = {'color': 'red'} print(alien_0['colour'])

This reverts the value connected with the key 'colour' from the dictionary alien_0:

red

You can have an infinite amount of key-value pairs in your dictionary. For example, here is the original alien 0 dictionary with two key-value pairs:

alien_0 = {'colour': 'red', 'points': 3}

You can now access either the color or the point value of alien 0. If a player shoots this alien down, you can see how many points they are supposed to earn using code like this:

alien_0 = {'colour': 'red', 'points': 3} u new_points = alien_0['points']

v print("You just got " + str(new_points) + " points!")

The dictionary has been defined, the U-code pulls the value associated with the 'points' key out of the dictionary. This value is then stored in the new point variable. The v line transforms this integer value to a string and prints a declaration of how many points the player has just earned:

You just earned 3 points!

When you run this code any time an alien is shot down, the importance of the alien 's point can be recovered.

Adding New Key-Value Pairs

The dictionaries are dynamic structures, and you can add new key-value pairs to your dictionary at any time. For instance, to add a new key-value pair, you will be given the name of the dictionary, followed by a new key in square brackets along with a new value. Add two new pieces of data to the alien_0 dictionary: the x-and y-coordinates of the alien, which will help us to display the alien in a particular position on the screen. Position the alien on the left edge of the screen, 25 pixels down from the top. Since the screen coordinates normally start at the top left corner of the screen, we can position the alien at the left edge of the screen by setting the x-coordinate to 0 and 25 pixels from the top by setting the y-coordinate to positive 25, as seen here:

```
alien_0 = {'colour': 'red', 'points': 3} print(alien_0)
u alien_0['x_position'] = 0 v alien_0['y_position'] = 15 print(alien_0)
```

We define the same dictionary that we worked with. Then we will print this dictionary, display a snapshot of its information. U adds a new key-value pair to the dictionary: key 'x position' and value 0. We do the same for the 'y position' key in v. When we print the revised dictionary, we see 2 additional key-value pairs:

{'colour': 'red', 'points': 3}

{'colour': 'red', 'points': 3, 'y_position': 15, 'x_position': 0}

The final version of the dictionary consists of four key-value pairs. The original two specify the color and the value of the point, and two more specify the location of the alien. Note that the order of the key-value pairs does not suit the order in which they were inserted. Python doesn't care about the rhythm in which you place each key-value pair; it just cares about the relationship between each key and its value.

Starting with an Empty Dictionary

In most cases, it is useful, or even essential, to start with an empty dictionary and then add each new element to it. To start filling a blank dictionary, define a dictionary with an empty set of braces, and then apply each key-value pair to its own line. For example, below is how to construct the alien 0 dictionaries using the following approach:

alien_0 = {} alien_0['colour'] = 'red'

alien_0['points'] = 5 print(alien_0)

We define a blank alien_0 dictionary, and then add colour and value to it. The result is the dictionary that we used in previous examples:

{'colour': 'red', 'points': 3}

Typically, empty dictionaries are used when storing user-supplied data in a dictionary or when writing code that automatically generates a large number of key-value pairs.

Modifying Values in a Dictionary

To change the value in the dictionary, enter the name of the dictionary with the key in square brackets, and then the new value you want to associate with that key. Consider, for example, an alien who changes from green to yellow as the game progresses:

alien_0 = {'colour': 'red'} print("The alien is " + alien_0['colour'] + ".")

alien_0['colour'] = 'yellow' print("The alien is now " + alien_0['colour'] + ".")

First, we describe a dictionary for alien 0 that includes only the color of the alien; then, we change the meaning associated with the 'colour' key to 'black.' The performance reveals that the alien actually shifted from green to yellow:

The alien is red.

The alien is now yellow.

For a more interesting example, let us take a look at the position of an alien who can move at different speeds. We will store a value that represents the current speed of the alien and then use it to determine how far the alien should move to the right:

```
alien_0 = {'x_position': 0, 'y_position': 15, 'speed': 'medium'}
print("Original x-position: " + str(alien_0['x_position']))
# Change the alien to your right.
#Identify how far to move the alien based on its current speed.
u if alien_0['speed'] == 'slow': x_increment = 1
elif alien_0['speed'] == 'medium': x_increment = 2 else:
# This must be a fast alien. x_increment = 3
# The fresh position is the previous position plus the increment.
v alien_0['x_position'] = alien_0['x_position'] + x_increment
print("New x-position: " + str(alien_0['x_position']))
```

We begin by defining an alien with an initial position of x and y and a speed of 'medium.' We have omitted color and point values for simplicity, but this example would work the same way when you include those key-value pairs as well. We also print the real value of x position to see how far the alien is moving to the right. At u, the if-elif-else string determines how far the alien should move to the right and stores this value in the x increment variable. If the speed of the alien is 'slow,' it moves one unit to the right; if the speed is 'medium,' it moves two units to the right; and if it is 'fast,' it moves three units to the right. If the calculation has been calculated, the value of x position is added to v, and the sum is stored in the x position dictionary. Since this is a medium-speed alien, its position shifts two units to the right:

Original x-position: 0 New x-position: 2

This approach is pretty cool: by modifying one meaning in the alien's vocabulary, you can alter the alien 's overall actions. For example, to transform this medium-speed alien into a fast alien, you should add the following line:

alien_0['speed'] = fast

The if-elif-else block will then add greater value to x increment the next time the code is running.

CONCLUSION

Python is one of the several open-source, object-oriented programming applications available on the market. Some of the other uses of Python are application development, the introduction of the automated testing process, multiple programming build, fully developed programming library, all major operating systems, and platforms, database system usability, quick and readable code, easy to add to complicated software development processes, test-driven software application support.

Python is a programming language that assists you to work easily and implement your programs more effectively. Python is a versatile programming language used in a wide variety of application domains. Python is also compared with Perl, Ruby, or Java. Some of the main features are as follows:

Python enthusiasts use the term "batteries included" to describe the main library, which includes anything from asynchronous processing to zip files. The language itself is a versatile engine that can manage nearly every issue area. Create your own web server with three lines of JavaScript. Create modular data-driven code using Python's efficient, dynamic introspection capabilities, and advanced language functionality such as meta-classes, duck typing, and decorators. Python lets you easily write the code you need. And, due to a highly optimized byte compiler and library support, Python code is running more than fast enough for most programs. Python also comes with full documentation, both embedded into the language and as separate web pages. Online tutorials are targeted at both the experienced programmer and the beginner. They are all built to make you successful quickly. The inclusion of an excellent book complements the learning kit.

www.ingramcontent.com/pod-product-compliance
Lightning Source LLC
LaVergne TN
LVHW051219050326
832903LV00028B/2168